AF518645

SALMAN RUSHDIE'S
Midnight's Children

A Reader's Companion

SALMAN RUSHDIE'S

Midnight's Children

A Reader's Companion

with

Exhaustive Critical Commentary

and

Edited Essays

TAPAN K. GHOSH

asia book club

Published by
asia book club
Post Box 9615, Janakpuri
New Delhi 110 058

ISBN: 81-7851-010-3

Copyright Author 2004

All rights reserved. No part of this book may be reproduced or utilized in any form or by any means, electronic or mechanical, including photocopy, microfilm, microfiche, recording, e-mail, web publication, or any information storage and retrieval system, without the written permission of the copyright owner.

Printed at Chaman Offset Press, New Delhi 110 002

CONTENTS

Section II

Critical Perspectives

Editor's Note

I first read *Midnight's Children* twenty years ago when I was a student of English literature in an Indian University. The time was early 1980s. India's first experiment with a coalition government at the centre had deplorably failed due to petty squabbles of methuselah and faddish leaders. Indira Gandhi had returned to power with a popular mandate and renewed vigour. The memory of the Emergency had already started fading from the collective consciousness of the people. At that time I did not know anything about the book's postcolonial and postmodernist perspectives. The critiques of nation and nationalism by Partha Chatterjee, Benedict Anderson, Eric Hobsbawn et al were still some way in the future. I read the book simply as an English novel about India by an expatriate Indian and was bedazzled by its brilliance. What struck me most was the author's irreverence to the hallowed conventions, history and fiction writing and his protagonist's sheer audacity to re-write the entire history of post-1947 India in order to place himself in a central role. I was also impressed by the confidence and ease with which he bent English, the rulers' language only a few decades ago, to his will and made it serve his purpose. I followed newspaper reports on the book's grandiose reception in the West and the debate it had generated in India among the literati as well as ordinary readers and realized that something very important had happened. I read the novel several times after that, sometimes in isolation and sometimes in association with the subsequent works of Rushdie. Each reading added to my appreciation of the text and reinforced my conviction that the book marked a turning point not only in Indian English novel but also in the history of twentieth century literature and ideas. I have come to believe, like many others, that the book's amazing success owed not simply to the post-Emergency timing of its publication and the Booker Prize (which no doubt contributed to its popularity, particularly in India), but also to its tremendous aesthetic energy, its rich wealth of imaginative and intellectual resources, and daring experimentation with the narrative medium that brought about a remarkable change in the very way in which Indian English novels had been written before its advent.

It is at once a privilege and a daunting task to introduce a much-decoded text like *Midnight's Children* to the readers of Salman Rushdie's fiction. Perhaps no other book by an Indian author had attracted such world-wide attention before. Critics have minutely dissected the novel and left not a single part of its anatomy untouched. Anyway, the plan of this volume was to give a brief overview of Rushdie's life and works and a general introduction to the text of *Midnight's Children* in the two chapters of the first section. The second section presents ten articles which discuss the novel from different angles with a view to providing the reader with a variety of perspectives and interpre tations.

It is my pleasurable duty to thank Dr. R.K. Dhawan for inviting me to edit the present volume. Dr Dhawan has always been affably helpful and co-operating and has patiently borne with my constant demands, some of which were very difficult to satisfy.

I should also take this opportunity to formally thank the scholars in India and abroad for their co-operation and timely contribution of well-researched articles to this volume.

I acknowledge my debt to Mr. Palash Samanta who painstakingly prepared the typescript from my illegible handwriting in his computer.

My wife and daughter encouraged me all along. But for their lively company, the whole process would have been a boring exercise for me. I also received my mother's blessings to complete the task. To them I shall remain eternally grateful.

Tapan Kumar Ghosh

Introduction

TAPAN KUMAR GHOSH
University of Burdwan

Salman Rushdie shot into international fame with the publication of his second novel, *Midnight's Children*, in 1980. The book won the prestigious Booker McConnell Prize for fiction in 1981 and was hailed as a literary masterpiece. The award gave it enormous publicity and media coverage, unlocking a flood of reviews and articles, radio-features and interviews. The novel was received, both in India and abroad, with enthusiastic and almost unanimous acclaim. Sceptical voices were silenced by exuberant rhetoric and hymnic panegyrics. Rushdie was accepted as a major writer and ranked with such widely diverse authors as Henry Fielding, Laurence Sterne, Rabelais, Charles Dickens, Franz Kafka, James Joyce, Gabriel Garcia Marquez, Gunter Grass and Milan Kundera. The book rode a wave of popularity unprecedented in the history of Indian writing in English.

More than twenty years have passed after that sensational event. Rushdie has published five more novels in the intervening period. One of them shook the world as no book had done before. But *Midnight's Children*, unlike many award-winning novels, continues to be read and discussed with interest not only by ordinary readers but by literary critics as well. The passage of time has sobered the uncritical enthusiasm and created a space for balanced critical judgement. The socio-economic and literary changes which have taken place both in and outside India and the tumultuous events of Rushdie's own life—particularly the controversy over *The Satanic Verses*—have made critics and scholars more guarded in their response to *Midnight's Children* and its author. Initially described as a comic-epic in prose about the picaresque journey of a fabulous hero whose birth coincided with India's Independence and whose life encapsulates the experience of the country, the novel has gradually been subsumed in a theoretical discourse on nation, nationalism and postcoloniality. It is now regarded as a foundational text of postcolonial novel which challenges the authority of imperial textuality and disrupts the cultural and linguistic stability of the colonizing centre. It shows an alternative way of conceiving history that breaks down barriers between cultures. Others have viewed the book as a fictional representation of the postmodernist celebration of fragmentation, multiplicity and self-reflexivity. Rushdie's perception that all narratives are susceptible to being re-written, his insistence on the 'provisional nature of all truths' and his narrativization of 'slices' in the form of 'fragments of broken mirrors'[1] also refurbish his disposition towards postmodernism. Critics have written about his multiple literary influences, his fusion of Indian oral tradition and Western novel genre, and his innovative use of language. Everybody in India was not, however, amused by the book's commercial success. Some severely criticized its 'chutnification' of Indian history while others challenged Rushdie's claim for radical innovations in language and style. It was argued that Rushdie could not be considered as an Indian author because of his outsider position and that the success of *Midnight's Children* was largely due to international publicity. But few people now deny its influence on younger writers for whom the book released a new spring of creativity and heralded a spirit of freedom. A whole generation of young, and largely male, authors (Amitav Ghosh, Allan Sealy, Shashi Tharoor, Mukul Kesavan, Rohinton Mistry, Vikram Seth, Vikram Chandra—to name only a few) followed in his footsteps. They were infected by Rushdie's confident use of English and inspired by his acknowledgement of multiple viewpoints and narrative modes as well as his audacious attempt to place the marginalized story of an individual or a family at the centerstage of national drama. *Midnight's Children* has been recognized as a landmark novel, an important turning point in post-Independence

Indian fiction in English. Its runaway success catalysed a spectacular resurgence of Indian English novel and brought about a remarkable change in the attitude of the reading public in India and abroad towards this phenomenon which had remained, until then, a largely walled-in literary entity.

Publicity and literary awards (the Booker, and subsequently the Booker of Bookers, the James Tait Black Memorial Book Prize and the American English Speaking Union Literary Award) no doubt contributed to the popularity of *Midnight's Children*. But the time was also most opportune for a dramatic change. Indian English novel had reached a stagnant stage, in terms of both content and form, by the end of the nineteen seventies. The old masters of the craft like Mulk Raj Anand, Raja Rao and R.K. Narayan, who had started writing in the 1930s, reached their peak by the 1960s. No new novelist drew the attention of serious readers after Arun Joshi and Anita Desai. Experimentation with either language or form was conspicuous by its absence. The readers were tired of the realistic portrayal of social ills, East-West cultural encounters, and individual's alienation from society and self which had been catered to them with unflagging regularity since Independence. At the end of the decade, Indian English novel reached an impasse and required a radical reformulation. The comet-like arrival of *Midnight's Children* with a stupendous aesthetic force galvanized the sluggish literary scene by reconceptualizing the novel—its form, content and narrative mode—and re-inventing its medium. It infused new life into Indian English novel and set the trend for a whole generation of writers. It broke the ground rules of the older form of fiction and created new rules without any apology or explanation, foreword or footnote. It broke away not only from the earlier tradition of Indian English novel but also from the Western depictions of India as one finds in the works of Paul Scott, E.M. Forster and V.S. Naipaul. Its thematic and stylistic concerns called for a new experimental strategy which is mirrored in its mode of narration, complex mixture of different narrative genres, novelty of metaphors and inventiveness of idiom. The novel brings together public and private events, history, myth and legends, realism and fantasy, hilarious comedy and scathing satire—within an imaginative and linguistic framework which is always under control. It flamboyantly crosses, fragments and parodies different narrative styles and perspectives, adopts—often subverts—Western genres and employs traditional local forms in a contemporary context to serve 'a huge purpose, namely the personification of India and the realization of Indian life'[2] with all its contradictions and its polyphonic plurality and cultural multiplicity.

Salman Rushdie: Life and Works

Like his hero Saleem Sinai, Salman Rushdie was born in Bombay in 1947, not on August 15 but on June 19, to a liberal and affluent Muslim businessman Anis Ahmed Rushdie and his wife Negin who had their origin in Kashmir. He grew up in a villa on Warden Road that resembled Methwold's Estate in the novel. Like Saleem, he attended the Cathedral School. When he was fourteen years old, his father sent him to England for higher education. He was enrolled in Rugby School where he had his first taste of British racism, an experience which he would later dramatize in *The Satanic Verses* and which would inspire him to wield his pen against racial prejudice and write polemical essays like 'The New Empire within Britain' (1982). In 1964, his parents migrated to Karachi, seventeen years after Independence. In 1965, he went to King's College, Cambridge, to study history. After Cambridge he returned to Pakistan for a brief period. But his stay in the country was far from satisfactory. Brought up in the 'highly-spiced non-conformity of Bombay,' Rushdie—like his narrator-protagonist Saleem—could never like Karachi, a city which exuded 'odours of acquiescence.'[3] He went back to England and tried a career first in acting and then in advertising. He joined Ogilvy and Mather as a copywriter and travelled extensively in the U.S., Canada and Europe. In 1969, he stopped work to write an unpublished novel, *The Book of the Pir*. He took up copy-writing again, working on a part-time basis which enabled him to continue writing. He finally settled in London as an expatriate and took to writing as a full-time vocation.

His first novel *Grimus* (1975) was a fantasy effort which defeated both critics and readers. Written for the Victor Gollancz Science Fiction Competition, the book is, in fact, a quest novel with an imaginary setting that uses certain key ideas of Sufi poetry in the context of Western fantasy genre. Modelled on Dante's *Divine Comedy*, Samuel Johnson's *Rasselas* and Farid ud-Din Attar's *Conference of the Birds* (*Mantiq al-Tayr*, a 12th century religious poem by the Sufi mystic), *Grimus* (an anagram of Simurg, the bird with reasoning power in Persian mythology) made little impact in India and abroad. Rushdie found his métier with his second novel, *Midnight's Children*, which brought him fame and recognition. A sprawling, humorous and aggressive book that mixes fact and fantasy with a linguistic extravaganza never seen in Indian writing in English before, it invented new metaphors of nationhood and a new idiom to interpret the multi-layered reality of the sub-continent. The book sold more than 500,000 copies world-wide and was translated in various European languages. It opened up a new era for the reception of Indian English novel in the West and brought it from the margin to the centre of the literary world. Its stunning reception in the West was an indication of the new status accorded to the margin. If *Midnight's Children* is about India, *Shame* (1983), his next novel, is about Pakistan and her evolution since 1947. As Rushdie claims: 'The country in this story is not Pakistan, or not quite. There are two countries, real and fictional, occupying the same space, or almost the same space.' (*Shame*, 29) He selects material from Pakistani history, fantasizes it and imposes it, like a palimpsest, on the existing country. Geography, history and persons are imaginatively re-created in the book to form part of a modern fairytale which is shaped by the controlling theme of shame and shamelessness. The book was banned in Pakistan but it won much critical acclaim. *The Jaguar Smile: A Nicaraguan Journey* (1987), a political travelogue which comes close to V.S. Naipaul's writings in this genre, resulted from Rushdie's visit to Nicaragua as a guest of the Sandinista Association of Cultural Workers in 1986. But it proved a tardy effort and was criticized for the author's naiveté. His fourth novel *The Satanic Verses*

(1989)—a capacious book with a convoluted plot and dazzling language and magic-realist effects—attempts to explore the questions of good and evil through the experience of two Indian actors, Gibreel Farishta and Salahuddin Chamcha. They fall from an air-crashed plane into Thatcherite England and metamorphose into Archangel Gabriel and the Devil respectively. Rushdie examines the nature of divine revelation from the viewpoint of a non-believer and weaves fantasies around traditional accounts of Prophet Muhammad's life. Gabriel's hallucinations call up passages that rocked the world. A send-up of history, myth, religion and film, the novel interweaves British racism, Islamic fundamentalism and the popular culture of metropolitan India to examine the failure, in this age of consumerism and cosmopolitan rootlessness, to achieve spiritual depth. It is this book which changed Rushdie's life and created a maelstrom unheard-of in literary history. He was trapped in the pincer of global and religious politics. The novel, banned in several countries including India, was charged with offending the religious sensibility of the Muslims and Ayatollah Khomeini of Iran issued a fatwa, on the Valentine's Day (14 February 1989), sentencing Rushdie to death. An U.K. £2 million bounty was put on his head by the Khordad Foundation of Iran and death squads were let loose to find out and kill the author of the blasphemous book. The controversy, which came to be known as the 'Rushdie affair,' split the world and triggered a civilizational clash between liberal humanism and Islamic fundamentalism. Writers and artists united to form the International Rushdie Defence Committee and pressure the Iranian authority to withdraw the threat. It did not work, nor did Rushdie's public apology to the Muslims. For ten years Rushdie lived in fear and under constant security, moving from place to place and house to house.[4] His second wife Marianne Wiggins, also a novelist, left him and he could not see his son. The experience of loneliness and incarceration began to take its toll but Rushdie refused to be silenced. He started writing again. In 1990 he published *Haroun and the Sea of Stories*. The book is about Rashid, a master raconteur who loves telling stories till Khattam Shud, the evil Prince of Silence and the enemy of speech, pollutes the very spring of stories itself. Rashid's son Haroun rescues his father and returns to him the gift of story-telling. Loved by children and adults alike for its delectable mixture of adventure, magic and fantasy, the book was read by many as an allegory of Rushdie's own predicament with a moving message to his ten-year-old son Zafar for whom he wrote the book. A protest novel written in answer to Imam Khomeini's fatwa, the book dramatizes, in the guise of an adventure story for children, the archetypal struggles between tyrannical regimes and the human longing for freedom of expression and the liberty of creative imagination. Around this time he also published a collection of literary criticism and essays significantly titled *Imaginary Homelands* (1991), an allusion to the expatriate writer's need to imaginatively reconstruct his roots. In 1993 *Midnight's Children* was adjudged the 'Booker of Bookers' i.e. the best book in the twenty-five years of Booker history. This was a recognition of the novel's worth and a tribute to the genius of Rushdie, one of fiction's finest practitioners. *East, West*, an anthology of short stories, came out in 1994. It brought nine scattered and earlier published pieces under three sections: 'East,' 'West' and 'East, West.' The stories reveal his competence and ease in dealing with both Indian and Western story material and his superb story-telling power. But this was an interim output of the author whose forte is clearly the large canvas. In 1995, *The Moor's Last Sigh* was published. The book marked the culmination of a long project, the fact-fantasy oeuvre of the sub-continent's peoples which began with *Midnight's Children* and includes *Shame* and *The Satanic Verses*. It is a spacious novel that stretches from Cochin to Bombay before a climactic ending in Spain. Rushdie once again tells the story of modern India through the fortunes of a family, this time a Christian-Jewish spice-trading family from the Malabar Coast. He explores the cultural diversity of India and the role minorities play in maintaining the country's rich cultural mix. Written in the wake of serial bombings and consequent communal riots in Bombay following the demolition of the Babri Mosque in Ayodhya by Hindu fundamentalists, who try to define a Hindu-dominated

Indianness to the exclusion of all other religious groups, the book nostalgically evokes the Nehruvian vision of a free, secular and hybrid India. (The genealogy of Rushdie's 'Moor,' Moraes Zogoiby, summons up the convoluted histories of such a hybridity. His identity is a synthesis of Catholic, Jewish, Arabic and Indian influences.) At the end of the book this mongrel figure escapes to Spain, impelled by the communally charged atmosphere of contemporary India.

The exceptional facts of Rushdie's altered life after *The Satanic Verses* have given a poignancy to his post-fatwa works which are invariably marked by displacement, despair and a profound sense of loss. Ever since the Moor's last sigh for the lost world, Rushdie has been singing an elegy for the India he knew. In an interview given to the BBC around that time, he categorically pronounced his irrevocable alienation from the country. The reasons for this separation had not only to do with his inability to visit the place of his birth but also with the demise of the Nehruvian idea of India which he cherishes and re-creates in his fiction. The new India which emerged in the last two decades of the twentieth century and was characterized by consumer capitalism, ethnic militancy and religious/cultural nationalism dismayed Rushdie who had been raised in an atmosphere of secularism and cultural multiplicity. 'This India,' he said in that interview, 'I suspect is not for me to write about.'[5] In 1997, Rushdie married Elizabeth West, an editor in her thirties who worked for the Bloomsbury publishing house. Rushdie and West edited *The Vintage Book of Indian Writing* for the 50th anniversary of India's independence. The anthology sparked off a controversy over his introductory remark that the best prose writing—both fiction and non-fiction—in India since Independence had been in English and not in the vernacular languages. It was trashed in India and Rushdie was severely criticized for his naïve comment.

Under continuous pressures from the international community and the frantic lobbying of IRDC, Iran finally lifted the death sentence on Rushdie. On 24 September 1998, the Iranian foreign minister, Dr. Kamal Kharazzi said at the United Nations that his government did not support the bounty on Rushdie and that it had no intention to threaten the life of the author of *The Satanic Verses*. Rushdie became a free man again. In the first interview after his emergence from the shadow of the fatwa, he told the London correspondent of the Calcutta weekly *Sunday*[6] that his biggest loss in those ten years was that his relationship with India had been thoroughly damaged. He expressed his anger and pain at having been rejected by the country. He had been denied entry not only into the land of his birth but also into Indian buildings and consulates abroad: 'I was informed I was persona non grata.' Even the permission to shoot a celluloid version of *Midnight's Children* was denied in India. He felt that the country was becoming a closed chapter and that he would soon have to say goodbye to it: 'It's like a divorce, in which one person doesn't want to get divorced and is left alone.' He said his next novel would be about leave-taking: 'I will never write about India again after this.' *The Ground beneath Her Feet* (1999) begins in India and then leaves the country. On the surface, it is a story of turbulent love between two Indian-born musical superstars, Vina Apsara and Ormus Cama that recaptures the crucial moments of the history of rock music. It also remakes the myth of Orpheus and Eurydice to explore the themes of damnation and tragedy which are essential to the condition of being an artist. But, above all, the book is about farewell to India, 'the fount of [his] imagination' (249), about the divorce between Rushdie and his 'imaginary homeland': 'In this particular divorce I was the party who didn't want the marriage to break up' (248), as Umeed Merchant, a.k.a. Rai, the photographer narrator who rejects the changes that have taken place in India after Independence, says before his forced departure from the country to the West in search of a new ground where bigger things happen.

But, fortunately, the marriage did not break up. Despite everything Rushdie refused to let India out of his system. He is emotionally shackled to India, not merely the idea or the dream which everyone agreed to dream half a century ago but the living India. That is why, ignoring all temptations to belong to other nations he still treasures his ancestral house in Solan near Shimla for which he fought and won a prolonged legal battle. He had imagined the nation and pined for reciprocity. His emotional outbursts on various occasions have been no more than the soulful cries of a man who feels displaced from and rejected by the country of his birth. The reciprocity came in April 2000. *The Ground beneath Her Feet* was short-listed for the Commonwealth Writers' Prize and Rushdie returned to India after twelve years to attend the prize ceremony held in Delhi. The book did not win the main prize but the author won a rapturous welcome and a five-year visa. An evidently pleased Rushdie told *India Today* that the visit was, for him, a renewal of links and that his 'real prize [was] India'; he did not 'care about the rest.'[7] His latest novel, *Fury* (2001), also reveals that he is willing to maintain a relationship, however tenuous, with the country of his origin. He writes once again about displacement and despair and a very personal search for peace and home. The book is about Professor Malik Solanka, a retired Cambridge historian and famous dollmaker with an eventful backstory in Bombay and London. Malik, a disillusioned academic, crosses the Atlantic, leaving behind his second wife and three-year-old son, and comes to New York to lead a solitary and celibate life. But the peace of his life is shaken by uncontrollable furies within and around him and by his encounter with a TV documentary producer of scintillating beauty, Neela Mahendra who draws him towards a different kind of fury on the other side of the world. The story of this dark enchantment, which ends in a fictitious South Pacific island, evinces that the new ground beneath Rushdie's feet (New York, which he had surveyed in his earlier novel) is still shaking and that he has not been able to forget Bombay, 'his damned Yoknapatawpha, his accursed Malgudi, which had shaped his destiny and whose memory he had suppressed for over half a lifetime.' (220) Bombay, Rushdie's synecdoche for India, still remains central to his imaginative reconstruction of the country as a symbol for her unity in diversity. As an interviewer aptly puts it, 'Take away India and there's no Rushdie.'[8]

Indianness of Rushdie

Anyone reading Rushdie's works is struck by his obvious attachment to his Indian roots. His education and his adult life have been British. But a strong part of him still identifies with India and his imagination continues to feed on the sub-continent. His works carry a deep imprint of the complex socio-cultural scene of India which has a significant bearing on the thematic as well as stylistic aspect of his fiction. It is this as well as his passionate involvement with the history and politics of his country which has induced many critics to consider him as an Indian writer in English. But in reality his novels provide a curious mix of Eastern and Western elements. Rushdie is a product of biculturalism which is regarded by many as the 'creative matrix' of his fiction. He is at home in the East and the West and the two diametrically opposite cultures have defined his identity and his writing. His split identity leads him to search for his literary ancestry in both the cultures (just as Saleem Sinai's obsession with the tracing of ancestry in *Midnight's Children* is an attempt to come to terms with his divided identity.) His novels have come to be viewed as a new kind of postcolonial writing in which a migrant, diasporic and cosmopolitan consciousness dominates. They are hybrid, multi-lingual and conversant with the cultural codes of the West, at the same time retaining their thematic connections with the country of his origin. This paradoxical dual position, as insider and outsider in the society he writes about, informs and animates his writing even today. Rushdie has discussed this problematic question of identity in several essays and interviews. He is not worried about the negative connotations associated with such a position and about criticism, both in India and in the West, that his works lack authenticity and are informed by political cynicism and lack of commitment, his hybridity being primarily an aesthetic device, a source of themes. He has stressed that assimilating Western and Oriental literary traditions should not be regarded as disloyalty towards one's cultural heritage but as a bridging of gaps. Rushdie has reiterated that for postcolonial migrant writers like him, who inhabit a fractured, hybrid world and are multi-lingual by necessity, the experience of cultural translation (he has called himself a 'translated man' and labelled postcolonial migrant literature in English as poly-cultural 'translated writing') is an aesthetic bliss. It not only supplies material for their works but also gives a valuable insight on the conditions of their home countries. The experience of 'straddling cultures' (*IH*, 15) provides the migrant writers with double perspective or, to use a metaphor from *Midnight's Children*, a 'stereo-scopic vision' on their dislocated world. A hybrid postcolonial text, *Midnight's Children* achieves a successful, and aesthetically satisfying, fusion of East and West in terms of both form and content. This hybridity or cultural mix, which is intrinsic to all of Rushdie's works and explains much of his versatility, has been valorized by postcolonial critical theory.

Critical Evaluation of the Novel

Midnight's Children had its genesis in a family joke: two months after Rushdie was born, the British ran away from India! As he recalls:

> This joke was always told to embarrass me at awkward moments, which gave me the idea to take a child and a country, and to join them comically. From that there was a short step to having the idea of a child that was born exactly at the moment of independence, and who believed himself to be connected to the country. Then, there was the story of the child growing up and the country growing up, so to say, in parallel, it began with that.[9]

This provides the central thesis of the novel, that the life of a midnight's child born on 15 August 1947 is analogous to that of the emerging history of the nation born at the same moment, and that the telling of the thirty-year-old story of the protagonist is the same as narrating the postcolonial history of the country. It allows Rushdie to relate private life and public events and examine the relationship between individual and history. By locking together the destinies of the man and the nation, he makes his narrator-protagonist, Saleem Sinai, a witness to the evolving history of the nation.

One way of connecting the individual member of society with the collective stream of history is writing history as autobiography. The very opening paragraph of *Midnight's Children* establishes Rushdie's narrative method, his interplay of history ('India's arrival at Independence'), autobiography ('I was born in the city of Bombay') and fantasy ('once upon a time'). This interplay is sustained throughout the narrative which has a tripartite structure, consisting of three books and thirty chapters which roughly correspond to the thirty years of Saleem's life and India's thirty-year course from Independence to Emergency. History provides the book with its narrative axis and the linearity of public events holds the novel together. All the important historical events in the sub-continent, from the Jallianwala Bagh massacre (1919) to the Emergency (1975) are ingeniously linked with the crucial turns in the story of Saleem and his family so that the autobiography of an individual reads like the history of a country and the odyssey of a family becomes the odyssey of a nation from 1915 to 1977, the period of Indian history Rushdie charts in the novel.

In his quest for individual identity, Saleem ventures to rewrite the entire history of his times from random shards of memory, all the while conscious of falling victim 'to the temptation of every autobiographer that since the past exists only in one's memories . . . it is possible to create past events simply by saying they occurred.' (443) He makes no distinction between official facts and gossips, history and legends because he believes that sometimes 'legends make reality, and become more useful than the facts.' (47) He takes liberty with chronology and blends history with fiction, allowing concocted stories to encroach upon recorded events, in order to preserve the correspondence between his life and the history of India and create the illusion of himself as a protagonist at the centre. Saleem knows that he cannot lay claim to objectivity and that the reconstitution of his history is bound to be largely fictive because of his egotistical and selective framework of reference, his fallible memory which constantly plays tricks and provides an excuse for factual errors and unreliability, and his partial, fragmentary vision represented by his mnemonic icon, the perforated sheet. Despite his intention to produce a comprehensive account of the past with its continuities and missing links, he is condemned by his heritage—his grandfather's perforated sheet—'to see [his] own life—its meanings, its structures—in fragments.' (107) Implicit in his statement is the admission that human beings are 'capable only of fractured perceptions,' (*IH*, 12) and that all reclamations of the past are bound to be provisional and incomplete. He attempts to re-imagine the past and restore it to himself with the aid of memory. What his narrative presents is not literal truth but 'memory's truth' which 'selects, eliminates, alters, exaggerates, minimizes, glorifies, and vilifies also; but in the end it creates its own reality, its heterogeneous but usually coherent version of events.' (211) Rushdie foregrounds memory as an inextricable aspect of his delineation of India and makes the subject of the novel 'the way we remake the past to suit our present purposes, using memory as our tool.' (*IH*, 10) *Midnight's Children* is an affirmation of the importance of memory in the reclamation of personal and collective history and the constitution of the individual's identity. Saleem compares his presentation of history through memory to the pickling process ('chutnification') which invariably leads to alteration and transformation: 'in words and pickles, I have immortalized my memories, although distortions are inevitable in both methods.' (459) The pickle metaphor suggests that history, reshaped ('chutnified') through the imagination of a creative artist, becomes a kind of fiction. Saleem's story is not authentic history; it only plays with historical shapes. *Midnight's Children* offers a fictional alternative to the official history of the country. As Rushdie says: "what I was actually doing was a novel of memory and about memory, so that my India was just that: 'my' India, a version and no more than one version of all the hundreds of millions of possible versions." (*IH*, 10) He presents the postcolonial history of India from the point of view of an individual. Rushdie seems to suggest that individual reclamation of the past provides a version of truth which is valid for the individual.

Saleem essays a revisionist history which destabilizes the certainty of the official version and offers a critique of authority. For example, the state truth of Pakistan about the Bangladesh War in 1971 and the official view of the Emergency—that no atrocities were committed by the Pakistani army in the East Wing and that there were no excesses like forced sterilization and slum clearance during the period of Indira Gandhi's authoritarian rule—are given the lie in Saleem's remembered version of the events. Rushdie believes that both writers and politicians 'try to make the world in their own images; they fight for the same territory.' (*IH*, 14) He uses the 'novel of memory' as a political weapon to disprove the politicians' version of truth and resist the forgetfulness which is induced by their distortion, even alteration, of history. In the first section of the novel that describes India's colonial past, Saleem's narrative debunks the myths which sustained the Empire ('Methwold') and shatters the idols of imperial history. A paradigmatic postcolonial text, *Midnight's Children* challenges the ideologically determined patterns of historical relationships. In this book, the natives of India do not play only side-roles or bit-parts in British history, as in the novels of M.M. Kaye and Paul Scott; they rather make history. It seeks to emancipate the formerly colonized people from the reverential awe in which they held the colonizers. The imposing figure of Mountbatten is reduced to insignificance ('Mountbatten with his extraordinary haste and his chicken-breast eater of a wife') and General Dyer is remembered only as a tyrant devoid of human emotions ('Mercurochrome'). The British transfer of power is parodied through the symbolic takeover of the intact Englishness of the Methwold's Estate. Rushdie ruthlessly attacks British colonialism through his caricature of characters like Methwold and attempts to link many of the ills which plague independent India to the mischief done by the British during their rule. What was invisible or forcibly silenced in the British history (like the story of the nationalist Muslims in 'Hit-the-Spittoon' and 'Under the Carpet') is brought to focus through an effective blend of fact and fiction. Saleem's oral narrative supplants the recorded British history of colonized India with a counter discourse that subverts and undermines the colonizers' view of the country. Rushdie's fabulism—his fusion of fact and fantasy—also contributes to this alternative version of history. Historical events, when viewed through the fractured lenses of a fallible memory and connected with myths and legends, lose their unidimensional veracity and appear fantastic. *Midnight's Children*, a novel about the textuality of history, replaces the unitary narrative of official history of India with a comprehensive and highly subjective version of the multi-dimensional reality of the sub-continent. It reads like a spoof on the traditional histories of the country which are no more than biographies of viceroys and generals, Presidents and Prime Ministers, and suggests that the autobiography of an ordinary individual can participate in, and significantly contribute to, the making of national history.

What gives *Midnight's Children*—which is chiefly about India, the country of Rushdie's own cherished childhood—its narrative breadth is the connection with autobiography. There is a close connection between the writer Salman and the narrator-protagonist Saleem. Rushdie himself acknowledges this identity: 'The fact that he is called Saleem and I am called Salman . . . it's not surprising that the identification is made.'[10] The narrative voice is put in Saleem's mouth and the first person narration lends the work an immense intensity. There is a lot of autobiographical material in the novel but it is sifted to suit the story's requirement. Rushdie's family, like Saleem's, hailed from Kashmir. His maternal grandfather was a doctor attached to the Aligarh University in U.P. As in the novel, the Partition split Rushdie's family. His parents migrated to Pakistan in 1964. Both the writer and his hero were born in 1947, within eight weeks of each other, and had an Anglicized upbringing in Bombay, a city nostalgically evoked in the novel. *Midnight's Children* is, like *The Moor's Last Sigh*, essentially a Bombay novel. Almost half the book takes place in this city. Rushdie has admitted in several interviews that he had always desired to write a long novel about Bombay of the 1950s and early 1960s. The cosmopolitan city with its composite culture and linguistic plurality becomes for him a metaphor of the multiplicity of urban India. The spirit of Bombay, both as a place and as an idea, permeates the book. Bombay cinema, the city's biggest cultural production and the most ubiquitous icon of India's popular culture, forms an important inter-text of *Midnight's Children*. This intertextuality is evident in the adoption of filmic terminology into the narrative. 'Nobody from Bombay should be without a basic film vocabulary' (33), says Saleem who has an insider's knowledge of the conventions of Hindi cinema. He uses this knowledge not only to construct his narrative but also to colour and interpret it for the readers. The novel simulates, and often parodies, the Bombay films' fantastic and melodramatic mode, incorporating formulaic devices like mistaken identities, changes of babies at birth, doubles, multiple parents, amnesia and accidental return of memory, and movie-trailers or previews involving anticipatory mention of events to come. The metaphor of a cinema screen is employed to discuss the question of perspective (165-66) while a film cliché—'a calendar ruffled by a breeze, its pages flying off in rapid succession' (346)—solves the problem of describing the passage of time. Saleem uses close-ups and long-shots to situate the reader in relation to the action. Dreams and fantasies, myths and legends—the stock-in-trade of Bombay cinema—are persistently used in the novel. Rushdie believes, very much like the Latin American magic realists, that the unreal and the bizarre are often a more accurate mirror of truth and that only the epic-fabulist mode can faithfully reflect the fantastic complexities of a vast country like India. Uncle Hanif succeeded as a film-maker when he adopted this unrealistic mode in 'Lovers of Kashmir.' But his naturalistic film about an ordinary pickle factory and its humble labourers flopped because, as Saleem says, 'in the temple of illusions, he had become the high priest of reality.' (244) Thus, in *Midnight's Children*, melodrama piles upon melodrama as Saleem's life acquires 'the colouring of a Bombay talkie.' (148)

Saleem sets out to write his autobiography near the end of his battered life in the hope that his mnemonic enterprise may achieve the significance which the events of his adulthood have drained from him. The act of recollection and recording becomes a sort of cathartic attempt to resist his fragmentation and regain control ('I must retain control as long as possible' [461]). His greatest desire is for meaning, and making sense of his marginalized life takes on the dimension of a life and death struggle: 'I must work fast, faster than Scheherazade, if I am to end up meaning—yes, meaning—something. I admit it: above all things, I fear absurdity.' (9) *Midnight's Children* begins and ends with explicit references to *A Thousand and One Nights* which provides Saleem with the organizing principle of his narrative—preservation and justification of life by story-telling. Like the imperilled Princess, Saleem tells his story, which is also the history of his time and place, within a framed narrative to a clearly defined listener (Padma) who functions as an implied reader within the text and as a continuous reminder of the present tense of the narrating time.

The narrative begins with an announcement of Saleem's portentous birth 'at the precise instant of India's arrival at independence.' (9) In order to account for it, he takes the readers back, with the help of his 'all-knowing memory,' (88) to his origin, his grandfather—the progressive doctor Aadam Aziz. Book One, consisting of eight chapters, traces the family's journey from Kashmir via Agra and Delhi to Bombay which becomes, synecdochally, the march of the country from colonial rule to Independence. All the major historical events from 1915 to 1947 are meticulously interlaced with Saleem's family saga: the Jallianwala Bagh tragedy, Muslim League and its communal politics, the role of the nationalist Muslims who opposed the idea of Pakistan, 'Quit India' movement, Cabinet Mission and its failure, the arrival of Mountbatten, the partition of the country and the consequent riots and bloodshed. Saleem's nativity marks the dividing line between the old world and the new. The dream of the nation born at the numinous midnight of August 15 amidst Nehru's legendary narration of postcoloniality in the Assembly Hall is embodied by the one thousand and one magical children. Born with miraculous powers between midnight and 1 a.m., they represent the unbounded optimism and marvellous promises of the nascent state. Saleem's autobiography is, in fact, the story of these children who are privileged to be both masters and victims of their time: 'The children of midnight were also the children of the time: fathered . . . by history.' (118) A sort of multi-headed monster, speaking in the myriad tongues of Babel, the midnight's children are a metaphor of heterogeneous Indian society, its very essence of multiplicity. Saleem is the spokesman of these children whom he unites in the parliament of his mind. By virtue of his synchronous birth with the nation at the exact stroke of midnight, Saleem claims 'a place at the centre of the things' (238) and feels responsible for the country's fate to which he is 'indissolubly chained.' (9) He is literally 'handcuffed to history,' (9) the circumstances of his birth making him analogous to the newly independent nation of India. His narrative is thus both a story of his own life and a mirror of the nation. Prime Minister Nehru's letter celebrating the illustrious moment of Saleem's birth identifies his life with the life of India itself and confers on him the 'role of the mirror of the nation.' (427) Book Two charts the dynamic growth of Saleem from childhood to adolescence which reflects the development of free India between 1947 and 1965. All the national and sub-continental events of consequence during this period of the country's postcolonial history are linked with Saleem's career: the assassination of Mahatma Gandhi, India's Five Year Plans, reorganization of Indian states and language riots, the imposition of Martial Law in Pakistan, the Chinese aggression, the theft of the holy relic in Srinagar's Hazratbal mosque, Nehru's death and the Indo-Pakistani War of 1965. At the autobiographical level, this section traces the ups and downs in the fortunes of Sinai family, the birth of Saleem's sister, the disintegration of Midnight Children's Conference, the death of Aadam Aziz and uncle Hanif, and the revelation of Mary Pereira's crime which exposes Saleem as an imposter and shatters his dream world. The Sinais migrate to Pakistan where Saleem reaches a tumultuous adulthood and witnesses the annihilation of his family in the war of 1965. Saleem's narration of the evolution of India since Independence is punctuated with many scandalous events which shook the nation while his treatment of the history of Pakistan is peppered with episodes of political grotesquerie. The ungainly shape that Independence took in the subcontinent and the deplorable developments of the twin nations which made Saleem and his family helpless victims meet with a severe indictment in his narrative. Rushdie noticed a downward slide in post-Independence India, particularly after the demise of Nehru. The euphoria of Independence lasted upto the first decade and then gradually gave way to despair. Progress of the country yielded to fanaticism and stunted growth and the body politic, like Saleem's fissured body, began to crack. With the decay of the myth of the nation, Saleem's sense of engagement was replaced by doubt, cynicism and withdrawal. Book Three deals with the Bangladesh war of 1971, the Emergency and its aftermath. This is a darker and more political section than the other two. The narrative in this part becomes less digressive and the political satire more devastating. Saleem, with his dream of saving the nation from her fate, is drawn into the vortex of politics which crushes him and leaves him impotent and marginalized. Rushdie is highly critical of Indira Gandhi's authoritarian rule between 1975 and 1977 (metaphorically described as an 'endlessly prolonged midnight' [419]) because it irreparably damaged Indian reality and betrayed the country's secular-democratic ideals.[11] The hopes of the nation generated at the moment of Independence were drained with the castration of the midnight's children by Indira Gandhi, called the 'Black Widow,' and her sinister minions. Disillusioned and impotent, Saleem retires to the privacy of a pickle factory and decides to preserve ('chutnify') his version of India's history for future generation before his demise. Saleem's progress from unlimited optimism to disenchantment, from illusion of centrality to marginalization and impotence, which parallels the journey of independent India from an optimistic and vibrant nation to a despairing and comatose state, is a telling comment on the postcolonial history of the country. The title *Midnight's Children*, drawn from the hour of India's Independence on 15 August, 1947, suggests both the promise of a new future that the one thousand and one children symbolized and the failure of the post-Independence generation to fulfil that promise and realize their potential to build 'the noble mansion of free India, where all her children may dwell,' (118) as Nehru had famously said in his speech at that momentous hour. The freedom's children betrayed the idea of a unified and secular India with their confusion, internal rivalry, divisiveness and parochialism. Their story is, in fact, about these 'broken promises; made to be broken.' (439) Rushdie himself admitted in an interview (1985) that if the novel had any purpose, it was to "say that the thirty-two years between independence and the end of the book didn't add up to very much, that a kind of betrayal had taken place, and that the book was dealing with the nature of that betrayal."

Midnight's Children has been criticized in India for its despairing tone. It has been alleged that the book's description of India is pessimistic. Rushdie, however, repudiates the charge of pessimism, claiming that the novel's structure itself indicates a forward-looking attitude. The ending of Saleem's narrative is no doubt bleak suggesting the defeat of the human spirit but, Rushdie thinks, the last pages of the book hint at the emergence of a newer, tougher and more pragmatic generation (represented by Saleem's strong-willed son Aadam Sinai) who takes over from the children of midnight. Distancing himself from the point of view of the narrator-protagonist, he says:

> What I tried to do was to set up a tension in the text, a paradoxical opposition between the form and content of the narrative. The story of Saleem does indeed lead him to despair. But the story is told in a manner designed to echo . . . the Indian talent for non-stop self-regeneration. That is why the narrative throws up new stories, why it 'teems.' (*IH*, 16)

The novel's multitudinous form, suggesting the inexhaustible possibilities of the country for rejuvenation, thus, counterbalances Saleem's personal tragedy and its textual plenitude offsets his dismal view of India's political impoverishment and historical grotesquerie.

Another remarkable aspect of the book is its rare, almost Dickensian, combination of realistic background and surreal foreground. In the novels of Charles Dickens, the details of place and social mores are 'skewered' by an unrivalled and merciless realism. Upon this naturalistic canvas, he introduces his outsize characters in whom the readers have no choice but to believe because the characters are inextricable part of the world they live in. Similarly, in *Midnight's Children*, Rushdie sets against a meticulously observed socio-historical background—the canvas of 'real' India—his 'unrealist' notion of 'midnight's children' which serves as the springboard for fantasy in the novel. Born at the midnight hour of India's liberation from colonial rule, and gifted with magical powers by the coincidence, the 'children' embody 'both the hopes and flaws of that revolution.' (2002: 71)

Saleem presents his narrative from a secular point of view. His India, like that of his creator, is based on a non-sectarian philosophy. His repulsion for fanaticism and communal violence is expressed through various incidents in the novel. Aadam Aziz, who rejects the authority of his faith, throws a religious tutor out of his house for teaching bigotry and hatred to his children. Like his friends, Mian Abdullah and the Rani of Cooch Nahin—two idealized characters in the novel who contest politically the communal policies of the Muslim League—Dr. Aziz opposes the idea of Pakistan. Ahmed Sinai, whose business in Delhi is destroyed by a Hindu revivalist group before Partition, distrusts Jinnah and rejects the Land of the Pure in favour of Bombay. Amina, Saleem's mother, makes a public announcement of her pregnancy to save the life of a Hindu peep-show man from Muslim communalists. In spite of his Islamic background, Saleem is 'enough of a Bombayite to be well up in Hindu stories.' (149) He eclectically draws upon the multiplicity of the country's intermingled faiths and cultures which creates a secular ambience in the novel. 'Eclecticism, the ability to take from the world what seems fitting and to leave the rest, has always been,' Rushdie thinks, 'a hallmark of the Indian tradition.' (*IH*, 67) In *Midnight's Children*, he attempts to delineate the eclectic hybridity of the country through its multiple narrative heritage: Hindu myths and legends, Sufi metaphors, Christian and Islamic motifs, folklores, oral tales and elements of popular cultures like film and magic. The philosophy of Maya co-exists in Saleem's narrative with the stories of Prophet Muhammad and Jesus Christ. (211) Out of such mélange is born Rushdie's hybrid tale of India, the 'new myth' which he describes as a 'collective fiction.' (112) 'There are so many stories to tell,' remarks Saleem at the beginning of his autobiographical enterprise, 'too many, such an excess of intertwined lives events miracles places rumours.' (9) *Midnight's Children* itself becomes a complex figure for the plenitude of India and it reflects the impossibility for any linear and homogeneous form of narrative to capture the variegated reality of the country.

This inevitably draws one's attention to Rushdie's intertextuality, his use of both Oriental and Western texts in the novel. His indebtedness to *A Thousand and One Nights* has already been mentioned. Among the other inter-texts, which comprise the mixed heritage of *Midnight's Children*, the most remarkable are Laurence Sterne's *Tristram Shandy*, Gunter Grass's *The Tin Drum*, Gabriel Garcia Marquez's *One Hundred Years of Solitude* and Rudyard Kipling's *Kim*. Rushdie himself has acknowledged his debt to the first two books in an essay on Gunter Grass, describing them as his 'passports' to become the sort of writer he had it in himself to be. (*IH*, 276) His book shares not only the digressive self-reflexivity, humour and linguistic wildness of Sterne's novel but also the poststructural literary practice foreshadowed in it. Like Tristram, Saleem narrates a large portion of his personal and family history before he actually gets round to describing his own birth. *Midnight's Children* has been called 'an Indian *Tin Drum*' because of its numerous allusions to the German novel which Rushdie had read in 1967 at the age of twenty. Both Rushdie and Grass have a migrant's vision; both 'pickle' the past in their respective books and create a fictional universe which is symbolic of historical reality. Like *Kim*, Rushdie's novel celebrates the vertiginous diversity of the subcontinent. Saleem's India is, like Kim's, 'teeming' (Rushdie's term borrowed, significantly, from Kipling) with stories and profusion of life. Fantasy plays an important role in both the texts which are multi-voiced and speak through a babel of tongues. Rushdie's narrative technique—'Matter of fact descriptions of the outré and bizarre, and their reverse, namely heightened, stylized versions of the everyday' which create 'a picture of the world of startling uniformity' (218-19)—resembles the magic realism of Marquez in *One Hundred Years of Solitude*. Like Marquez, Rushdie models his story-telling on oral narration and deploys fantasy elements in his novel to talk about the reality of a country where incredible things happen constantly and quite plausibly and where the fantastic and the supernatural form an inextricable part of the lived human experience. Much of the magic effect of *Midnight's Children* derives from such Marquezean techniques as multiple fantasies, hyperboles, exaggeration, taking liberties with causality, with facts and chronology, and turning metaphors and symbols into the real things. But Rushdie adapts and embellishes these techniques for his particular needs and grounds his magic realism—his use of myth, memory and fantasy—in the larger context of the Indian view of reality. The closely-knit structure of multiple shorter narratives in *Midnight's Children* manifest a non-western, specifically Indian, form of non-mimetic narration. This form of narrativization, derived from the *Ramayana* and the *Mahabharata* (two important intertexts of Rushdie's novel), exemplifies what Raja Rao has aptly described, in his famous 'Foreword' to *Kanthapura*, as 'the characteristically Indian penchant for obsessive digressions and the telling of an interminable tale.'[12]

The interpenetration of multiple realities—the improbable and the mundane, the actual and the marvellous, past and present—within the textual confines of *Midnight's Children*, again, betokens an Indian 'urge to encapsulate the whole of reality.' (75) Saleem suffers, like Lifafa Das (74-75) and the painter friend of Nadir Khan (48-49), from this Indian mania to 'get the whole of life into his art.' His heterogeneous but subjectively coherent version of the events of his life does not thus exclude the world: 'To understand just one life, you have to swallow the world.' (109) This inclusive mode of writing, which disregards the arbitrary distinction between fact and fiction and stresses the interrelationship between the individual and the world around him, distinguishes *Midnight's Children* as an Indian work of art despite the wild profusion of its inheritance from the Western novel genre. The novel appropriates some ingredients of European novel, e.g. realism, psychology, law of causation, structural unity, satire and fantasy. But these are intermixed with some characteristically Indian features which Rushdie has highlighted on several occasions. He referred to the capacity of Indian oral story-tellers to draw huge crowds and arrest their undistracted attention and remarked that he had wanted to capture the feel of such oral performance in the book (*Kunapipi*, 1985, 1-19). The novel is infused with a sense of orality and Saleem's seemingly endless narrative with its digressions and metronomic swings through time and space, its analogy and repetition, corresponds to the form of the traditional oral tales. Saleem's story of modern India follows the structure of ancient Indian narratives, the epics and other popular collections like *Panchatantra* and *Kathasaritsagar*, in all of which a teller narrates his story to a listener/ group of listeners through a frame tale which usually describes how the various stories had come to be written. These seemingly endless tales, like Saleem's own stories in the novel, have a way of leaking into each other. They constantly transgress into the unreal—the bizarre and the fantastic—questioning thereby the very nature of reality.

Rushdie constantly invokes the mixed and pluralistic tradition of Indian culture which has a remarkable bearing on the novel. Saleem is a product of the truly hybrid Indian society. He is partly Hindu, partly Muslim and partly Christian, suggesting thereby the intermixing of various religions and cultures which make up the India Rushdie writes about. *Midnight's Children* marked a departure from the metaphysical (Hindu) world-view of earlier Indian English novelists like Raja Rao, R.K. Narayan, Sudhin Ghose and Arun Joshi who perceived Indian society as a homogeneous one. This was almost a paradigm shift which ushered in novels about individuals and families belonging to minority communities and marginalized groups in Indian English fiction. Saleem is, like Rushdie, familiar with Hindu myths which he interweaves with the thematic concerns of his autobiography. He incorporates a number of mythical characters and incidents in the text. There is an interplay between contemporary Indian reality and its mythical parallel in his narrative (for example, 'Kolynos Kid' and 'Commander Sabarmati's baton') and the characters often assume the identities of mythical archetypes. Both Saleem and his adoptive son Aadam are related to elephant-headed Ganesh for their gargantuan nose and enormous, flapping ears respectively. His arch-rival and destructive alter-ego Shiva represents the Hindu god of procreation and destruction who together with his consort Parvati creates a progeny. In *Midnight's Children,* myth 'functions as a kind of shorthand to convey concepts'; it is not 'elaborately worked out' (Goonetilleke, 19) as in Joyce's *Ulysses* and Eliot's *The Waste Land* which employ myth as a framework. Rushdie also significantly differs from writers like Narayan and Rao in his use of myth. Whereas these authors share the mythical consciousness of the people which tends to perceive the temporal in the light of the timeless, Rushdie does not participate in the myth-ridden world. He assumes a parodic stance towards his mythic material. His use of mythical allusions in the novel is playful and ironic in a postmodernist way. For example, Rushdie invokes Shiva in his destructive role, born to remove evil from the world. But in the book the most powerful child of midnight evolves into an evil force, determined to destroy Saleem for depriving him of his birthright. This is Rushdie's way of interpreting a myth: constantly playing on the meaning of words (as he does with the name of Padma), referring to the original associations of a myth but, in the process, turning it upside down.

Throughout his narrative Saleem gives numerous hints that his way of looking at the world is typically Indian. At a crucial point in his story ('Drainage and the desert'), he speaks of a 'national longing for form'; "As a people, we are obsessed with correspondences. Similarities between this and that, between apparently unconnected things, make us clap our hands delightedly when we find them out" (300). It is this overpowering desire for form that saves the novel from falling apart. The vast narrative, which encompasses the country's history over a period of sixty-three years, is held together by an elaborate pattern of interlocking metaphors and interlaced motifs which Rushdie calls a 'non-rational network of connections.' (1985: 6) The metaphor which is central to Rushdie's imaginative reconstruction of the country, is the metaphor of birth: that of the nation (India) and its body (Saleem). This organic metaphor equates Saleem with India herself. His face represents the whole map of India and he takes on in his person the joys and sorrows of the entire nation. The history of the country from Independence to Emergency is virtually written on Saleem's body and continuous parallels are drawn between the growth, maturity, decay and disintegration of the individual and the body-politic. The most important structural motif in the narrative is the relationship between Saleem and Padma—the narrator and the narratee. Padma is Saleem's reader-surrogate within the text and the purveyor of his pickle (Rushdie's metaphor for history). At once a character and a listener, she not only serves as an index of Saleem's narratorial successes and failures but also plays a significant role in the creation of his fictional universe. With her ignorance and superstition, her 'paradoxical earthiness of spirit' and constant demand for a linear narrative, Padma provides the 'necessary counterweights to [Saleem's] miracle-laden omniscience.' (150) She checks his wild flights of fancy and keeps his feet firmly on the ground, ensuring thereby the formal integrity and progression of the story. Her temporary departure from his narrative reduces it to the 'narrow one-dimensionality of a straight line.' (150) In response to the incessant queries of Padma, the spur and judge of his fictional autobiography, Saleem explains to her the art of constructing the novel. This is how Rushdie compels the reader to share his creative travails and increases his responsibility to understand the text. By continually focussing attention on its artifice—the very process of its construction—*Midnight's Children* becomes an allegory of artistic creation, a novel about writing a novel; in short, a metafiction.

The political events narrated in the book are symptomatic of the centrifugal pull of history. But throughout the novel Saleem strives to resist fragmentation—his own and the nation's—and provide a contrary current of inclusiveness by using narrative devices like chronological progression, analogy and parallelism, repetitive imagery, summaries of past events and previews of events to come. Certain key objects like the perforated bedsheet, the silver spittoon, the *Times of India* baby snap, Prime Minister Nehru's letter and the fisherman's pointing finger, which map out Saleem's memory of growing up with the newly independent nation, are recurrently used in the story and thus made to form a complex pattern of leit motifs which link persons and events wide apart in time and space. The narrative thrives on this dynamic of form and formlessness, drift and control, fragmentation and inclusiveness which generates an astonishing energy in the novel and accounts for its tremendous success.

Equally important are the dynamics of Rushdie's language in the novel. *Midnight's Children* has been praised for its innovative use of English as a creative medium. In fact, it is its language which has contributed, more than anything else, to the popularity as well as controversiality of the book. In his famous essay entitled 'The Empire Writes Back with a Vengeance,' (*London Times*, 3 July, 1982, 8) Rushdie wrote about the decolonizing of the English language by writers like Chinua Achebe, Ngugi wa Thiong'o, Derek Walcott, Raja Rao and G.V. Desani. These writers have, like him, loosened English from its colonial past and forged it 'into new shapes' as they have moulded the formal shape of the European novel to indigenous realities. G.V. Desani (whose influence on his work Rushdie acknowledges), for example, has shown in *All about H. Hatterr* (1948) 'how English could be bent and kneaded until it spoke in an authentically Indian voice.' The disruption of English in Desani's novel is an exemplary gesture of defiance, on the part of a postcolonial writer, towards the cultural superiority of the West. Published in the year following India's emancipation from British rule, *All about H. Hatterr*, with its 'rigmarole English' (Desani, 37), provides Rushdie with a model for a linguistically hybrid text. Rushdie makes a claim (in 'Imaginary Homelands') to conquer English postcolonially by reformulating the language and using it innovatively, even subversively. English is 'conquered,' he writes in this seminal essay, by acculturation. In

Midnight's Children he has tried to indigenize English by subjecting it to a process of verbal and syntactic dislocation and adapting native idioms and cultural referents. What he has done, like Desani, is to 'break up the language and put it back together in a different way . . . to dislocate English and let other things into it.' (qtd. in Goonetilleke, 43) This disruption/subversion through infiltration as a strategy for decolonizing English is reflected in the diction and syntax of Rushdie's language. He frequently incorporates Hindustani (Hindi and Urdu) words, phrases and collocations into his flawless English sentences (e.g. 'angrez,' 'baba,' 'chamcha,' 'duniya,' 'ekdam,' 'feringhee,' 'godam,' 'hai hai,' 'jehad,' 'khichri,' 'lassi,' 'muhalla,' 'sab-kuch,' 'talaaq,' 'yaar,' 'zenana' etc.). Such audacious mixing of English and indigenous lexical items results in a creative hybridization that defies the purity of the imperial language. Rushdie's 'chutnification' of the narrative medium is also illustrated by other devices, such as: (a) transliteration of vernacular idioms (e.g., 'donkey from somewhere,' 'madman from somewhere' etc.); (b) invention of new forms of existing English words and Indian lexical items (e.g., 'writeri,' 'doctori,' 'unbeautiful,' 'dupattaless,' 'chutnification' etc.); (c) translation of Indian concepts into corresponding English expressions (e.g., 'piece-of-the-moon,' 'four hundred and twenty,' 'whatnextism' etc.); (d) linking a vernacular and an English word to form a phrase ('hennaing ceremony') or a name ('Picture Singh') and (e) introduction of nonsense neologisms (e.g., 'tea-cup-kissery,' 'funtoosh'), back-up words ('club-slub,' 'joke-shoke,' 'writery-shitery' etc.) and habitual linguistic mannerism ('whatsitsname'). The novel's syntax also evinces similar disruptiveness. There are sudden, dramatic changes of tense (e.g., 'night is falling has fallen,' 'we were are shall be the gods you never had' etc.) and person ('the boy soldiers waited for the man-dog to die; but I was stronger than the snake-poison') and abrupt shift from direct to reported speech and vice versa in a single sentence. Like Desani, Rushdie strings together groups of nouns, adjectives and verbs for the sake of emphasis and joins unpunctuated words to give the narrative greater fluency. Again, the surfeit of punctuation marks (dots, dashes, commas, hyphens, colons, capitals, etc.), which Rushdie, following G.V. Desani and Laurence Sterne, introduces in his syntax, is a deliberate attempt to disrupt the natural rhythms of the English language and represent certain aspects of Indian speech in written form. Disruption also takes place at the level of narrative voice. Saleem's story constantly negotiates between different registers, between high and low voices, elite and mass cultures. The gossip of the spittoon-hitters in Agra and the susurrus of the Bombay crowd are intermingled with advertising doggerel ('Keep Teeth Kleen And Keep Teeth Brite, Keep Teeth Kolynos Super White' [240]), quotations from religious and filmic texts, newspaper reports and the street trader's lingo. One hears a noise of voices speaking through narrator Saleem. The resulting polyphony has induced many poststructuralist critics to see in the text an illustration of the dialogic quality espoused by Mikhail Bakhtin.

All these are not mere literary pyrotechnics or linguistic gymnastics, as it is often alleged. They form parts of a conscious anti-colonial strategy: adulteration of 'proper' i.e. colonial English with the tempo and cadences of Indian speech so that the measured sound of the imperial language is accented in the text through an unrecognizable babel of native tongues. Like Raja Rao, he tries to filter Indian speech rhythms into 'alien' English in order to 'reflect the spirit that is one's own.'[13] The deployment of linguistic hybridity in the novel is also an attempt to forge a multi-lingual medium for evoking the complex, polyglossic and multi-cultural reality of India which no single language can adequately represent. But Rushdie's success in conquering English through acculturation is not beyond question. It has been argued that his bi-lingualism is playful but superficial; it lacks 'any complex meditative or mediative engagement between two languages and cultures,'[14] which one finds in the novels of Raja Rao, R.K. Narayan and G.V. Desani. Since most of the Hindustani words, used in the text as a badge of authenticity or native informancy, are immediately translated or parenthetically explicated in English, this bi-lingual strategy does not work for an Indian reader who is proficient in both the languages. It is true that the transcription of nuances and idioms of the native tongues into English is, to some extent, an exercise in artificiality, even redundancy. But Rushdie has shown a way, through his own experiment in *Midnight's Children*, to give these languages a convincing imaginative presence. His unapologetic exuberance has enthused a whole generation of Indian writers in English—known as the post-Rushdie generation—to use the language with more confidence and ease and with less echo of the Empire. At once a celebration and an elegy of India and her pluralistic culture, this trailblazing novel remains, with its multifoliate texture and innovative style, a source of inspiration as well as a challenge to future novelists to emulate its success.

NOTES

1. Salman Rushdie, *Imaginary Homelands: Essays and Criticism 1981-1991* (London: Granta, 1991), pp. 10-12.
2. William Walsh, "India and the Novel," *The New Pelican Guide to English Literature*, ed. Boris Ford (Penguin, 1983), p. 257.
3. Salman Rushdie, *Midnight's Children* (London: Picador, 1981), p. 308.
4. Rushdie records the traumatic experience in the second section, called 'Messages from the Plague Years,' of his recently published book *Step across this Line: Collected Non-Fiction 1992-2002* (London: Jonathan Cape, 2002), pp. 229-83.
5. Qtd. Sanjoy Iyer in 'East, West: No Home is Best,' *Indian Review of Books*, vol. 4, No. 3, 16 January-15 February 1995), p. 2.
6. 'Free At Last,' Salman Rushdie's interview with Shravani Basu, *Sunday*, 11-17 October, 1998.
7. 'My Real Prize is India,' Salman Rushdie's interview with Swapan Dasgupta and Ashok Malik, *India Today* (May 1, 2000), pp. 71-74.
8. Swapan Dasgupta, 'Return to Eden,' *India Today*, 1 May 2000, p. 71.
9. M.L. Pandit, 'An Interview with Salman Rushdie,' *New Commonwealth Writing* (New Delhi: Prestige, 1996), p. 44.
10. Rani Dharkar, 'An Interview with Salman Rushdie,' *New Quest*, 42 (November-December 1983), p. 351.
11. Rushdie's views on the excesses of Emergency are depressing. He represents Indira's unmitigated villainy in misogynistic terms. No

wonder that *Midnight's Children* provoked the anger of Nehru's daughter who brought and won a libel suit against the author. Some offending remarks were expunged from the novel.

12. Aijaz Ahmad, 'Salman Rushdie's *Shame*,' *In Theory*: *Classes, Nations, Literatures* (Bombay: Oxford University Press, 1992), p. 126.
13. Raja Rao, Foreword to *Kanthapura* (Delhi: Orient, 1971), p. 5.
14. Harish Trivedi, 'Salman the Funtoosh: Magic Bilingualism in *Midnight's Children*,' *Rushdie's 'Midnight's Children': A Book of Readings*, ed. Meenakshi Mukherjee (Delhi: Pencraft International, 1999), p. 86.

Midnight's Children: The Text

TAPAN KUMAR GHOSH
University of Burdwan

Midnight's Children is a sprawling novel with an epic sweep that extends in time and space. It covers six decades (1915-1977) and the whole sub-continent and its history. The book has a tripartite structure—of eight, fifteen and seven chapters. The chapters, which correspond to the pickle jars arranged on the shelf in Saleem's room in Braganza Pickle Factory where he writes down his experience while supervising large-scale production of condiments, add up to thirty—Saleem's age when he completes his narrative. Each chapter has an appropriate title which symbolically captures a key object or a situation. Book One covers the time from Jallianwala Bagh massacre (1919) to the birth of the narrator protagonist on the fateful midnight of August 15, 1947. Book Two ends with the Indo-Pakistani War in September, 1965. Book Three carries the narrative forward to the end of the Emergency rule in March 1977 and the electoral defeat of Indira Gandhi. Within this time span, the narrative encompasses the vertiginous kaleidoscope of India, the country's multitudinous opulence of life and variegatedness of culture, her anti-colonial struggle and the colonial aftermath.

Chapter I: The perforated sheet

The book opens with Saleem's declaration of his celebrated moment of arrival, the coincidence of his synchronic birth with the new nation at the stroke of midnight hour on August 15, 1947. The opening paragraph, with its fairy-tale beginning, firmly establishes the reordination of time and character, history and individual and sets up the style. The book links individual history with the larger, episodic account of the nation's roller-coaster progress towards adulthood and presents it in the vein of magic realism. Right from the beginning, Saleem is conscious of his historical centrality: "I had been mysteriously handcuffed to history, my destinies indissolubly chained to those of my country." (9) This grandiloquent claim—itself a comic inversion of the relationship between individual and history—provides the central metaphor of the novel and its basic premise that the accident of the protagonist's birth made him analogous to the newly independent nation of India and inextricably chained his destiny to the history of the country. Saleem's narrative is at once an account of his own life and a mirror of the life of India. This device of interlocking the destinies of individual and the nation through the process of zeugmatic synchronicity not only solves the problem of form but also supplies the novelist the structural base from which his tragi-comic hero launches into interlacing planes of fact and fancy, history and fantasy. Saleem is aware that it is 'a dangerous sort of involvement' (9) but with his tremendous imaginative feat he turns this danger into an advantage. The narrative is held together by Saleem's search for meaning and form. Making sense of his life with all its complexities assumes the proportion of life and death struggle. His prophetic awareness of his impending demise spurs him on to reach toward the meaning of his life; 'I must work fast, faster than Scheherazade, if I am to end up meaning—yes, meaning—something.' (9) He narrates because he is afraid of absurdity. *Midnight's Children* begins and ends with explicit references to Scheherazade's tales. *A Thousand and One Nights* provides Saleem with the organizing principle of his narrative—physical self-preservation and justification by story-telling. Like the imperilled Princess, he tells his story within a frame narrative to a clearly delineated listener who serves as a reader-surrogate and a continuous reminder of the present tense of the narrating time. As narrator Saleem realizes that his life as protagonist consists in 'an excess of intertwined lives, events, miracles, places, rumours, so dense a commingling of the improbable and the mundane' (9) from which, with the help of memory and imagination, he will have to reconstruct the farm of his life. He admits that his narrative will be a promiscuous blend of various kinds of stories and narrative modes and it will unfold in series of episodes spiced with myths and legends, gossips and rumours.

The chapter begins with an announcement of Saleem's portentous birth and then travels back in time to the story of his, and his family's, origin in Kashmir. Saleem starts remaking his life with random shards of memory from the point it actually began, thirty two years before his 'clock ridden, crime-stained birth,' (10) with the story of his grandfather, Aadam Aziz. Aziz—named after the nationalist Indian in Forster's *A Passage to India*—embodies Saleem's origin. He was a Western educated and progressive Kashmiri who rejected ancestral ways in favour of modernity. Son of a gemstone merchant, Aadam had spent five years in Germany to study medicine. His German experience, particularly the association with his anarchist friends, upset his Islamic and Indian presuppositions. At the same time they distanced him with their orientalist notions that "India—like radium—had been 'discovered' by the Europeans . . . that he was somehow the invention of their ancestors." (11) He returned home with a void in his head—Europe had unsettled his faith in his place of origin and his religion. The void soon changed into a space for desire; he became 'vulnerable to women and history.' (10) During his absence from Kashmir, Aadam's father had suffered a stroke which severely affected his brain. His mother, a traditional housewife who had spent her life in purdah, was compelled to go out of home and run the family business which put Aziz through medical college. His stay in Germany had altered his vision but on his return Aziz made an attempt to re-unite himself with his earlier self which ignored the European influence. But the attempt suffered a setback after an accident at prayer-time (10) which drew blood from his legendary nose and led to his loss of faith in the family religion of Islam. Dr. Aziz 'resolved never again to kiss earth for any god or man.' (10) The decision created a permanent hole in him, 'a vacancy in a vital inner chamber.' (10) The years in Germany returned Aziz to a hostile environment. The progressive doctor's home-coming was looked upon as evil intrusion into paradisal Kashmir by boatman Tai who represented that part of India which was changeless. To Tai, Aziz's pigskin briefcase that

Aziz's pigskin briefcase that contained his medical equipments, represented 'an alien invader, progress.' (19) A 'living antithesis' of the belief of Aziz's German friends in 'the inevitability of change,' (15) Tai was a 'quirky, enduring familiar spirit of the valley. A watery Caliban, rather too fond of cheap Kashmiri brandy.' (15) His brandy induced magical chatter which was fantastic and ceaseless and which interwove, like Saleem's own narrative, history, fable, myth and imagination, used to leave Aadam spell-bound in his boyhood days. He insisted on possessing an antiquity which defied both logic and numbering. Boatman Tai claimed not only to have seen Jesus Christ on his supposed visit to Kashmir but also to have transcended time and history; 'I have watched the mountains being born; I have seen emperors die.' (16) Tai epitomized an oriental world-view. His view of an ageless, changeless, organic cosmos was lost by his protégé Aadam whose Western education had dispossessed him of his faith, replacing it with a belief in material science and history. His Kashmir stood for wholeness as against Aziz's—and later Saleem's—fragmented world-view. The character of Tai provided a symbol, and a moral framework for the subsequent periods of strife, bloodshed and fragmentation that the novel encapsulates. It was Tai who, on the morning of Aziz's prayer-time accident in the spring of 1915, brought from the blind landowner Ghani an urgent summons which set history in motion and catapulted the Heidelberg-returned doctor into his future. Ghani's nubile daughter, Naseem, had fallen sick and Tai came to ferry his earlier protégé to the wily landowner's house, to the strange tableau of the perforated sheet which would alter his life. Naseem, being a decent girl from a conservative family, would not flaunt her body under the noses of strangers. Hence the doctor—with a hole in him waiting to be filled—was obliged to examine his patient in segments through the perforated centre of a white bed-sheet held over her by two enormous women.

Chapter II: Mercurochrome

Padma, Saleem's interlocutrix, is introduced. Plump, strong, jolly and down-to-earth, Padma, who is 'named after the lotus goddess,' (24) works in the Pickle Factory managed by Saleem. Apart from giving Saleem's story a necessary ear, she looks after his more mundane needs—'a consolation for my last days,' (24) as Saleem admits. The narrative thread is picked up in the second paragraph as Saleem, ignoring Padma's attempt to distract him returns to the story of his grandfather which he left 'hanging in mid-air—just as Scheherazade, depending for her very survival on leaving Prince Shahryar eaten up by curiosity, used to do night after night,' (24) Aadam Aziz had fallen under the spell of the perforated sheet and the patient behind it, much to the resentment of his mother who construed the whole thing as landowner Ghani's clever ploy to trap the promising doctor into marriage with his daughter. Because in those days Naseem Ghani suffered from an extraordinary number of ailments and each time the young doctor was summoned to treat her. On each occasion he was allowed a partial glimpse, through the perforated sheet, of the young woman's body. Aziz's prolonged treatment of his invisible patient coincided with World War I: 'Far away the Great War moved from crisis to crisis. While in the cobwebbed house [of Ghani] Dr. Aziz was also engaged in a total war against his sectioned patient's inexhaustible complaints.' (25) As he treated her in parts, he began to imagine her as whole. This synecdochic process of discovering a woman's body led to Aziz's reintegration. With the imaginative construction of the partitioned patient over the years, Aziz 'had fallen in love, and had come to think of the perforated sheet as something sacred and magical' (27) because the sheet had permitted him glimpses of things which filled up the hole in him created by his loss of religious faith. On the day the World War ended (in 1918), Naseem developed a headache which Aziz had longed for with an almost illicit desperation because it would allow him a glimpse of his patient's face. ('Such historical coincidences,' Saleem says, 'have littered, and perhaps befouled, [his] family's existence in the world.' [27]) The mutual look of the doctor and the patient put an end to the charade of the sheet and completed Aziz's 'fall.' In the meantime, boatman Tai had inexplicably stopped cleaning his body and washing his clothes as a 'gesture of unchangingness in defiance of the invasion of the doctori-attaché from Heidelberg.' (28) The malodorous fumes of his body killed the flowers in the valley and drove away all its birds. He lost work and contracted a skin disease (King's Evil) of which he would be cured only after the doctor left the valley. In 1918, when the Indian regiments returned home from the War, Aziz's parents died in quick succession, leaving him orphaned but free. He landed a job as the doctor of Agra University and married Naseem Ghani whom he had discovered and loved in parts. His wedding dowry included, apart from a large sum of money, a perforated sheet—stained with three drops of blood after marriage—which would condemn his family to a life of fragments. When the newly married doctor left Kashmir for India, he had the feeling of a Fall, a loss of Eden. Banished by Tai from changeless Kashmir, he entered the linear narrative of colonial India.

After a brief interruption by enraged Padma who takes umbrage at Saleem's light-hearted remarks about her name ('Dung Goddess') and whom he placates by a mock-serious paean to dung, the narrative shifts to April 6, 1919 in the holy city of Amritsar where Dr. Aziz and his newly married wife were stranded, on their way to Agra, due to political agitation. It was India in the heyday of Gandhian nationalism and the people all over the country were observing, in obeyance of his call, 'hartal'—a day of mourning—as a protest against the infamous Rowlatt Act. Aziz, with Tai in his head, still did not feel Indian—Kashmir being an independent princely state was not part of the British India—and he was not sure whether the protest against the colonizers was his fight also. But he could not ignore the overwhelming pull of Indian nationalism: "Doctor Aziz notices a soldierly young man in the street, and thinks—the Indians have fought for the British; so many of them have seen the world by now, and been tainted by Abroad. They will not easily go back to the old world. The British are wrong to try and turn back the clock." (33) Even as Aziz was forging his national identity from the regional by his participation in the anti-colonial protest, his wife Naseem—exposed to the multiplicity of the Indian subcontinent—struggled between traditional inhibitions and the demands of secular modernity that her husband made on her by his exhortation to her to come out of purdah and behave like a modern woman: "This was a struggle my grandfather never won; and it set the tone for their marriage, which rapidly developed into a place of frequent and devastating warfare." (34) In exasperation, the progressive doctor dragged all her purdah-veils and set fire to them saying: 'Forget about being a good Kashmiri girl. Start thinking about being a modern Indian woman.' (34) Meanwhile Mahatma Gandhi's design of non-violent protest against British rule was subverted by rioting mobs who ransacked shops and railway stations leading to the imposition of Martial Law. Dr. Aziz, leather bag in hand, roamed the streets, bandaging wounded people and disinfecting them with mercurochrome, red medicine which looked like real blood. Mercurochrome became a metaphor of the real blood shed in inhuman violence inflicted on thousands of peaceful demonstrators in Jallianwala Bagh by Brigadier Dyer and his fifty soldiers on 13 April, 1919. The prosaic, unemotional description of the incident brings out the callousness of the British towards the Indians: "Brigadier Dyer's fifty men put down their machine-guns and go away. They have fired a total of one thousand six hundred and fifty rounds into the unarmed crowd. . . . 'Good shooting,' Dyer tells his men, 'We have done a jolly good thing'." (36) The deliberate killing of innocent people and the total lack of human feelings on Dyer's part evoke indignation against the colonial rule. The blood that flowed in Jallianwala Bagh on that ill-fated day was the blood of sacrifice that baptized Aziz who witnessed the infernal massacre and received a severe bruise on the chest which would not fade until after his death. The event infused him with patriotic feelings and made him Indian. It filled the space in his heart, left empty by his loss of religious faith, with the new faith of nationalism. Unlike Tai, the boatman, who had wanted Kashmir to retain its separate identity and remain free of all political/ historical affiliations to either India or Pakistan and who would be killed in 1947 while fighting all alone against Indian and Pakistani armies marching into the valley, Aziz threw in his lot with India and embraced Indian nationalism and secular ideal.

Chapter III: *Hit-the-Spittoon*

The chapter begins with Saleem's admission of his disintegration. Having been 'buffeted by too much history, subjected to drainage above and drainage below,' (37) his body is falling apart. This disintegration, which is slow at first, accelerates with the progress of the tale until he crumbles into 'six hundred and thirty million particles of anonymous dust.' (37) It is this apprehension of his eventual demise that compels him to recollect and record his history. Saleem, who possesses a rare 'mastery of the multiple gifts of cookery and language,' (38) spends his latter days in the pickle factory preserving condiments and memory. During day-time he supervises large scale preparation of pickles and through his nocturnal scribbling he preserves his memory from the corruption of time for his amnesiac nation. Whenever he appears to digress, Padma, his fellow purveyor of pickle and the conduit for his narrative, pulls him up and keeps his tale on track by her demand for 'linear narrative.' (38) The tension between Padma's desire to know 'what happened next,' (38) which is routinely satisfied by periodic previews of events to come, and Saleem's need to digress propels the narrative. Saleem, confident of his virtuosity as a storyteller and his ability to keep Padma on the tenterhooks, explains to her that he must go back two generations to tell his own story because 'the past has dripped into [him]. . . . So [he] can't ignore it' (38) just as he cannot ignore Mian Abdullah, the doomed Hummingbird, and Nadir Khan, the rhymeless poet and impotent idealist, who made an important contribution to his narrative. The story leaps forward to 1942, the year of the Quit India movement (as the narrative space shifts to Agra where Saleem's grandparents had settled) to narrate the tragedy of nationalist Muslims who opposed the Partition and a separate Muslim state, and whose hope of a unified India, based on the concept of plurality and religious tolerance, was foiled by the colonial policy of divide and rule and the communal politics of the Muslim League. In the late summer of that year a highly infectious 'optimism disease' broke out all over India despite a severe drought and a World War. The 'optimism epidemic' (40) was caused by an individual named Mian Abdullah, popularly known as the Hummingbird because of his strange habit of humming without pause (symbolizing the joyful ecstasy in his work). He had emerged from the magicians' ghetto in Delhi to become the hope of millions of India's Muslims. He had almost single-handedly united dozens of Muslim groups, representing widely varying social strata, into 'a loosely federated alternative to the dogmatism and vested interests of the [Muslim] Leaguers.' (46) His party, named Free Islam Convocation, opposed the idea of Pakistan. The second convocation of the party was to be held in Agra in the summer of 1942. Aadam Aziz, like thousands of nationalist Muslims, was infected by the optimism of Mian Abdullah. With his deep-seated distrust of religious bigotry he whole-heartedly supported the Hummingbird's cause. As he told Abdullah's benefactress and his friend, the Rani of Cooch Nahin (an intralinguistic pun meaning the Queen of Nothing after the real queen of Cooch Behar, a princely state): "I started off as a Kashmiri and not much of a Muslim. Then I got a bruise on the chest that turned me into an Indian. I'm still not much of a Muslim, but I'm all for Abdullah. He's fighting my fight." (46) Aziz, now fifty, was himself fighting a losing battle at the home front. His conjugal life had long turned into a site for devastating warfare with gradual estrangement of the husband and the wife. Naseem, whom he had loved in parts and imagined as a whole, eventually transformed into an altogether different being. She emerged as the stronger partner in the relationship, defying her husband's desires by becoming fat and refusing to do his sexual biddings. She had become a pre-maturely old woman and come to be known as 'Reverend Mother.' Having been forced to live in unveiled shamelessness, Naseem had barricaded herself within 'an ironclad citadel of traditions and certainties' (40) where politics and progress were denied entry. They had five children: three girls—Alia, Mumtaz and Emerald—and two sons—Hanif and Mustapha. Ten years earlier, Aziz had taken upon himself the control of the children's education. He taught them foreign languages and instilled in them his liberal, progressive ideas. To balance this, Naseem made one educational stipulation: religious instruction. One day he overheard the children being taught bigotry and hatred and threw the maulvi out of his house. Horrified by her husband's blasphemous act, she retaliated by denying him food. But Aziz stood by his decision even to the point of starvation. Having failed to storm her fortress, Aziz left Naseem alone to rule her domain and turned to politics. He preferred the company of the Rani of Cooch Nahin and her 'brilliant circle of friends' (47) who were secular and cosmopolitan in their attitudes. The Rani herself suffered from pigmentation disorder (her skin went white in blotches) which she humorously explained as 'the outward expression of the internationalism of [her] spirit' (45) and her 'cross-cultural concerns.' (45) It was here that Aziz met the Hummingbird and his personal secretary, Nadir Khan, a rhymeless poet who, like his boss, hated the Muslim League. They discussed politics and poetry and played the commoners' game of 'hit-the-spittoon.'

Much of what happens in this chapter is narrated in the language of gossip, rumour and everyday talk of common people—old superstitious men at pan-shops who chewed betel leaf and practised the nawabi game of hitting the spittoon with betel juice (which gives the chapter its title). Gossip is, like fantasy, a subversive medium which provides an alternative view of history. The official history of the country remains silent about the tragedy of nationalist Muslims and highlights Muslim League as the sole representative of Indian Muslims before Independence. The memory of those Muslims who supported a secular state and rejected partition has been 'swept under the carpet.' (48) Saleem, thus, depends more on legends and gossips than on officially certified facts ('Sometimes legends make reality,' he says [47]) to record this unwritten episode in India's anti-colonial struggle and to narrate how Mian Abdullah was murdered by unknown assassins a few days before the second convocation of his party in Agra, a Muslim League stronghold. The Rabelaisian manner in which Saleem describes the atrocious incident reveals the fantastic and the grotesque inherent in the actual: 'Six new moons came into the room, six crescent knives held by men dressed all in black, with covered faces. Two men held Nadir

Khan while the others moved towards the Hummingbird.' (47) The high-pitched hum of Mian Abdullah shattered the glass windows of his office, a glass eye of a killer and was heard by thousands of pie-dogs who rushed to the spot and tore the murderers into pieces. Nadir Khan managed to escape and fled to hide in a cellar under the carpet in Aziz's house. The legacy of the Hummingbird provides Saleem with two important narrative threads which lead to the heart of his story: 'the thread that leads to the ghetto of the magicians; and the thread that tells the story of Nadir the rhymeless, verbless poet and a priceless silver spittoon.' (45)

Chapter IV: Under the carpet

This chapter is a straightforward continuation of the narrative without any digression. Saleem, eager to trace his origin and parentage, flouts 'the halal portions of the past' (59) to record the unspeakable part of family as well as national history which has been swept under the carpet. The 'optimism disease' was cured by the violent shock of disillusionment. The gruesome murder of the Hummingbird put an end to the hope of a unified, secular nation. The Rani of Cooch Nahin took to her bed. Doctor Aziz, terribly shaken by the unexpected turn of events, immersed himself in his work, taking upon himself the care of the sick and the dispossessed. Nadir Khan, Abdullah's lieutenant, fled from the assassins and with the help of Rashid, a rickshaw boy, secured asylum in the basement of Aziz's house.[1] His request for sanctuary was granted by Aziz, thus precipitating a storm in the family. Aadam Aziz resolved to hide the mortally afraid optimist in the underground cellar defying his wife's objections to giving shelter to a man in the house which was 'full of young unmarried girls.' (53) In protest, Reverend Mother sealed her lips curtailing communication through determined muteness. A grim silence descended upon the house filling it 'from wall to wall, from floor to ceiling' (53) leaving all its inhabitants including the fugitive tongue-tied. But in that 'bog of muteness' (54) in the house where 'life [had] been transmuted into grotesquery by the irruption into it of history,' (57) romance burgeoned. Major Zulfikar, an unattractive army officer with a future, called on Doctor Aziz to tie up a few loose ends of Abdullah's murder and fell in love with Emerald, the youngest but the most beautiful and precocious of the three Aziz sisters popularly known as the 'Teen Batti.' Emerald, not yet fifteen but with an impossibly adult gaze in her eyes, understood Zulfikar's future, and despite his ungainly appearance, agreed to marry him. Alia, the eldest (she was twenty-one) and most brilliant of the Aziz sisters, was wooed, during that 'marshy time without words,' (54) by a young leather cloth merchant, Ahmed Sinai. Ahmed, who had been divorced at twenty, met Alia at the university and seemed intelligent enough for the grave and bookish girl. Everyone expected him to propose Alia but the profound silence in the house seemed to infect him too and he could not ask for her hand. Mumtaz, Dr. Aziz's nineteen-year-old second daughter, also fell in love. Mumtaz, whom her mother could never love because of her dark complexion, was neither intelligent like Alia nor beautiful like Emerald. But she was good, dutiful and lonely. Her gifts of tenderness, care and assiduity endeared her to her father. Mumtaz took upon herself the duty of looking after the needs of their guest under the carpet. Everyday she descended into the cellar to carry his food and clean his latrine, and in murkiness of the underworld she was courted by the long-haired, rhymeless bard whom her father's persuasions had failed to bring overground. Nadir Khan asked Dr. Aziz for his daughter's hand, more as a bargain for his safe refuge. In the summer of 1943, Mumtaz married Nadir in a secret ceremony, which was attended by the family members except the mother who had 'chosen to remain immured in her room with her web of silence,' (57) and started living a strange, double life. During day-time she was a single girl living with her parents and studying at the University. But at night she descended into her marriage chamber which her husband fancifully called Taj Mahal. In the lamplit seclusion of the subterranean Taj the couple played an ancient game with a silver spittoon which the dying Rani of Cooch Nahin had sent them as a wedding gift. Meanwhile the Reverend Mother began to swell under the pressure of unspoken words and the dumb house of the

Azizes, 'infected with the listlessness of the times,' (59) drifted to August 1945 when things dramatically changed. In August 1945, the Rani of Cooch Nahin took leave of the world amid torrential rain, bequeathing Saleem's story a silver spittoon. Also in August, when Subhas Chandra Bose's Indian National Army was fighting a pitched battle with the British soldiers in rain-soaked Burmese forests and the Satyagrahis in India were staging non-violent demonstrations against the retreating power of the Raj, Mumtaz fell seriously ill in her damp, underground cellar. A physical check-up by Dr. Aziz revealed that his daughter's two-year-long tryst with Nadir Khan had remained unconsummated, that the impotent idealist had failed to hit her spittoon and redeem his pledge. The shocking revelation led to the explosion of Reverend Mother whose pent-up words burst in a storm over her embarrassed husband. While she was pouring out her long-suppressed grievances against her husband whom she held responsible for her daughter's plight, Emerald ran unveiled to Major Zulfikar to divulge the carefully guarded family secret. On that day (9 August 1945), when America was dropping an unheard-of weapon on Japan, Emerald used her secret weapon, Zulfikar (whose name meant the two-pronged sword used by Prophet Mohammed's nephew, Ali), against the 'fountainhead of her family's troubles.' (61) Nadir Khan successfully eluded Zulfikar and his soldiers, leaving a message of divorce. In January 1946, when the storm subsided, Major Zulfikar married Emerald. In the meantime, Ahmed Sinai had discovered in newly divorced Mumtaz a kindred spirit. Mumtaz stole her sister's fiancé and in June that year married him. Ahmed reinvented Mumtaz who became Amina for him. The newly married Sinais shifted to Delhi to make a fresh start, leaving behind a sad, embittered Alia who felt 'bruised even more badly than her father in Jallianwala Bagh.' (64)

Chapter V: A public announcement

From her unproductive tryst with the impotent idealist in the cellar under the carpet Amina, re-invented by Ahmed Sinai, resurfaced as wife and mother-to-be in the communally charged atmosphere of pre-Partition Delhi to make a public announcement of her motherhood. Amid the grinding of historical machineries forcing events toward the inevitable finale of the colonial rule and the birth of a new nation—the failure of the Cabinet Mission to implement its scheme for the transfer of power that paved the way for the last viceroy, Earl Mountbatten, who would appear shortly (invested with 'plenipotentiary powers' and a soldier's knife to vivisect the sub-continent)—Amina had journeyed with her new husband to old Delhi to settle down in life.

After a brief interruption by Padma—a listener to Saleem's autobiographical past but a witness to his corporeal self and narratorial present—who gets irritated whenever Saleem's narration becomes 'self-conscious' and who, being alarmed by his references to his cracks, calls in a quack to have him examined (the physician finds no cracks and declares him whole but casts doubts on the stability of his mind and, thus, on his 'reliability as a witness' [65]), the story picks up the narrative thread to describe Amina's new life as Ahmed's wife. With her gifts of assiduity, forbearance and meticulous care, she transformed the orphan's dwelling of Ahmed Sinai into 'something gentle and loving.' (67) Though Amina, with her mind still clogged up with the memory of Nadir Khan, could not give her husband unquestioning devotion, she began to train herself to love him. In the process, she fell victim to the legacy of her father—the fragmentation of the perforated sheet. Since she was unable to love her husband in full, she assiduously learned to love the different parts of him separately, to love him in segments: 'she resolved to fall in love with her husband bit by bit.' (68) Under the magic influence of her painstaking care with which she effected transformation in Ahmed's life and which helped her in her stupendous task of accepting and loving him in fragments, Ahmed came to resemble—and to live in a place that resembled—'a man he had never known and an underground chamber he had never seen.' (68-69) Meanwhile, in the geographical space of Delhi national unity and the liberal, secular ideals, espoused by Aadam Aziz and his optimist friends, were being threatened by the anarchic forces manifested in the form of religious fanaticism and pre-Partition communal violence. Ahmed's own business became a prey to the ravages of racial hatred. Ahmed, who was doing well in his leather-cloth business with the help of Major Zulfikar (now a highly placed military officer in Delhi), shared a go-down with two other Muslim businessmen, Mustapha Kemal and S.P. Butt (two grotesquely drawn characters) at the industrial estate on the outskirts of the city. On a January morning in 1947, when Amina was preparing to reveal the secret of her pregnancy to her husband, Ahmed received from Butt and Kemal the horrible information of arson in the industrial estate. The outrage had been perpetrated by a fanatical Hindu-revivalist group named (after the many-headed puranic demon-king) 'the Ravana gang' which terrorized and blackmailed Muslim businessmen and burnt down their factories and shops if they failed to give it protection money. When the three businessmen left in panic for their warehouse leaving Amina with her undisclosed secret behind, a peep-show man named Lifafa Das arrived at the scene in the Muslim neighbourhood near Chandni Chowk (where the Sinai house was situated) to precipitate the annunciation of Saleem which gives the episode its title. Lifafa Das, a non-descript Hindu youth with a beautiful smile, used to frequent the Muslim neighbourhood with his mobile 'Dunia dekho' machine. By the magical rattle of his 'dugdugee' he attracted children as well as grown-ups into the street to show them the collage of a unified India: 'Inside the peepshow . . . were pictures of the Taj Mahal, and Meenakṣhi Temple, and the holy Ganges . . . untouchables being touched, educated persons sleeping in large numbers on railway lines.' (75) Lifafa Das seemed to suffer, like a painter friend of Nadir Khan (48-49), from the strange Indian urge 'to encapsulate the whole of reality.' (75) He stuffed his magic box with more and more pictures to make good his promise to the customers to show the whole world. He posed an image of unity and harmony. On that ill-fated morning, a petty quarrel among a group of children about who should put his/her eyes first at the hole in his peepshow box turned communal as the 'insanity' and 'disjointed unreality of the times' (76) seized the neighbourhood and the violent Muslim crowd turned on the lone Hindu. Amina, with her parental gift of secularism and hatred for religious prejudice, rushed to the rescue of Lifafa Das with the public announcement of her pregnancy even before her husband had heard about it: 'Listen well. I am with child. I am a mother who will have a child, and I am giving this man my shelter. Come on now, if you want to kill, kill a mother and show the world what men you are!' (77) The announcement of Saleem's arrival, which turned him into 'public property' (77) much before his birth, and the spectacle of Amina's motherhood, which presented a nationalistic image of unity and wholeness, saved Lifafa's life. In return, she was offered by the grateful youth the gift of a prophecy about her unborn child.

Chapter VI: Many-headed monsters

While reconstructing incidents remembered from long ago, from several generations prior to his own birth, narrator Saleem finds reality to be assailed by the unchanging duality of things and acknowledges the intervention of chance in the process of causality. 'A filmy curtain of ambiguities,' (87) thus, pervades the events leading to his nativity to which he imputes an ineluctable fatalism: 'My mother's pregnancy, it seems, was fated; my birth, however, owed a good deal to accident.' (79) This coupling of contrasting perspectives turn the incidents at once serious and trivial, ordinary and bizarre and raises questions about their veracity. Debunking the idea of chronometric time ('time has been an unsteady affair, in my experience, not a thing to be relied upon. It could even be partitioned.' [79]), Saleem reflects on the relationship between 'reality' and 'truth' and enunciates his narrative philosophy: 'Truth, for me, was . . . something hidden inside the stories Mary Pereira told me.' Truth is, for Saleem, what is concealed in the story/fiction of his foster-mother and reality is contingent. By privileging the truth hidden in fiction, Saleem's story offers a self-conscious fictional alternative to the linearity of historical narrative.

Prefaced by Saleem's reflection on the meaning of reality and truth, the episode narrates Amina Sinai's visit to the fortuneteller Ramram Seth and Ahmed's encounter with the demonic forces of racial hatred on a cold January evening in 1947. Both the journeys had far-reaching consequences: 'One foretold the future; the other settled its geographical location.' (80) And at the end of both the roads, many-headed monsters—representing, respectively, the fanatical anti-Muslim group named the Ravana gang, the many-headed crowd, and Saleem's monstrous suspicion about the truth of the prophecy about him ('Suspicion, too, is a monster with many heads,' 88)—lurked menacingly, giving the chapter its title.

Amina's journey, which began at Red Fort, led her to the gift of a prophecy while Ahmed's expedition, which took him to the Old Fort, resulted in disaster. Having received anonymous telephone calls from the Muslim-hating blackmailers, the three businessmen—Ahmed, Kemal and Butt—reached the ruins of an antique time, each carrying a grey bag stuffed with money. Ahmed, like his friends, left his bag in the turret of the crumbling fort and began to wait in its shadow, with his head full of money worries, his unfulfilled ambition of rearranging 'the Quran in accurately chronological order' (82) and the dilemma of choosing between the offer of Major Zulfikar (to decide for Pakistan) and that of his old friend, Doctor Narlikar (to shift to Bombay and property business) with promises of fortune. Before the appointed representative of the Ravana gang, a ragged creature with 'the head-dress of a demon,' could arrive to collect the booty, something bizarre happened. A monkey, enraged by the intrusion of humans into his territory, pounced on the bags, tore them and sent the bundles of currency notes down in the ditch, amid the obscene imprecations and threats of revenge from the grotesque money collector. While the panic-stricken businessmen were engaged in scooping rupees from the pools of urine and animal waste, Amina embarked upon a journey to Ramram Seth. She cruised in a taxi, through the narrow, crowded streets of Old Delhi where people (like 'some terrible monster, a creature with heads and heads and heads,' 81) led their 'invisible lives,' to a broken-down tenement building and climbed a dark stair-well towards the levitating soothsayer surrounded by monkeys, snakes and vultures. Before the amazed eyes of the peep showman and his cousins—a bone-setter, a monkey dancer and a snake charmer—Amina received the oracular predictions about her child from the hysterical seer who found 'history speaking through his lips.' (87) Ramram predicted a son: 'A son . . . who will never be older than his motherland. . . . There will be two heads—but you shall see only one—there will be knees and a nose, a nose and knees. . . . Newspaper praises him, two mothers raise him! . . . Washing will hide him—voices will guide him! Spittoons will brain him—doctors will drain him—Soldiers will try him—tyrants will fry him. . . . He will have sons without having sons! . . . And he will die . . . before he is dead.' (87-88) Ramram fell down on the floor and frothed at the mouth after making 'too much damn prophecy.' (88) The cryptic prophecy of Ramram Seth, which is a kind of movie-trailer foreshadowing future events, is veiled in narrative uncertainty. The entire narration of the weird incident is dotted with questions regarding its authenticity. It leaves a lingering doubt in Saleem's mind. Saleem even suspects his mother of adultery with the fortune-teller who resembled her ex-husband, Nadir Khan. His suspicion undermines the reliability of the prophecy implying that its truth is equivalent to what is concealed in Mary's story.[2]

Ahmed Sinai returned home that night from the ruins of his gutted godown with a ditchy reek and an ash-streaked face. He declared, amid 'a wifely tantrum' (90), his decision to leave Delhi and move to Bombay to invest in real estate. The experience had hardened him to fanaticism and communal politics so much so that he, with his distrust for Jinnah, made up his mind to think no more about 'Pakistan claptrap.' (90) On 4th June, 1947 when Earl Mountbatten—the last viceroy—was holding a press conference to announce the partition of India and his count-down calendar, Saleem's 'ill-matched parents,' (91) pushed by many-headed monsters, left for Bombay to start their own countdown to the fulfilment of an enigmatic prophecy.

Chapter VII: Methwold

From Delhi, the place of public announcement, the narrative shifts to Bombay, the city of Saleem's birth. Although Rushdie stalks the entire subcontinent in the book to reclaim the undivided heritage of his 'imaginary homeland,' *Midnight's Children* is, like *The Moor's Last Sigh*, essentially a Bombay novel steeped in the spirit of the city. Almost half the book takes place here. Rushdie has admitted in various interviews that his original plan was to write a long, sprawling 'city' novel with Bombay of the 1950s and the early 1960s as its fictive space. In this autobiographical novel he reclaims his 'lost home in a lost city in the mists of lost time,' (*IH*, 9) the reclamation of Bombay, a city of seven islands, by foreigners being the springboard for this rich metaphor.

Saleem identifies himself with the city of his birth and childhood ('Our Bombay, Padma!' [93]) and he evokes it nostalgically both as a physical reality and as an idea. This hybrid and cosmopolitan city with its composite and secular culture becomes, for Saleem, a metaphor for the multiplicity of India. He becomes emotional as he describes the city and his home: 'We are entering my kingdom now, coming into the heart of my childhood; a little lump has appeared in my throat.' (94) The many-faced city is brought alive by narrator Saleem as much through its topographical details, local myths and legends (its numen Mumbadevi from whom the city derived its present name, Ganapati—its chief festival—and the equestrian statue of Shivaji) as through the historical fact of the city being part of the marriage dowry when Catharine of the 'Portuguese house of Braganza' was betrothed to Charles II of England. Bombay in its pristine beauty is resuscitated in his narration. Saleem regretfully describes how this primeval world was occupied by successive invaders, from the Portuguese to the East India Company, who changed the complexion of the city and displaced its earliest inhabitants, the Koli fisherfolk.

It was this city where Saleem's parents came in June 1947, two months before the end of British dominion, and entered into a strange bargain with a departing colonial, William Methwold who had lost his stomach for India and decided to sell his properties at a low price before returning home. Methwold, a tall and attractive Briton, with a prominent nose and centrally parted hair, claimed descendance from an officer of the East India Company who had dreamed the city of Bombay into existence. Having been left with no other option but to accept the historical inevitability of the transfer of power ('I'm dead against it myself, but what's to be done' [96]), Methwold played an imperialistic 'game' by staging his own allegory of 'transfer of assets': 'Select suitable persons . . . hand everything over absolutely intact: in tiptop working order.' (97) His estate ('the conquerors' houses,' as they are called) consisting of four identical houses built in European style and named after the royal palaces of Europe (he was simply unable to acknowledge the existence of any culture other than his own), was sold to select members of Indian elite on two conditions. The conditions, which displayed his reluctance to discard his hold, were that the houses should be purchased with every last thing in them and the 'entire contents' were to be retained by the 'new owners,' and that 'the actual transfer should not take place until midnight on August 15.' (95)

Methwold is a grotesque caricature who stands for the evil and moral depravity of British colonization. Rushdie uses him to express his views about the history of colonial exploitation in the subcontinent. Through this untrustworthy and degenerate imperialist, he exposes the sinister colonial game the British had played since Macaulay's time to create Indians who were English at heart. The conditions imposed by Methwold on his Indian heirs were absurd and none but Amina protested against them, though she was effectively silenced by her husband. But, as Rushdie suggests, this was the price the country had to pay for its freedom. Methwold's Estate symbolizes colonized India—once possessed by the British who had super-imposed European culture on Indian consciousness—which was now transferred to the Indian rulers intact with the colonizers' political and economic systems.

The 'transfer of assets' is a parody of the transfer of power. The allegory of this passage debunks the myths that sustained and justified the Empire ('you'll admit we weren't all bad: built your roads. Schools, railway trains, parliamentary system, all worthwhile things,' Methwold says to Ahmed Sinai [96]) and suggests the perpetuation of the colonial system and psychology through the legacy handed over. It implies the passing on of the colonial mantle to the Indian elite who inherited political power from the British masters and shamelessly aped their arrogance and airs (like Ahmed Sinai who changed his voice into a 'hideous mockery of an Oxford drawl' in the presence of an Englishman [96]). The caricature drives home the unsavoury fact that the change of rulers never made Indians free from psychological attachment to the West.

Carefully chosen by Methwold, his Indian heirs moved into his estate: the Sinais in Buckingham Villa (named after the seat of British royalty); Homi Catrack, a film magnate and racehorse owner in Versailles Villa; the Ibrahims (old Ibrahim, a sisal farm owner, his sons Ismail and Ishaq, and Ismail's pregnant wife, Nussie) in Sans Souci. Escorial Villa was divided into flats and sold to the nuclear physicist Adi Dubash and his wife, the child-hating gynaecologist, Dr. Narlikar, and Naval Commander Sabarmati and his wife Lila. These people, who would form the centre of Saleem's world, found themselves gradually changing by the 'subtle magic' (100) of the place. They adapted themselves to colonial accoutrements and life-style and celebrated cocktail hours, while the retiring imperialist, who ensured the continued slavery of the Indians through planned psychological conditioning, supervised their transformation and mumbled with satisfaction a parody of the Hindustani expression: 'Sab Kuch ticktock Hai.' (99) Trapped in a web of worries caused by her gravidity, Amina somehow escaped the change that overtook the new inhabitants of the colonial myth-world. She felt that 'time in which the ticktock of countdown calendars was rushing everyone towards August 15th' (101) had stopped for her. But when the *Times of India*, searching for a human interest story for Independence celebrations, announced a prize to any Bombay mother who would 'give birth to a child at the precise instant of the birth of the new nation,' (99) Amina, in whom the skepticism of her father had been replaced by the credulity of her mother and the prophecy of Ramram Seth had sunk very deep, was absolutely certain that she would win the prize. Her certainty was based on intuition even though she knew that she had, apart from Nussie, another serious contender for the prize, Vanita, the wife of a poor, low-caste Hindu clown and street entertainer named (after the eponymous hero of a Kipling story) Wee Willie Winkie. Vanita's pregnancy was the result of Methwold's guilt. She had been seduced by the profligate Englishman in the absence of her husband. His seduction of Vanita is a metaphor for appropriating and exploiting what rightfully belongs to another; this is what is also meant by colonialism. If the parents and the children of midnight came, the midwife could not be left behind. Mary Pereira, a virgin midwife at Dr. Narlikar's Nursing Home, had, 'like every Mary . . . her Joseph.' (104) Joseph D'Costa, her communist lover, hated the rich. He was, like Aadam Aziz, sensitive to the winds of change. He had sniffed the air blowing from the north (India) and concluded: 'This independence is for the rich only; the poor are being made to kill each other like flies. In Punjab, in Bengal.' (104) Enraged by the Partition riots, Joseph turned his attention from plump, virginal Mary to the 'patriotic cause of awakening the people' (103) to the fakery of Independence.[3] The unfulfilled love of distraught Mary motivated her to commit a crime on the night of 15 August and, thus, to make the 'most important contribution to the history of twentieth century India.' (104)

The chapter—significantly titled 'Methwold'—brings Saleem's prenatal stories to a close (his birth being the dividing line between the old world and the new) and ends with the steady, 'metronomic beat of a countdown to an 'inevitable midnight.' (106)

Chapter VIII: Tick, tock

The title of this chapter connects the idea of a countdown, with which the previous chapter ended, to its opening line: 'Padma can hear it: there's nothing like a countdown for building suspense.' (106) Saleem, who had promised Padma that he would finally reveal the secret of his birth, launches into a lengthy synopsis of the previous events. This deferral of promise fulfilment creates suspense while the summary serves as a recapitulation of the plot. It also gives the impression that the story is all of a piece coming from a single witness and suggests the simultaneity of the past, which has been carried in memory, with the present. The intertwined lives and events from the time of Aadam Aziz's loss of faith and his synecdochic discovery of Naseem through a perforated sheet to the moment before Independence are Saleem's inheritance, 'part of the luggage [he] brought into the world.' (108) They are 'the parents of the child born on that midnight.' (108) The details of his diverse inheritance mention a number of factors responsible for his temperament, though all of them do not originate in his genetic make-up. He tries to establish the belief that the history of his life is the history of the country and that he is India and India is Saleem. Saleem, with his encyclopedic taste, has been a swallower of lives. His heterogeneous but subjectively coherent version of the events of his life also includes the world: to understand just one life one has to swallow the world—as Saleem puts it—even though that makes the individual appear somewhat grotesque. Rushdie has always stressed that his books are related to the world. This inclusive mode of writing which defies the arbitrary distinctions between fact and fiction and between the individual and the world around him, distinguishes *Midnight's Children* as an Indian work of art, despite the 'wild profusion' of his inheritance from the Western novel genre. Saleem, thus, rationalizes the multiplicity of strands which have been woven into his life as well as his narrative: 'If I seem a little bizarre, remember the wild profusion of my inheritance . . . perhaps, if one wishes to remain an individual in the midst of the teeming multitudes, one must make oneself grotesque.' (109) Saleem's grotesquerie is a clever ploy of Rushdie to endow his narrator-protagonist with omniscience. It enables him to see, know and report, more than any normal human being can, things and events, a considerable number of which took place in his pre-natal past and were connected with the country's history.

The summary is followed by an elaborate description of the preparations for the simultaneous birth of the nation (India) and its body (Saleem Sinai) between August 13 and August 15.

There is an hour to hour progression towards the numinous midnight. The relentless countdown ('tick, tock') captures all the euphoria, tension and trauma of Independence through allusions to public drama and private rituals. The protestations of astrologers to the would-be rulers, the 'mass bloodletting' (112) on the frontiers of the divided Punjab, the communal violence and Mahatma Gandhi's peace march in Bengal are reported in Saleem's narration of Amina's enigmatic dream (of being glued to flypaper), Ahmed's invention of imaginary ancestors and family curse to impress the retiring Englishman, William Methwold, and Aadam Aziz's discovery of his 'moth-eaten' (111) history (the perforated sheet). On 14th August, Vanita—the wife of Wee Willie Winkie—entered into a prolonged, unproductive labour in the charity ward of Dr. Narlikar's Nursing Home. The first pangs hit her when, 'hundreds of miles away, M.A. Jinnah announced the midnight birth of a Muslim nation.' (111) At that time, across the border, hectic preparations were going on, despite ill-omens, 'moth-eaten memories' (115) and rituals of blood, to celebrate the birth of a 'new myth,' the myth of a nation. India was a myth because it was an imagined construct. Echoing Benedict Anderson,[4] Saleem writes: 'a nation which had never previously existed was about to win its freedom, catapulting us into a world which, although it had five thousand years of history, . . . was nevertheless quite imaginary; into a mythical land, a country which would never exist except by the efforts of a phenomenal collective will—except in a dream we all agreed to dream.' (112) Saleem would be, by virtue of his synchronous birth, a living proof of this 'collective dream.' (112) Six hours before midnight on 15 August William Methwold finally transferred his assets to his Indian heirs and departed for good after revealing the deception (his brilliantined hair-piece with a neat centre-parting) which had tricked poor Vanita into an illicit liaison. At the same hour Amina went into a 'prophecy-ridden' (114) labour (Saleem was prophesied for the second time by a sadhu who mysteriously came to Buckingham Villa that evening) and was driven to Narlikar's clinic. Saleem's arrival into independent India was framed by the optimism and promise of Nehru's legendary narration of postcoloniality. The hour of Independence was projected through the celebrations of the 'many-headed monster of the crowd,' (115) the refraction of the national tri-colour (saffron fireworks, green flames of burning trains and the whites of the eyes of the women in travail) and snippets of Nehru's speech in the Assembly Hall. These were interspersed with the mothers' labour-pains, partition riots, ravaging fires and police haunts. The montage represents Rushdie's multiple vision which replaces the uni-linear version of official history by an alternative view that takes into consideration contrasting realities and displays the varying impact of the event on different sections of the people. When the twin children of midnight were finally born, a somewhat crazed midwife, Mary Pereira, committed, out of a wrong sense of revenge, a 'private revolutionary act.' (117) She changed the name-tags of the babies of Vanita (who died in child-birth) and Amina, 'giving the poor baby a life of privilege and condemning the rich-born child to . . . poverty.' (117) Thus Saleem, who became 'the chosen child of midnight' to win the *Times of India* prize and receive Prime Minister Nehru's congratulatory letter, turned out to be an Anglo-Indian, the illegitimate son of a reluctantly departing colonizer and a poor Hindu woman. The shocking revelation of Saleem's alternative genealogy ("'An Anglo?' Padma exclaims in horror" [118]) debunks the established narrative of Indian history and repudiates the newly born nation-state as an illegitimate product of the colonial violation of the Indian sub-continent. Narrator Saleem, however, insists that the accident is an inescapably allegorical condition of the inheritors of the colonial state: 'In fact, all over the new India, the dream we all shared, children were being born who were only partially the offspring of their parents—the children of midnight were also the children *of the time*: fathered, you understand, by history.' (118) He, therefore, declines to acknowledge any guilt of trickery or inauthenticity and withhold his flawed, crime-stained genealogy. When the Sinais eventually discovered the betrayal of Mary Pereira (who, being consumed by remorse, gave up her job in the Nursing Home and devoted her life to bringing up baby Saleem as a surrogate mother), they reconciled themselves to the fact of Saleem's hybridity or miscegenation: 'We all found that *it made no difference*! I was still their son: they remained my parents. In a kind of collective failure of imagination, we learned that we simply could not think our way out of our pasts.' (118)

Book Two

Book Two charts the growth of Saleem Sinai from childhood to adolescence, which also mirrors the development of the newly independent nation between 1947 and 1965. All the major historical events of the period are alluded to: the assassination of Gandhi, the Suez crisis, the conquest of Everest, India's Five year plans, the linguistic reorganization of Indian states and consequent language riots, the imposition of Martial Law in Pakistan in 1958, the Chinese aggression in 1962, the theft of the sacred relic from Hazratbal Mosque in Srinagar, Nehru's death and the Indo-Pakistani War in 1965. At the autobiographical level, this section—consisting of fifteen chapters—traces the ups and downs in the fortunes of Sinai family: Ahmed's financial bankruptcy consequent upon the collapse of his dream project of land-reclamation, the birth of Saleem's sister, the discovery of Mary Pereira's midnight crime, the successive deaths of Saleem's uncle (Hanif) and grandfather (Aadam Aziz), and the family's migration to Pakistan where Saleem reaches a tumultuous adolescence and witnesses the destruction of his family in the war of 1965. The euphoria created by Independence lasted into the first decade and then gradually gave way, from the early Sixties, to disillusionment caused by ubiquitous corruption and the government's failure to live upto its promise. The myth of the nation was in fast decay and progress yielded to stunted growth. With cracks appearing in the body politics, the immense possibilities and promises of Independence, embodied by one thousand and one midnight's children, were closed off. Optimism was replaced by cynicism, illusion of centrality by withdrawal. Throughout Book Two, Saleem is on a slide towards disintegration (he loses his hair, finger, telepathic power and memory), which is conflated with the cracking up of the nation.

This section delineates a disappointing series of retreats from Saleem's initial enthusiasm to his premature disenchantment.

Chapter IX: The fisherman's pointing finger

Having waited impatiently for Saleem to arrive at the moment when his story began, the moment of his auspicious birth, Padma is shocked by the seeming irrelevance of his flawed genealogy which he has presented in a digressive and fragmentary manner from the scraps and shards of his memory. This fragmentation, in narrative style, with which narrator Saleem puts his fractured vision of the history of his life and nation into perspective, is his legacy from his grandfather. Aadam Aziz's experience with the perforated sheet condemned Saleem to a 'life of fragments.' But, while Aziz 'remained the victim of the sheet,' (121) Saleem has become, by virtue of his supreme narratorial skill, its master. And Padma has fallen under its spell. She has been, Saleem claims, 'captivated by love.' (121) But this self-conscious flaunting of his virtuosity as a story-teller and his propensity to digress exasperate Padma who desires a straightforward narrative. Moreover, the mention of the word 'love' by impotent Saleem triggers a violent reaction from her. She points a finger at Saleem's dysfunctional organ, calls him a 'mad man' and departs, briefly, from his narrative, abandoning him to his 'auto-biographical enterprise' and 'cracked digression.' (123) Padma's accusing finger reminds Saleem of another, and more significant, pointing finger—that of a fisherman which is the focal point of a picture hung on the wall of baby Saleem's bedroom in Buckingham Villa. The picture of an old, net-mending fisherman pointing his finger to the western horizon where the sun is setting while a young European is listening to his 'liquid tales,' (122) is a prophetic image of Saleem's future. The pointing finger, itself a symbol of quest (because Saleem is a quester for the meaning and purpose of his life), is a continuous reminder of the invisible presence of boatman Tai, with his oriental worldview and vision of wholeness, in Saleem's life which is condemned to fragments and handcuffed to history. It is also a warning of his 'special doom' and 'inescapable destiny' of which narrator Saleem is aware from the beginning.

Saleem had begun his life with unbounded optimism and absolute confidence in his centrality, a position ratified by the Prime Minister himself. In his congratulatory letter to the 'midnight's child,' phrased with all the hopes and promises of the newly independent nation, Nehru identified Saleem with India itself and linked the unlimited potential of the newborn infant with that of the nascent state: 'you are the newest bearer of that ancient face of India which is also eternally young. We shall be watching over your life with the closest attention; it will be, in a sense, the mirror of our own.' (122) Assured of his role as the 'mirror' of the nation, baby Saleem arrived home from Narlikar's clinic with his umbilical cord preserved in a pickle jar and embarked on a 'heroic programme of self-enlargement' (124)—described in a comically exaggerated manner which is reminiscent of Rabelais, Swift and Gunter Grass—under the supervision of his twin mothers—Amina and Mary. This ugly baby with a grotesque figure—a round face disfigured by birthmarks, bulbous temples, and a colossal nose—was a child prodigy who gave proof of his magical powers from the cradle. He had a huge appetite and a fantastic growth rate and his dry, unblinking eyes could receive incredibly large number of impressions (a reference to India's ambitious five-year plans and the large amount of national resources and foreign aids they devoured). He started taking his place 'at the centre of the universe' (126) and gave meaning to it. Raised by twin mothers, he became a very popular child, highly in demand at Methwold's Estate. The heirs of William Methwold, who had settled into English life style, wanted Saleem in their houses to fulfil a prophecy of Wee Willie Winkie that the first birth would make the place appear real to its inhabitants. Willie Winkie, now a bereaved widower and a victim of throat cancer, continued to visit Methwold Estate with his son named (after the Puranic god of procreation and destruction) Shiva. As the minstrel tried to entertain Methwold's successors with sad, nostalgic songs in a harsh, bitter voice, his son—a large infant with knobbly knees—sat at his feet 'silently bearing the burden of being the cause of burden of being the cause of his father's slow decline.' (128) Gradually his eyes would fill with an unspeakable rage and he would throw pebbles dangerously 'into the surrounding emptiness.' (128) While Shiva whom Mary's crime had deprived of birthright and doomed to a life of poverty, was waiting for his eventual descent into the dark labyrinths of Bombay's underworld from where a war would save him, Saleem 'began a triumphal progress around the red-tiled palaces, gracing each in turn with [his] presence' (129) and learning a lot of things. This clairaudient child voyeur eavesdropped on the secrets of his adult neighbours—their crookedness, infidelities, untidiness and betrayals—because 'the grown-ups lived their lives in his presence without fear of being observed.' (129) Saleem's role as a witness to his place and time and his prodigious capacity for imbibing things, thus, provide a rationale for his account of both private and public lives for which he felt responsible: 'I lay in my crib and listened; and everything that happened, happened because of me.' (133) His presence exerted an influence on history and worked changes on the people around him including his father. Saleem's birth altered the life of Ahmed Sinai. His position in the family was undermined by his son's arrival, as Amina's assiduity and meticulous care found a different target. Deprived of his wife's attention and angry at her preoccupation with the child, Ahmed took to boozing and womanizing. At night he drank wine and battled with the bottled 'djinn' and during day-time he flirted with his Anglo-Indian secretaries in his ground floor office from where he ran his property business. The 'convolutions of his life' (133) eventually made him yield to Dr. Narlikar's 'entrepreneurial dream' (134) of back-bay reclamation with concrete tetrapods, which offered him a chance to 'restore his position in the world.' (134) With his propensity for taking wrong turning, Ahmed invested huge sums in the fantastic project which led to the freezing of his assets and, literally, his balls. (After Partition, the government of India froze the assets of many affluent Muslims to force them to flee to Pakistan. Rushdie here presents a social-realist, though a little stylized, version of the historical fact, like the blackmailing of Muslim businessman in pre-Partition Delhi by Hindu revivalist groups.) But at the dramatic reversal of family fortunes, Amina's wifely dedication 'rose to new heights' (136) and brought about a fleeting warmth in their conjugal life. It was at that time Saleem's sister, Brass Monkey, was conceived.

Chapter X: Snakes and ladders

In the winter of 1948, when Ahmed Sinai was reeling under the impact of state-endorsed freeze and the threat of penury, Dr. Schaapsteker, an aged European snake-expert, came to rent the upper storey of Buckingham Villa. The arrival of the humanitarian scientist, who had devoted his life to carrying out valuable research on snake-poison for medicinal purposes, initiated the charade of snake and ladder in the Sinai family. The blow of the freeze had been too hard for Ahmed; he had lost the nerve to fight back and taken to bed. Not knowing what to do, Amina sought the advice of her parents who arrived at Methwold's Estate to stand by their daughter in the hour of crisis. Dr. Aziz had turned prematurely old, fading with the passing years and losing the strength to fight the fanaticism and intransigence of his burgeoning wife. (Amina even discovered a hole in the center of her father's body.) Two of their daughters had gone to Pakistan: Emerald with her husband Zulfikar who was laying the foundations of an immense fortune, and Alia who was teaching in a Karachi school. Their elder son, Hanif, had rejected Pakistan and arrived in Bombay to become the youngest director in Hindi cinema. He had married, to the disapproval of his mother, one of the brightest stars of the celluloid world, 'the divine Pia, whose face was her fortune.' (142) The youngest son, Mustapha, had joined the Indian Civil Service. Relieved by Reverend Mother of the 'exigencies of running her home,' (139) Amina rediscovered within herself the adventurous spirit of his father and went to gamble in the racecourse. With the money won in the horse races (and she won, despite her ignorance of horse and rules of the race, with surprising regularity) and the help of the crooked lawyer Ismail Ibrahim she fought Ahmed's legal battle against the discriminating 'secular' state. But no sooner had Amina climbed the ladder to success, 'represented by her racecourse luck,' (141) than she discovered a snake waiting around the corner. The game of snakes and ladders (which supplies the chapter its title and a clue to the fluctuating fortunes of the Sinai family) captures the eternal verity that one falls but to rise, and for every snake that pulls one down there is a ladder to lift one up, and vice versa. It implies the unchanging duality of things in the world: good against evil, luck against misfortune, success against failure. But the game lacks the crucial dimension of ambiguity. Because, 'snakes can also lead to triumph, just as ladders can be descended.' (148) And it was this 'ambiguity' that Amina, like others in her family, learnt. One evening, in the midst of her racecourse victory, Amina and Ahmed went to the premiere of Hanif's first feature film 'The Lovers of Kashmir' which was starred by his wife, Pia. While they were watching Hanif's revolutionary technique of 'indirect kiss' (a parody of the prudishness of Bombay films in 1950s where direct physical contact between the hero and the heroine could not be shown) which would help him climb the ladder to a spectacular, though short-lived, success, a terrible announcement by the hall manager brought the show to an abrupt end: 'This afternoon, at Birla House in Delhi, our beloved Mahatma was killed.' (143) The snake of religious fanaticism had snatched away the life of the nation's father. The Sinais, being Muslims, apprehended communal troubles and remained confined in their house until the radio disclosed the name of the murderer, Nathuram Godse, to the relief of everybody except Aadam Aziz 'upon whom the news of Gandhi's death had placed a new burden of age.' (143) Meanwhile, the quarrel between Mary and Musa, the ayah and the servant who had always been at daggers drawn with each other, reached the point of explosion. Mary, proud of her superior status in the Sinai household, had insulted the aged and devoutly Muslim bearer in a thousand different ways to engineer his departure from Methwold's Estate. Humiliated by the Christian ayah and abused by his master Ahmed whom whisky had goaded into excesses of rudeness, Musa committed, out of his fear of dismissal and sense of injured pride, a theft in the house.

The police detected Amina's precious possessions from his belongings. Musa left Buckingham Villa discovering the ambiguity that ladders could go down as well as up. But Mary's victory was short-lived as she presently learnt that even when ladders operated in her favour, she could not avoid a snake. Joseph D'Costa, the absconding terrorist who had secretly taken shelter in the inoperative clock tower at Methwold's Estate, died of snake-bite before the police, tipped off by Amina, could arrest him. When his poisoned body was carried out from the tower which was filled with home-made explosives, Mary, fearing discovery of her crime, fell 'like a sack of potatoes to the floor . . . in a sudden and dramatic faint.' (147) In the midst of all these melodramatic incidents which followed each other in quick succession as in a Bombay film, Baby Saleem fell seriously ill. He contracted typhoid which nearly stopped his life. When Dr. Aziz's attempt to save his grandson failed, Schaapsteker appeared with a bottle of diluted snake poison and asked him to administer it. The venom of King Cobra miraculously saved the baby's life, bringing his temperature to normal and giving him 'an early awareness of the ambiguity of snakes' (149): that their venom could save life as well. Saleem recovered but lost his phenomenal growth rate. His recovery was followed by the uneventful birth of his sister, Brass Monkey (so called because of her red gold hair) and Ismail's victory in the court case. While the lawyer was announcing the news to Ahmed and Amina at Nurlikar's Nursing Home, Saleem, aged exactly one year and fifteen days, won his own battle against gravity: he dragged himself erect in his cot.

Chapter: XI: Accident in a washing chest

The departure of Padma, Saleem's 'necessary ear,' (149) from his narrative upsets his balance. With her superstition, ignorance and 'paradoxical earthiness of spirit,' (150) she served as a 'counterweight to [his] miracle-laden omniscience' (150) and kept his feet firmly on the ground. But her exit has disturbed the balance between the past and the present and between digressiveness and linearity. No longer able to traverse the entire continuum of time, Saleem has to be reconciled to the 'narrow one-dimensionality of a straight line' (150) which cannot project a multi-dimensional reality. Seized by anger at his unreasonable treatment at the hands of his disciple, he boasts about his erudition and the multiplicity of his cultural heritage. (In spite of his Muslim background, he is well up in Hindu myths.) But in doing so, he commits a factual error: 'When Valmiki, the author of the *Ramayana*, dictated his masterpiece to elephant-headed Ganesh, did the god walk out on him half-way?' (149) His mistake about the myth—the erroneous attribution of the scribe's role to Ganesh in the writing of Valmiki's *Ramayana* instead of Vyasa's *Mahabharata*—which is central to his story (Ganesh's elephantine nose and dubious parentage prefigure his own) deflates his narratorial pomposity and casts a doubt on his reliability as a chronicler. He, therefore, decides to speak plainly and continue his Padmaless narrative which leaps to the year 1956, the year of the Suez crisis, to record the larger than life experience of nine-year-old Saleem and of his sister who was seven. Brass Monkey had grown into a beautiful but mischievous girl. Her 'unprophesied' (150) life had been at struggle from the beginning. Deprived of parental affection by the 'overpowering shadow' (150) of her elder brother, she was desperate for love. But she would become furious if anybody spoke to her loving words. She had inherited her great grandfather's gift of talking to birds and beasts: 'From birds she learned how to sing; from cats she learned a dangerous form of independence.' (151) Uninhibited like an animal, Brass Monkey developed a strange habit of burning shoes to draw others' attention. Amina was exasperated by the unfeminine ways of the 'problem child' (152) and obliged to sentence her to silence (echoing the war of silence with which her own mother, Naseem Aziz, had punished her husband). But there was a perfect understanding between the siblings. Saleem treated her as an 'ally' and Brass Monkey never blamed her brother for his pre-eminence in the family. It was she who catalyzed Saleem's accident in the washing chest by answering a mysterious telephone call in the unusually hot summer of 1956.

Even at that early age, Saleem was assailed by doubts about the purpose of his existence and perplexed by its meaning. He had a premonition that his much trumpeted life, like the freedom of the newly born nation, might 'turn out to be utterly useless . . . without the shred of a purpose.' (152) To escape from the terrible misgiving, he started hiding in his mother's washing chest which provided him with a refuge from the unbearable pressures of reality. Outside the chest, he found himself surrounded by people who possessed a clear sense of purpose. His friends and schoolmates had absolute certainty about their future: 'they knew what they were for.' (153) He buried himself in fairytales and comic books to avoid the nagging sense of purposelessness. In the world outside, Saleem, with his stunted growth and lack of certitude, worried about the meaning of his life: 'Where do you find it? I pleaded at my window; the fisherman's finger pointed, misleadingly, out to sea.' (154) But in his hiding place he felt 'safe from all pressures . . . from the demands of parents and history' (156) and could forget his times (the conquest of Mount Everest, the Suez Crisis and the country's Five Year Plans). The fisherman's pointing finger, the rude jokes of friends and teachers about his ugliness, the parental and grandparental expectations of greatness were all muffled by the dirty laundry. And it was from this womb-like place of concealment that Saleem spied on and discovered maternal duplicity which led to an accident and a revelation. During the summer of that year, Amina began to receive a series of 'wrong-number' telephone calls. Brass Monkey answered one such call in her absence and heard the soft, fleshy voice of a poet. It planted in Saleem's mind a suspicion that his mother might have a secret. The suspicion turned into certainty a few days later when she gave him an irrefutable evidence of her infidelity. From the washing chest Saleem heard his mother answering a 'wrong number' call. Then she came to the 'spied out privacy' (161) of her bathroom and cried while repeating a long forgotten name, Nadir Khan. The shattering exposure to maternal perfidy coincided with an accident. A pajama cord, inserted into his left nostril, caused a violent sniff. The accumulated mucus of his gargantuan nose with upward thrust painfully burst through to the frontiers of the brain to bestow on him the power of telepathy. Saleem heard 'a headful of gabbling tongues' (163) and discovered that, like a radio-receiver, he could hear unspoken words, select individual voices and control their volume. He lost a refuge (banished for good from the washing chest by his guilt-ridden mother) but received the gift of a revelation: 'like Musa or Moses, like Muhammad, the Penultimate, I heard voices on a hill.' (163) But the absolute certainty of his sublime gift and the profound confidence in his newly discovered greatness—when disclosed to unbelieving family members next morning—resulted in parental wrath (he received a mighty blow from his irate father and went permanently deaf in the left ear) and perpetual self-doubt: 'I was doomed . . . to be plagued by constant doubts about what I was for.' (165) The accident grotesquely fulfilled a part of Ramram Seth's prophecy: 'washing will hide him . . . voices will guide him.'

Chapter XII: All-India radio

The more Saleem's narrative comes closer to the present, the more it loses its deep perspective and becomes fragmentary and grotesque. Using the metaphor of a cinema screen, narrator Saleem reflects on this question of perspective:

> Suppose yourself in a large cinema, sitting at first in the back row, and gradually moving up, row by row, until your nose is almost pressed against the screen. Gradually the stars' faces dissolve into dancing grain; tiny details assume grotesque proportions; the illusion dissolves—or rather, it becomes clear that the illusion itself is reality. (165-66)

The movement towards the movie screen suggests the narrative's progress through time towards the present. As it nears the contemporary events, it becomes partial or fragmentary showing only the blobs on the screen and not the whole picture. The reflection stems from Saleem's confusion and lack of certainties which Padma's absence has generated in him. His memory also plays tricks so much so that he discovers, while re-reading his story, a chronological error in dating the assassination of Mahatma Gandhi. He attributes the error to his failing memory and mental confusion. Still, he clings to this imperfectly remembered version preferring it to literal facts of history: 'in my India Gandhi will continue to die at the wrong time.' (166) The error, like many such factual inaccuracies in the book, provides a clue that Saleem is capable of distortion and that his story is not an authentic guide to the history of his nation. Saleem is not a dispassionate chronicler. He shapes his material according to his need and tampers with chronology to preserve the correspondence between his life and the history of his country and to create the illusion of himself as a protagonist at the center of things. He is aware that this will raise questions about the reliability of his chronicle. He, therefore, asks: 'Does one error invalidate the entire fabric? Am I so far gone, in my desperate need for meaning, that I'm prepared to distort everything—to re-write the whole history of my times purely in order to place myself in a central role?' (166) Leaving the question to posterity for an answer, he resumes his narrative and describes the consequences of his accident in the washing chest. In the summer of 1956, the summer of the language march demanding the partition of the state of Bombay on linguistic basis, Saleem discovered that he had become a sort of radio which could receive and control voices. But afraid of parental wrath, he kept his knowledge a secret. At midnight, he would wake up and tune his inner ear to the gabbling, disembodied voices which, he discovered, were not sacred but 'profane . . . and . . . multitudinous as dust.' (168) What he heard telepathically were the 'inner monologues of all the . . . teeming millions, of masses and classes alike.' (168) Rushdie skillfully weaves the multi-lingual texture of Indian life and the country's language problem into Saleem's miraculous power: 'The voices babbled in everything from Malayalam to Naga dialects, from the purity of Lucknow Urdu to the Southern slurring of Tamil,' (168) On deeper probing Saleem learnt that beneath the 'polyglot frenzy' of the voices language was 'replaced by universally intelligible thought forms' (168) which signalled the existence of the children of midnight. But he did not put his prodigious gift to any vital use, for the betterment of the impoverished country, for example. Afraid of 'parental ostracism' (172) and withdrawal of their love, he chose to conceal his faculty and fritter it away on meaningless voyeurism and cheating. He misused his talent to help himself out with his schoolwork (by picking information out of the minds of his more intelligent class-mates) and to eavesdrop, first on the people he knew and then, as his daring grew, on filmstars, politicians and cricketers. His strange behaviour at that crucial point in the history of the child-nation resulted from his 'confused thinking' (172) and desire for popularity which spoilt much of his career. In order to seek refuge from his inner turmoil (reflected in a long, breathless passage without any full stops [170-71)] and the confusion of adult voices which poured into him, Saleem eventually retreated into the empty, inoperative clock tower and took his 'first tentative steps towards . . . involvement with mighty events and public lives.' (173) From the privacy of the dilapidated tower, he discovered, first like a tourist, the country's geography and then, as tourism ceased to satisfy him, politics: exploitation, corruption, bribery, electoral malpractice and political grotesquerie. The telepathic power of 'mind hopping' (174) gave him the 'illusion of the artist' as omniscient creator (he felt he was creating a world and making things happen) and filled him with pride: 'I can find out any damn thing.' (174) But the 'spirit of self-aggrandizement' (175) which possessed him at that time and made him invent a world where he could take the central position was, as Saleem-the narrator admits with a bitter hindsight, 'born of an instinct for self-preservation.' (175) He wanted to protect his individuality from 'the massed identities' of the teeming multitudes which threatened to engulf him and which, he arrogantly believed, he could control from a distance. But Saleem, the perennial victim suffering from the illusion of the protagonist, could not control the tides of his father's ebbing fortunes. The last days of 1956 witnessed the revival of Ahmed's dream of land reclamation. Having lost his interest in sex-life in the aftermath of the freeze, he found—at the proddings of Dr. Narlikar—a surrogate for sexual activity in the fantasy of the tetrapods. He was cautious this time. He took a lesson from the freeze and avoided publicity. He invested money without keeping any record of his involvement in the scheme. But Narlikar's sudden death in mob-violence[5] led to Ahmed's financial ruin. He began to decline and within a few months turned completely white. In short, Ahmed fell victim to 'pigmentation disorder' whose first casualty had been the Rani of Cooch Nahin, and which afflicted a large number of Indian businessmen in the years following Independence. Puffed up with black money in the wake of the first Five Year Plan, India's business community turned white. The pigmentation disorder, suggesting the metaphorical process of westernization, thus, served as a moral allegory for a collective, historical phenomenon. The episode ends with a preview of the following chapters and a report of Wee Willie Winkie's death.

Chapter XIII: Love in Bombay

From his psychic travels and voyeurism in the broken-down clock tower, Saleem's story progresses to his involvement in public life through a brief but disastrous love affair. His love with Evie (Evelyn Lilith) Burns in Bombay at the time of language march led to the enactment of his historical role in the partition of the state and his discovery of the midnight's children. During the 1950s India had a short-lived romance with America and received large quantities of American aid—a historical fact which corresponded to Saleem's brief infatuation with the American girl. Motherless Evie came to Bombay on the New Year's Day of 1957 to stay with her father in an apartment block built exclusively for foreigners near Methwold's Estate. She was a tough, knife-sharp girl with a grotesque figure: 'her hair was made of scarecrow straw, her skin was peppered with freckles and her teeth lived in a metal cage.' (181) On her first appearance at Methwold's Estate the imperious kid served notice to her Indian neighbours that an invincible power had come among them. Armed with an air pistol she arrived at the circus ring on a bi-cycle and by a fantastic display of her cycling skill and sharp-shooting established her supremacy over the Indians who 'stood frozen in open-mouthed attitudes' (182) and accepted the new boss without any arguments. For Saleem, it was love at first sight. But tongue-tied in the presence of Evie, who was half a year older than him, he could not directly express his feelings to her. So, 'in a grotesque mimicry of European literature' (185) he approached his best friend Sonny Ibrahim to entreat her on his behalf. Sonny, a handsome boy with forcep-hollows on his temples, had fallen in love with Saleem's tempestuous sister Brass Monkey and had been badly bruised in his attempt to woo her. Enraged by his nagging protestations of love, Brass Monkey had publicly disgraced him with the help of her European schoolfriends. They had turned upon Sonny on his way to school and stripped him before immobilized Saleem who could not take sides between his sister and his friend. Sonny, however, forgave his friend for his passive role in his humiliation and agreed to plead his case before Evie. It was early in 1957 and the run-up to the general election had begun. As the political parties all over India—from Hindu Jan Sangh and secular Congress to equalitarian Communists and regionalist D.M.K.—were speeding up their election campaigns (Saleem's narrative adopts the campaign rhetoric to describe his indirect courtship), Sonny canvassed his friend's 'chosen constituency' (185) and failed. Evie scornfully turned down Saleem's offer of love: 'That sniffer? He can't even ride a bike!' (185) She reached out towards his cute electoral agent instead. Unperturbed by his voter's rejection, Saleem changed his approach and resolved to share her interest in cycle riding. The 'siren temptations' (186) of Evie Burns irresistibly drew him to the circus ring where she taught the hillock-top children her bi-cycle arts. During a trial run, Evie pushed Saleem roughly and the cycle flew uncontrollably across the ring to collide with Sonny Ibrahim. Saleem fell on the ground and received a severe injury in the head. The accident completed what the mishap in the washing chest had begun; it unlocked the door to the midnight's children: 'they were there in my head, in the front now . . . sending their here-I-am signals, from north south east west . . . the other children born during that midnight hour.' (187)

After a short break, introduced to describe an unpleasant family reunion in the old, decaying house of Saleem's grandparents in Agra during which he learnt from rickshaw-puller Rashid the techniques of cycle-riding and discovered the moth-eaten perforated sheet of Dr. Aziz, the narrative returns to Bombay to give a straightforward, journalistic account of the language riots of 1957. The passage that describes the historical event begins like a newspaper report:

> It is a matter of record that the States Reorganization Committee had submitted its report to Mr. Nehru as long ago as October 1955; a year later, its recommendations had been implemented. India had been divided anew, into fourteen states and six centrally-administered 'territories.' (189)

The boundaries of the new states were defined not by any mountains or rivers but by 'walls of words.' The Committee somehow overlooked the problem of Bombay province and the omission led to violent protest and mass demonstration. The supporters of Gujarati and Marathi languages organized mammoth processions under the aegis of Maha Gujarat Parishad and Samjukta Maharashtra Samiti to press the demand for a linguistic division of the state. The cold, dry facts of history are introduced in the story to explain Saleem's involuntary interference in it. In February 1957, soon after Saleem's return from Agra, Methwold's Estate was cut off from the city by a two-day long protest march of Marathi supporters. The children of the estate followed their American chief to sneak a look at the parade from the hill-top disobeying parental ban. While wide-eyed Evie was immersed in the spectacle of 'chanting humanity,' (189) Saleem incurred her wrath by his enthusiastic attempts to impress her with a demonstration of his newly learnt cycling skill. She gave him a shove and he hurtled down the slope to make his first foray into history, crashing into the procession on a runaway bicycle. When some hoodlums in the Marathi-speaking mob asked Saleem, 'the little laad-sahib . . . from the big, rich hill' (191) who knew none of the two languages, to speak some Gujarati, he inadvertently repeated a facetious rhyme designed to make fun of the speech-rhythms of the language:

> Soo che? Saru che!

Danda le ke maruche! (191)

The nonsensical jingle ('How are you?—I am well—I'll take a stick and thrash you to hell!') was taken up as a war-cry by the Marathi supporters against the Gujarati demonstrators. Thus, a major historical event was triggered off by Saleem's seemingly trivial intervention: 'the two parties fell upon one another with no little zeal, and to the tune of my little rhyme the first of the language riots got under way, fifteen killed, over three hundred wounded.' (192). He, however, acknowledged his responsibility for the violent incident which resulted in the partition of Bombay and, ironically, cured him of Evie Burns.

Chapter XIV: My tenth birthday

Padma, who had stormed out of Saleem's narrative following a quarrel, returns and this chapter begins with her story. Driven to craziness by her unconsummated love, she makes an attempt to resuscitate Saleem's manhood with 'herbs of virility' (193) which she had collected on the advice of a holy man during her absence. The herbs fail to awaken his masculinity and drives him to delirious fever for a week. Saleem does not blame Padma for the misadventure because her return has a salutary effect on his narrative. He regains his balance and 'lost sense of proportion' (194). Padma's excursion in the world of magic and folklore in search of love-potions briefly connects him with the 'world of ancient learning' (194) which, despite his Muslim background, he claims to share. Saleem introduces the Indian concept of time and the myth of cosmic creation, referring to Padma—the Lotus Goddess—as 'one of the Guardians of Life, beguiling and comforting mortal men while they pass through the dream-web of Maya.' (194) In *Midnight's Children* 'Maya' becomes a metaphor for the illusory nature of reality delineated by Saleem as well as the wild flights of imagination, the atemporal fancies which he, as an omniscient narrator with a non-linear or cyclical concept of Time, indulges in. But Padma, with her superstition and earthiness of spirit, her preoccupations with love and marriage, forces Saleem back into the world of linear narrative—into the spatio-temporal reality. She, thus, becomes 'the

Mother of Time' (195) and a co-producer of Saleem's fictive universe. This bases Rushdie's magic realism—his use of myth, memory and multiple fantasies—on the Indian view of reality. And out of this juxtaposition of western narrative mode and the mythic/folkloric tradition of India is born Rushdie's hybrid tale which incorporates a number of Hindu, Islamic and Christian motifs and, thus, undermines the purist representation of the world and creates a secular ambience in the novel.

Having exhausted the 'strain of old time fabulism,' Saleem comes to the 'fantastic heart' (195) of his story which provides the novel with its title—the midnight's children. During the first hour (between midnight and 1 a.m.) of 15 August, 1947, the hour of the nascency of free India, one thousand and one children were born within the country's frontiers. What made the event remarkable was not the number but the nature of those children each of whom was born with a miraculous gift or talent. Fathered by history, they represented the promise of a new future: 'as though . . . history, arriving at a point of the highest significance and promise, had chosen to sow, in that instant, the seeds of a future which would genuinely differ from anything the world had seen upto that time.' (195) Out of the total one thousand and one children, four hundred and twenty died soon after their birth due to malnutrition and disease. Of the surviving five hundred and eighty one, two hundred sixty six were boys and three hundred fifteen were girls. The children, who were completely ignorant of one another's existence, were nearing their tenth birthday in January 1957 when Saleem became aware of them as a consequence of the bi-cycle accident. Another noteworthy feature of the children, who were normal human beings despite their miraculous gifts, was that the closer to midnight their times of birth were, the greater were their powers. The children born in the last seconds of the hour were no more than 'circus freaks,' (198) like Siamese twins and bearded girls. Those born towards the half hour were gifted with more useful faculties like the powers of healing and remembering. To the children, who arrived in the first minute after midnight, were given 'the highest talents of which men had ever dreamed,' (199) like the gifts of transformation, prophecy, time-travelling and, as in the case of Parvati-the-witch—a girl in Old Delhi's ghetto of magicians—sorcery. Two of them, Saleem and Shiva who were born on the stroke of midnight, were endowed with the greatest talents of all. Shiva, blessed with powerful knees, received the 'gift of war' while Saleem, with his prodigious nose, was given the gift of telepathy—'the ability to look into the hearts and minds of men.' (200) The children with their miraculous talents and varied tongues became a metaphor of 'a thousand and one possibilities' (200) offered by the freedom and of the multiplicity of Indian society, its one thousand and one ways of looking at things. They suggested the new direction which the country was supposed to take: 'Midnight's children can be made to represent many things . . . they can be seen as the last throw of everything antiquated and retrogressive in our myth-ridden nation . . . or as the true hope of freedom.' (200)

Padma is amazed by the story. Her incredulous response to the fantastic account of midnight's children ('O baba! You are sick; what have you said?') engages Saleem in a passionate defence of his narrative. He reminds her: 'Reality can have metaphorical content; that does not make it less real.' (200) What he has narrated to her is literal truth, not the 'bizarre creation of a rambling, diseased mind' (200) or the hallucination of a lonely child. But the time preceding his tenth birthday was hallucinatory with nothing but troubles outside his miracle-laden head. As a result of Narlikar's death and of increasing addiction to alcohol, Ahmed Sinai 'had taken flight into a dream world of disturbing unreality.' (201) His behaviour began to border on abnormality: he withdrew from family life and entered into a profound solitude. He divested himself of all human ties and took refuge in a world of fiction and make-believe. Saleem's ayah, Mary Pereira, too, entered a world of unreality that blurred the margins between waking and dreaming. Consumed by her long-suppressed guilt, she began to be haunted by the phantom of Joseph D'Costa until she realized that only by making a clean breast of her crime to the world she could free herself from 'the ghost of her conscience.' (205) But her love for the ten-year old boy proved too powerful; she could not bring herself to make a confession. Saleem's tenth birthday, which coincided with the tenth Independence Day, was marked by national disasters—drought, storms and floods—which played havoc with the much trumpeted Five Year Plan. On his tenth birthday, a chance mention of the communists by Hanif Aziz made Saleem's mother inexplicably blush. It aroused a suspicion in Saleem's mind and he decided to spy on her. His birthday party was boycotted by the hilltop gang because an embittered Evie Burns had put a ban on festivities. On his tenth birthday, they stormed and occupied his private hideout in the clock tower. Expelled from one gang, ten-year old Saleem formed his own group—'Midnight Children's Conference'—whose headquarters were located in his brain.

Chapter XV: At the Pioneer Café

This chapter begins with Saleem's feverish dream[6] of a witch-like woman sitting on a high chair and killing, one by one, a group of screaming children with her long, serpentine hands amidst hideous laughter. The murderous woman with green and black hair who gathers the children in her hands, rips them apart and rolls them into little balls which are hurled into the night, resembles Kali, the mother goddess in her destructive role. The ominous dream, rendered with lyrical intensity and occurring immediately after Saleem's introduction to the midnight's children, foreshadows their inevitable doom at the hands of the unidentified woman called 'the Widow.' The fever, induced by Padma's potion of unknown herbs, breaks two days later and Saleem foils an attempt by Padma and Mary (who visits him in the pickle factory with his son) to take him to an insane asylum with tricky offers of an outing. His account of the midnight's children has shaken Padma's faith in his narrative and made her suspicious of his sanity. Her suspicion compels Saleem to embark on an eloquent justification of his narrative, his alternative—and highly subjective—version of reality. He holds that personal experience is the only authentic version of history and, therefore, memory becomes the only representative of truth. He insists that he has told her the truth. It is 'memory's truth' which 'selects, eliminates, alters, exaggerates, minimizes . . . but in the end . . . creates its own reality, its heterogeneous but usually coherent version of events.' (211) Saleem thus foregrounds memory as an inextricable feature of his reclamation of the past and re-creation of history. Despite the vagaries of memory, he values his remembered version of events more than the literal facts of history. Only a mad man would prefer somebody else's version to his own, he tells Padma. He brings her round by talking about his son, for whom he is writing his autobiography, and by waxing rhetorical on theology (Hindu, Islamic and Christian alike). By his show of erudition he eventually succeeds in persuading Padma of his sanity and his narratorial right to be unreliable: 'Padma, if you're a little uncertain of my reliability, well, a little uncertainty is no bad thing.' (212) But the whole incident teaches him a valuable lesson: that it is very dangerous to 'impose one's view of things on others.' (212) He, therefore, brackets the subsequent event, his discovery of maternal adultery, with the soothing overtures of a fairy-tale: 'Once upon a time there was a mother who, in order to become a mother, had agreed to change her name.' (213) Shortly after Saleem's tenth birthday, his mother Amina resumed her practice of disappearing, always after receiving a wrong number telephone call, on mysterious shopping trips. He suspected her of harbouring secrets (a suspicion confirmed by his telepathic incursion into her thought processes) and resolved to prove her perfidy with the evidence of his own eyes. He followed her, hidden like 'a stowaway' (214) in the boot of the family car which he had learnt to open with a strip of plastic from his friend Sonny Ibrahim, and arrived at Pioneer Café, 'a rutputty joint' (215) situated near the film-studios in north Bombay. Pioneer Café was a favourite haunt of film extras and a 'notorious Communist Party hangout' (216) where Amina made her rendezvous with her ex-husband Nadir Khan who had been transformed from a rhymeless poet into a political leader. Like his ex-wife, he had acquired a new name, Qasim Khan, an official candidate of the Communist Party of India in the general election. Saleem watched through the 'glassy cinema screen' (216) of the Pioneer Café's window as Amina and her ex-husband played out their love-scene. He spied on the lovers who were engaged in strange hand-dance ('hands longing for touch, hands outstretching tensing quivering demanding to be—but always at last jerking back' [217]) and 'glass kissery' (Amina kissed a glass of lassi and passed it to Nadir Khan who planted on its opposite side his passionate mouth) in grotesque travesty of Hanif's filmic technique. The farcical scene of impotent love convinced Saleem of his mother's treachery and he began to think of revenge. He did not confront her with the evidence of her duplicity, nor did he return to the Café. Instead, he lodged himself in her thoughts and followed her through the byways of Bombay as she moved among the destitutes to campaign on behalf of Lal Qasim and his party. Shocked by the painful experience of maternal infidelity and banished from his private hide-out by Evie Burns and her gang, Saleem began to visit the midnight's children and commune with them telepathically in the secrecy of night. It was during one such nightly meeting of the M.C.C. held in the parliament of his brain, Saleem encountered Shiva, his fellow changeling and alter-ego. Shiva, the genetic son of Ahmed and Amina Sinai, had been raised in extreme poverty and was filled with violent resentment against the unjust world. He had to fight for survival from his childhood and defend himself against the 'parental zeal' (221) of his putative father, Wee Willie Winkie. By the time Saleem met him, Wee Winkie had died and Shiva had become the leader of a notorious gang in Bombay's underworld. Shiva reacted to the presence of Saleem with utter rage and claimed the joint-leadership of the Conference by virtue of his birth on the stroke of midnight: 'my father said I got born at exactly midnight also—so don't you see, that makes us joint bosses of this gang of yours!' (220) But Saleem, with his idea of the Conference as 'a sort of loose federation of equals,' (220) turned down the proposal. Shiva mocked at the rich boy from Methwold's Estate whose head was full of 'crazy stuff' like reason and purpose: 'What purpose, man? What thing in the whole . . . world got reason. . . ? For what reason you're rich and I'm poor?' (220) The encounter initiated a rivalry between Shiva and Saleem (between 'knees and nose') which would have far-reaching consequences in their lives as well as in the life of the nation. Shiva embodied the force of chaos which posed a threat to the notion of liberal freedom represented by Saleem. It was this force which was let loose by the ruling Congress Party, under the leadership of 'Boss Patil' (a fictional equivalent of S.K. Patil), to rig the election of 1957 in Bombay. Shiva and his gang threatened the voters to keep them away from the polling stations on the election day. Qasim Khan was defeated but the Communists emerged as the largest single opposition party in the Parliament.

At the end of the episode, Saleem discovers yet another factual error: the election of 1957 had taken place before, and not after, his tenth birthday. He realizes that his memory has again played a trick on him. But his brain stubbornly refuses to unscramble itself and 'alter the sequence of events.' (222) He clings to the imperfectly remembered version, preferring it to mere literal happenstance.

Chapter XVI: Alpha and Omega

Saleem's narrative reaches the half-way point in this chapter which is significantly titled 'Alpha and Omega.' He thinks of several alternative headings in keeping with the events taking place in this episode but sticks to the one he has given because 'there are beginnings here, and all manner of ends.' (223) The chapter begins with the end of Evie Burns' dominion over the children of Methwold's Estate. There was widespread political turmoil in Bombay soon after the general election of 1957. The Central Government's failure to take a quick decision about the future of Bombay led to riots between the supporters of Marathi and Gujarati languages. A severe drought made the situation worse. There was also a series of explosions at the city's central reservoir and the main fresh-water pipes resulting in an acute scarcity of water and a 'great cat invasion.' (224) The stray cats began to congregate in the relatively better-off areas of the city where water was still available. Methwold's Estate was invaded by an army of thirsty cats and its alarmed inhabitants began to think that it was 'the end of the world.' (224) But Evie Burns, the American tom-boy, came to their rescue with her air-gun and put an end to the feline assault in return for bounty money. She became rich and very popular at the Estate. But her moment of triumph proved to be short-lived; it was quickly followed by her downfall. Enraged by Evie's persecution of the cats, Brass Monkey—with her fondness for feline life and hatred for her brother's tormentor—challenged her to a fight. In a fierce battle fought on the circus ring, Monkey vanquished Evie Burns. She broke her teeth, her spirit and her unquestionable sway over the hill-top children. Evie's father sent her home for good to 'get a decent education away from these savages.' (225) A few months later she knifed an aged woman for objecting to her assault on a cat and was sent to a reform school. The ending of Evie's story was followed by the beginning of the M.C.C. network and the midnight parliament. Evie's fall put an end to Saleem's exclusion from the hill-top gang. But he found it difficult to forgive them and for a while kept himself aloof. He immersed himself in the miraculous events inside his head and like the mythical gander—the 'parahamsa'—began to inhabit two worlds: 'Awake I was obliged to face the multiple miseries of maternal perfidy and paternal decline, of the fickleness of friendship and the varied tyrannies of school; asleep, I was at the centre of the most exciting world any child had ever discovered.' (227) With the increase of his telepathic power, Saleem discovered that he could not only pick up the children's transmissions and broadcast his own messages but also 'act as a sort of national network.' (227) He could turn his mind into a forum where all the children could talk to one another through him. Thus, the surviving five hundred and eighty one children began to meet, from the early days of 1958, for one hour (between midnight and 1 a.m.) in the 'lok sabha' of his brain. From the very beginning of the association, there was rivalry between Saleem and Shiva over the question of leadership. Saleem never liked the rough-tongued and impenetrable son of Wee Winkie for the 'crudity of his ideas.' (226) The issue of leadership was eventually decided in Saleem's favour because he had not only discovered the children and there was rivalry between Saleem and Shiva over the question of leadership. Saleem never liked the rough-tongued and impenetrable son of Wee Winkie for the 'crudity of his ideas.' (226) The issue of leadership was eventually decided in Saleem's favour because he had not only discovered the children and founded the conference but also provided them with the meeting place. He introduced the notions of meaning and purpose to the conference: 'We must think what we are for' (228). In the ensuing debate widely divergent, even contradictory, views about the aims and philosophies of the association were put forward by the child members, ranging from 'collectivism and individualism,' 'capitalism and altruism,' 'science and religion.' The debate reflected the typically Indian dissension and division of opinions. Their magical faculties notwithstanding, the children remained 'a sort of many-headed monster, speaking in the myriad tongues of Babel . . . the very essence of multiplicity.' (229) With their natural exuberance and youthful optimism, they refused to look at the darker side of reality and ignored the warning of the time-travelling member, Soumitra, that they would be destroyed by the adult world before long. None of the prodigious children could think that 'the purpose of Midnight's Children might be annihilation; that [they] would have no meaning until [they] were destroyed.' (229) Even at that early stage of his life, Saleem was haunted by a diffuse sense of 'destiny, historical role, numen.' (229) But he was constantly distracted from the marvellous world inside his head by the small incidents of everyday life and the 'painful, engrossing torture of growing up.' (229) He was forced to stop his imaginative flight and come down, like the legendary swan, to the quotidian world of strife and stress to experience mutilation and bloodshed. Saleem's first mutilation was the contribution of Emil Zagallo, the geography teacher of his school. Zagallo was an Anglo-Indian and, probably, a bastard although he claimed himself to be a Peruvian. He was a living terror to his students and had earned notoriety for his bullying tactics and hatred for the Indians whom he called 'savages' and 'bead-lovers.' (230) In a geography class, Saleem incurred his wrath by protesting against his harassment of a poor but brilliant student, Jimmy Kapadia, who suffered from a heart disease. The crazy teacher dragged him by his hair to the front of the class and unleashed his wit on him. Displaying Saleem's hideous face to the students he taught them human geography: 'In the face of the ugly ape you don't see the whole map of India?' (231) Saleem's chin, Zagallo mischievously said, stood for the southern peninsula and the disfiguring birthmarks on his face represented the two wings of Pakistan because Pakistan was 'a stain on the face of India!' (231) The crude joke, which equated Saleem with India and his misshapen body with the national map, culminated in his loss of hair. Writhing in agony beneath Zagallo's violence and black humour, Saleem inadvertently dropped a blob of nose goo on his hand. The furious teacher seized a tuft of his hair and pulled it out creating a blood-filled patch on his head. The incident put an end to Zagallo's service. He left the school bequeathing Saleem his legacy: 'a monkish tonsure' and a couple of taunts, 'baldie' and 'map face,' (232) which his friends would fling at him. The first mutilation was quickly followed by a second in which two of Saleem's classmates became 'instruments of destiny.' (233) At the School Social, held soon after the class-room drama, a beautiful European girl, Masha Miovic, who was Brass Monkey's friend and a champion breast-stroke swimmer, agreed to dance with Saleem. Envious of his luck, two bullies in his class, Glandy Keith Colaco and Fat Perce Fishwala, taunted him and divulged the secret of his bandaged head to Masha. Enraged by his friends' betrayal and goaded by his dance partner, Saleem rounded on them. In the skirmish that ensued, he lost the middle finger of his right hand and was admitted to a hospital. Saleem needed an emergency transfusion and an analysis of his blood performed on that occasion revealed that it was neither Alpha nor Omega, neither A (his mother's blood group) nor O (his father's), and that it was, unlike his parents' blood, rhesus-negative. The startling disclosure that he was not the genetic son of Ahmed and Amina Sinai had devastating effects on his private life. It put an end to all certainties: 'Suddenly you are forever other than you were; and the world becomes such that parents can cease to be parents, and love can turn to hate.' (237) The chapter ends cinematically with the image of ten-year-old Saleem—sitting on the hospital bed with a bandaged finger, brooding over the mystery of blood and listening to the radio-borne voice of Tony Brent singing 'The Clouds Will Soon Roll By' and snatches of an altercation, outside his cabin, between a hateful father casting aspersions on his wife's character and a distraught mother protesting her innocence—which zooms out slowly into long-shot.

Chapter XVII: The Kolynos Kid

This chapter, which describes Saleem's first exile from home consequent upon his accidental loss of finger and the discovery of his genetic difference from his parents, begins with a playful explication of his claim for the central position in his story and the multiple modes of his engagement with the nation. Saleem who has always been a victim, more acted upon than acting, persists in viewing himself as protagonist and, 'against all indications to the contrary,' (237) explains his grandiose claim to a 'place at the center of things,' (238) a position ratified by the Prime Minister. In his congratulatory letter, Nehru had identified baby Saleem with the newly born state and written that his life would mirror the life of the nation. How can the life of a single individual be said to influence and reflect the fate of a country? asks narrator Saleem thirty years later as he tries desperately to preserve his version of India before complete fragmentation. He provides a pseudo-scientific answer to the question: "I was linked to history both literally and metaphorically, both actively and passively, in what our (admirably modern) scientists might term 'modes of connection' composed of dualistically-combined configurations' of the two pairs of opposed adverbs." (238) He was related to his country 'actively-literally' (by which he means his actions which directly influenced the course of history, like his intervention in the language riot); 'passively-metaphorically' (the socio-political events which impinged on his life metaphorically; for example, the connection between child Saleem's programme of self-enlargement and the infant nation's heroic attempt at growth). He was entwined with his country 'passively-literally' (by which he suggests the national events that directly affected him and his family; for instance, the freezing of Ahmed's assets by the state) and 'actively-metaphorically' (the things done by or to Saleem which were mirrored at the macrocosmic level; for example, the mutilation of his finger which corresponded to the cracking up of the state). What is significant in this rational analysis of the interaction between individual and national lives is Saleem's recognition of the passive-metaphorical mode of connection. He, like the other children of midnight, has no place in the active-literal mode where he is a victim, 'handcuffed to history.' It is only in the passive-metaphorical realm that he assumes his central position as a witness to and chronicler of national events.

The accident irreversibly changed Saleem's life. The discovery that he was not his parents' son left him shattered. When his uncle Hanif and his ayah Mary came to collect him from the hospital, he realized that something had gone wrong with his world. He was taken to the small apartment of Hanif and his wife Pia near Marine Drive. Saleem guessed that he was in exile. His parents had lost their interest in him and loaned him out for some indefinite period. He bore his banishment uncomplainingly and blamed himself for it. He looked upon himself as the Kolynos Kid, a gleamtoothed elf on a hoarding near Kemp's corner proclaiming the virtues of Kolynos toothpaste by squeezing an 'inexhaustible tube.' (240) Saleem, 'an involuntary Kolynos Kid,' had been 'squeezing crises and transformations out of a bottomless tube . . . on to [his] metaphorical toothbrush.' (240) Childless Hanif and Pia accepted the abandoned boy graciously and enlivened his life with their affection. For them, he acted out 'the part of the surrogate son.' (243) He basked in their delight, enjoyed Mary's cookery and began to grow in height. To live in his uncle's house was, for Saleem, to 'exist in the hot sticky heart of a Bombay talkie.' (243) By that time both Hanif's and Pia's career in the cinema had fallen into a decline. Deprived of movie roles, Pia had turned her life into a feature film in which she played the role of a star-crossed tragedienne railing against an unjust and ungrateful world and pouring out her grievances against her husband and his family. She sought refuge in nostalgia while Hanif crusaded against the cult of fabulism and fantasy in Bombay cinema. Although he had begun his career in the fabulist mode, Hanif soon remembered his father's legacy and dedicated himself against the unreality and fantastic preoccupations of the film world. He began to despise the 'myth-life of India' (244) which provided sustenance to Bombay cinemá. During Saleem's stay in his house, Hanif was busy writing the script of a realistic film about a pickle factory created, run and worked in entirely by women. He declaimed against the pernicious effects of fantasy in the presence of his miraculous nephew who was still unaware of the future significance of a pickle factory in his life.[7] But in the 'temple of illusions,' nobody had time for the 'high priest of reality' (ibid). Hanif besieged Homi Catrack with his scripts. The film magnate produced none but, for some reasons, paid him a regular salary. Hanif and Pia, once popular film director and actress, thus, survived on the charity of a man who would soon be 'murdered by mushrooming Saleem' (ibid). Meanwhile, Mary was in the grip of a panic. The ghost of Joseph D'Costa did not follow her into exile. Still, she constantly suffered from a fear that during her absence from Buckingham Villa he might appear before Saleem's parents and reveal to them the secret of her crime. Every morning she would leave Hanif's house for Methwold's Estate to check if Joe had betrayed her and return to Marine Drive with strange rumours of 'supernatural invasion' (245) she heard during her bus journey. She relayed the rumours—of the re-enactment of Kurukshetra war, the re-appearance of many-headed demons, and the discovery of the bleeding tomb of Jesus Christ in Kashmir—to wide-eyed Saleem. While Hanif, with his distrust of the supernatural, laughed at them, Saleem remained half-convinced. He could not ignore them as the superstitious ideas of a guilt-crazed ayah. For him, the rumours reflected a grave crisis in the nation. As he says with the benefit of hindsight:

> in that time of accelerated events and diseased hours the past of India rose up to confound her present; the new-born secular state was being given an awesome reminder of its fabulous antiquity . . . so

> that people were seized by atavistic longings, and forgetting the new myth of freedom reverted to their old ways, their old regionalist loyalties and prejudices, and the body politic began to crack. (245)

Saleem, like Rushdie, believes that many of the problems which plagued post-Independence India and threatened its secular-modernist structure can be traced to the unwholesome habit of the people to occasionally lapse into the myth-ridden and retrogressive past. Independence had provided the country with an opportunity to emerge from the shadows of the 'fabulous antiquity' of Hindu India and become a land of promise and dream by espousing the notions of modernity and multiplicity and embracing secular, democratic ideals. But the dream was shattered because the people soon forgot 'the new myth of freedom' and 'reverted to their old ways' and 'regionalist loyalties' which created cracks in the country's democratic fabric. The act of nostalgically reminding the newly born secular state of its religio-mythical traditions was fraught with danger. It resulted in a nation which was divided along linguistic, regional and communal lines. The fissure in the state coincided with Saleem's amputation and he found a connection between the two. It was at that diseased time he was possessed by a strange lust for revenge. Despite his declining career, Hanif's house remained a popular place frequented by the well-known artists, politicians and journalists of Bombay. They would arrive in the evening to play cards, gossip and exchange rumours. In one such 'card-evening,' (245) when Saleem was alone on the balcony, Homi Catrack pressed a note into his hand and asked him, in a sibilant voice, to deliver it secretly to his aunt. He even threatened to cut the boy's tongue if he disclosed it to anybody else. That night Saleem dreamed the murder of his classmate, Jimmy Kapadia, and screamed in panic. When Pia took the yelling boy to her bed to comfort him, he discharged his duty, thus precipitating a crisis in the conjugal life of his beloved uncle and aunt. Pia Aziz, who had been Homi Catrack's 'fancy woman' (250) for many years, was informed by the film producer that he had tired of her charms. Saleem realized that he had been tricked by his neighbour and he began to hate him for seducing and, then, abandoning his beautiful aunt. Next day, he returned from school (where he learnt that Jimmy Kapadia had suddenly died of heart-seizure and felt responsible for his death because he had dreamed it) to witness the histrionics of his film-actress aunt whose lover had discarded her. Saleem went to Pia's room to cheer her up but, with his budding sexuality, he got 'indiscreetly carried away.' (251) The incident put an end to the exile of the 'Kolynos Kid.' His mother came to take him back without offering any explanation for his banishment. Saleem's loathing for his adulterous mother was linked with his newly born hatred for his treacherous neighbour. Possessed by this two-headed monster, he began to devise a terrible revenge which would have grave consequences for both his family and the nation.

Chapter XVIII: Commander Sabarmati's baton

Throughout the novel national history is entangled with the family history of the narrator-hero who, in spite of being a victim, claims to influence the historical process sometimes directly and sometimes by his passive presence. In this chapter, which describes the disintegration of Midnight Children's Conference and Saleem's revenge on Homi Catrack, he fancies himself acting upon Indian history at a scandalous point and, thus, engendering the Sabarmati affair, a send-up of the famous Nanavati case of the late 1950s in which a handsome, epicurean youth named Prem Ahuja was murdered by Commander Nanavati, a promising officer of the Indian Navy, for seducing his wife. The incident, which shook the nation, is given a fictionalized form in Saleem's narrative. Rushdie parodies the Nanavati case viewing it as a kind of farcical re-enactment of the story of abduction and retribution in the *Ramayana*.

After her return from exile, Mary found it increasingly difficult to suppress her crime. During her absence the ghost of Joseph D'Costa had begun to decay. The sight of the crumbling spectre heightened her sense of guilt and brought her very close to a confession. But, once again, her love for the disgraced boy delayed the revelation which would expose him as a fraud.

While Mary was caught on the horns of a dilemma, Saleem tried to come to terms with the changes which had occurred in his family during his banishment. He returned home in 'an atmosphere of confusion and distrust' (253) and found that his primacy in the family had been usurped by his sister. She was now the sole recipient of parental affection of which her brother's overpowering shadow had so long deprived her. With Brass Monkey's pre-eminence in the household, even her 'flirtation with Christianity' (253), under the influence of her Christian ayah and European school-friends, was tolerated by her parents. She donned a nun's outfit and a rosary and went around the house singing Christian hymns. She even fasted in the period of Lent, instead of Ramzan, thus 'revealing an unexpected streak of fanaticism' (253) which would later dominate her personality. Saleem accepted the change in his fortune as a painful and inevitable price of growing up. But he could not enjoy the freedom which his altered position in the family had provided him because he was distracted by a series of transformations which were taking place in his life. He was transforming physically with the symptoms of adolescence appearing on his body which had already attained its full adult height. Unexpected change was occurring in his inner world as well. The Midnight Children's Conference had started disintegrating. The initial excitement of the discovery of each other had worn off. The novelty of meeting in the midnight parliament was replaced by growing boredom and dissension which widened the cracks in the association. The miraculous children were not immune to the influence of their parents and as a result 'the prejudices and world-views of adults began to take over their minds.' (254) The poison of the grown-ups leaked into the children's council and drew its members apart: 'I found children from Maharashtra loathing Gujaratis, and fair-skinned northerners reviling Dravidian 'blackies.' (254) The regional hatred bred other hatreds based on religion and class: 'there were religious rivalries; and class entered our councils.' (254) The children's conference, thus, fulfilled Nehru's prophecy and became 'a mirror of the nation,' It fell victim to the paradoxes of Indian nationalism, its 'endless duality of masses-

and-classes, capital-and-labour, them-and-us.' (255) Saleem's desperate pleas to overcome the differences, to forge an identity peculiar to themselves and break through the unproductive dualisms inherent in such social divisions to another level of truth, to a 'third principle,' were ignored by the squabbling children. Their magical gifts seemed powerless to prevent the conflict that broke out among them and Saleem felt the children slipping away from him. The duality persisted, as did the rivalry between idealistic Saleem and pragmatic Shiva (for whom the world was not 'ideas' but 'things' and 'there [was] no third principle; there [was] only money-and-poverty . . . right-and-left . . . me-against-the-world' [255]) leading inevitably to the disintegration of the conference. In utter disappointment, Saleem bade adieu to his hope of putting things in a different way: 'If there is a third principle, its name is childhood. But it dies; or rather, it is murdered.' (256) Childhood was killed by the poison of the adult world and the increasing discord and cynicism of the children who, despite their prodigious talents, found it impossible to mould things differently.

Amidst all those troubles Saleem was continually impelled by the two-headed monster lurking inside him to teach his hypocritical mother a lesson and avenge the treachery of his promiscuous neighbour, Homi Catrack. Consumed by his lust for revenge, he went up-stairs to the top floor of Buckingham Villa and learnt from the senile European snake-expert, Schaapsteker, about the 'occult powers of snakes' (257) and their ways of attacking an enemy: 'Imitate the action of the snake . . . strike from the cover of a bush.' (258) Having discovered how to proceed, Saleem used his telepathic powers to spy on his enemy, Homi Catrack, and his new fancy woman, Lila Sabarmati, the beautiful wife of the 'heir apparent to the title of Admiral of the Fleet' (258) Armed with the details of their weekly rendezvous in an apartment near Colaba Causeway, Saleem struck secretly like a snake. Cutting pieces out of newspaper headlines and reshaping them on a sheet of paper, he prepared a cautionary but anonymous note and sent it to Commander Sabarmati. His absurd action reflects the absurdity of the historian's claim of presenting history as an objective truth and shows that history can be manipulated to constitute a new view of reality and serve dangerous and individual designs. He was not proud, as he admits retrospectively, of what he did: 'Cutting up history to suit [his] nefarious purposes.' (259) Driven by maternal hypocrisy and the grief of his aunt, he only wanted to teach 'a lesson to all unfaithful wives and mothers.' (262) But his 'first attempt at rearranging history' (260) caused the greatest scandal of the time. Proceeding on his clue, Commander Vinoo Sabarmati reached the place of assignation with a gun and shot his faithless wife and her lover. Homi died on the spot while Lila was seriously injured. Having accomplished his mission, the gun-waving naval officer surrendered himself to a traffic sergeant. As the policeman fled in panic leaving him in the midst of a traffic confusion, Sabarmati mounted the podium and 'began to direct cars, using the smoking gun as a baton.' (262) This was how he was found at the time of his arrest. The incident created a tremendous uproar in the country and captured the people's imagination. Sabarmati became 'the most popular murderer in the history of Indian jurisprudence.' (262) During the trial, public opinion swung dramatically in favour of the cuckolded husband. His murder of his wife's seducer was compared to Rama's slaughter of Sita's abductor, the many-headed monster, Ravana: 'If Rama himself were alive, would we send him to prison for slaying the abductor of Sita?' (264) Saleem's 'vengeful irruption into . . . history' (264) precipitated a national crisis. The country found itself having to choose between the rule of heroism and the rule of law, between its mythical past and its democratic present. The crisis ended with the President's refusal to pardon Sabarmati and the latter's imprisonment. Saleem's revenge had its desired effect on his mother (she stopped answering wrong-number telephone calls) but it brought the world of his childhood to an end. In the aftermath of the Sabarmati affair, all the heirs of William Methwold, except Ahmed Sinai, sold their houses to the Narlikar women and left the Estate for good.

Chapter XIX: Revelations

Saleem's story picks up speed to keep pace with his accelerating decay. With the narrative rush comes a jarring alteration in tone. He relies more and more on his ministrant Padma and her reactions to avoid the risk of error and unreliability and keep himself on the rails as his story enters into the worst period of his eleven-year-old life when 'revelations flowed faster than blood.' (271) The chapter begins with an account of the transformation of Saleem's most brilliant friend, Cyrus Dubash, into the richest child guru in India. After the accidental death of his father, the nuclear physicist Dr. Dubash, during the hue and cry of the Sabarmati scandal, Cyrus' mother unleashed on him her long-suppressed religious fanaticism. With her keen business acumen, she reworked the Superman comics (which boy Saleem had given to Cyrus as a fee for the latter's lectures on female anatomy) to invent a potent modern myth, the advent of Lord Khusro Khusrovand Bhagwan. The metamorphosis of Cyrus from a 'school prodigy' into 'the most successful holy child in history' (269) who lectured rich American disciples, owned a luxury liner and an aircraft, and eventually drowned at sea while attempting to walk on water—is a parody of the scandal of fake Balguru Jogeshwar in the late 1950s.[8] The revelation of Cyrus' apotheosis was followed by the startling disclosure of Aadam Aziz and the confession of Mary which shattered Saleem's dream world. The series of unsettling revelations began with a dust storm in Methwold's Estate and the death of Hanif Aziz. Towards the end of 1957, the Narlikar women started razing the colonial palaces of William Methold to erect a dream mansion in its place and to force Ahmed Sinai to sell his house. Clouds of dust enveloped Buckingham Villa making life miserable for the Sinais. It was at that time they received from Pia the shocking news of Hanif's suicide. Deprived of an income by Homi Catrack's murder, he had jumped off the roof of the Marine Drive apartment block. The entire Aziz family, including the bereaved widow, gathered at Buckingham Villa to observe the forty-day mourning period. But in the 'ghost haze' (271) of the dust which besieged the family for forty days, 'things were said and seen and done from which none of [them] ever recovered.' (272) Everybody had expected Pia, an 'accomplished tragedienne,' (272) to orchestrate her misfortune with a forty-day raga of howling pain. But she remained surprisingly calm, refusing to give a theatrical display of her grief like her hair-rending and breast-pummelling in-laws. She did so in honour of her husband who had died for his hatred of melodrama. Enraged by the unusual behaviour of her film-actress daughter-in-law whom she had never liked, Reverend Mother berated her and, echoing her old war of starvation with Aadam Aziz, threatened to fast until the shameless widow shed tears for her deceased spouse. The stalemate was broken on the twentieth day of the mourning period when Saleem went to Pia to apologize for his indiscreet conduct during his exile. She was about to reply when dust entered her nose and made her sneeze, breaching the walls of her self-possession. The sneeze brought tears to her eyes and the family witnessed the much-hoped-for display of sorrow. Tears fell from Pia's eyes like 'Flora Fountain' (273) and she shaped the irresistible flood with great éclat. Pleased by the performance, Reverend Mother joined her, 'turning the solo into a duet, mingling the music of reconciliation with the unbearably beautiful tunes of grief.' (273) She broke her fast and announced her decision to migrate to Pakistan with her husband and her widowed daughter-in-law. Two days later, Aadam Aziz made an astounding revelation that he had 'seen with his own eyes the God in whose death he had tried all his life to believe.' (275) Dr. Aziz, sixty-eight years old at that time, had declined over the decades. His loss of optimism after the death of the Humming-bird and his disappointment with the new nation had taken a heavy toll on his body. With his growing submission to the fanaticism of his wife, the progressive doctor's body had begun to crack like Indian Independence and all that it stood for him. His bones had started disintegrating, creating fissures on his leathery skin (a disease which would leak into Saleem, along with his unbelief and vulnerability to women). When he announced in a rambling voice to the members of his family that he had seen someone with perforated hands and feet in his room the previous night, and that the apparition had asked him: 'You're the one whose son died,' (276) nobody, except Mary Pereira, believed him. They dismissed his disclosure as the confusion of a bereaved father. But Aadam Aziz never forgot the vision and with the passing years the bitter idea struck root in the depths of his senility that God had snatched his son from him. It filled his mind with a hatred for God and a passionate desire for revenge. He refused to go to Pakistan, as his wife had planned, because it was a God-ridden country. The narrative moves forward in time to describe his terrible revenge and death which coincided with the theft of the holy relic from the Hazratbal Mosque of Srinagar in the winter of 1963. Saleem suggests that the bizarre incident, which resulted in communal and political disturbances in the whole sub-continent, might be an 'attempt at revenge upon God by a father who had lost his son.' (277) In December 1963, Dr. Aziz left his house in Agra alone and boarded a Srinagar-bound train. On December 27, a man corresponding to his description was found near the Hazratbal Mosque. Next morning, the theft of the Prophet's hair was detected and it led to widespread riots and a massive search to retrieve the valley's most sacred treasure. On 1 January 1964, five days before the relic was recovered, Aziz climbed the hill on which stood the temple of Sankara Acharya. But before the stick-waving old man could enter the inner sanctum to wreak vengeance on God, his cracking sickness claimed him. His bones disintegrated beyond all hope of repair and he died. Aadam Aziz, who had once left the valley with a hole at the centre of his body created by his loss of faith, thus ended his story where it had begun. The death of the patriarch was accompanied by a national tragedy. Nehru, 'the father of the nation,' (279) succumbed to a fatal illness on 27 May, 1964. By a convoluted logic, Saleem claims the responsibility for Nehru's death.

The narrative returns to 1958 to allow Mary to make her shocking revelation which irreversibly changed the course of Saleem's life. Three days before the end of the mourning period, Mary saw the ghost of Joseph in the shape of an old man, whose disfigured body was filled with sulphurous stench, walking towards the office of Ahmed Sinai. Unnerved by the sight, she rushed to Amina, threw herself at her feet and cried for mercy.

When the family members assembled, at her request, in Ahmed's office, Mary made a public confession of her long-suppressed crime. Her disclosure that Saleem was not the genetic son of Ahmed and Amina and that his real parents were Wee Winkie and Vanita, left the family astounded. As they reeled under the 'horror of the truth' (280) which had pulled them out of the make-believe world invented by Mary with the change of name-tags eleven years ago, Ahmed drew their attention to the apparition who had precipitated the crisis. The deformed creature was none other than Musa, the old servant of the family who had been dismissed from service on charges of theft. Musa had contracted leprosy and returned, 'across the silence of the years,' (280) to beg for Ahmed's forgiveness so that he could be released from what he believed to be a curse. It was his decayed body which Aadam Aziz had mistaken for God and Mary had taken for the ghost of her communist lover all along. Mary left Buckingham Villa for good and went back to her mother in Goa. But her confession forced Saleem to enter into his second exile, this time in Pakistan.

Chapter XX: Movements performed by pepperpots

Mary Pereira's confession had a stunning effect not only on Saleem's family but on his inner world as well. With the discovery of the secret of his birth, he stopped convening the midnight conference and avoided his fellow children. He excluded Shiva from the parliament of his mind for fear that his destructive alter-ego might claim his birth-right. But his deliberate expulsion of the most powerful of midnight's children closed off the possibility of regaining harmony in 'the increasingly fractious councils' (282) of the M.C.C. Having banished Shiva from the forum, Saleem found himself thrown across the border and lost his connection with the children. His exile was expedited by the violent reaction of Ahmed Sinai to Mary's disclosure. At the end of the mourning period for Hanif, Ahmed emerged from his 'private world of abstraction' (283) and encountered his wife with an indefinable rage. He reviled Amina for hours and held her responsible for what Mary's confession had revealed. But Reverend Mother defended her daughter against her irascible and intoxicated son-in-law and legitimized Saleem in the face of his 'lunatic temper.' (283) Her recognition of Saleem as the son of Amina ended all opposition to his rightful place in the Sinai household. She instructed Emerald and Zulfikar to take Amina, her children and Pia with them to Pakistan and await her migration to the country with Aadam Aziz. Emerald was displeased but she could not defy her mother. To Saleem, the whole incident was a maturing experience; it meant the end of innocence and childhood. He left his life-long home with empty hands and the knowledge of his birth and went to Pakistan to accept the 'grudging hospitality' (284) of his aunt. For him, it was a change from the warmth and exuberance of Bombay to the coldness of Rawalpindi and the listlessness of General Zulfikar's lavishly decorated military bungalow. He never felt at ease in the stifling atmosphere of the dull and lifeless house where the Sinais and Pia Aziz were constantly reminded of being useless, 'non-productive members' (286) and whose most interesting inhabitant was not human but a dog. Saleem describes—as a trailer to the 'pepperpot revolution' and the formation of the Cutia Unit of Pakistani army during the Bangladesh War—the exploits of General Zulfikar's aged beagle bitch named Bonzo. She had demonstrated, in a travesty of military exercise, her marvellous gift of smelling out mines in a specially prepared minefield on the Indo-Pakistani border and was drafted into the army as a 'four-legged mine-detector with the courtesy rank of sergeant-major.' (286) But the most embarrassing member of the Zulfikar household was the General's enuretic son Zafar who wetted his pants throughout his adult life and, thus, brought shame on his family. Saleem went to school with Zafar and watched his mother withering in her exile and struggling hard, like his sister, to rebuild her relationship with him. But neither Amina nor Brass Monkey entirely succeeded in their re-imaginings of Saleem as a son and a brother because he detected a distance behind their apparent gentleness towards him. The pain of personal life and the angst of forced migration were, however, compensated by the thrill of public events. Saleem witnessed, as an eleven-year-old boy, Pakistan's momentous transformation from a parliamentary democracy, which had already become a farce with the erosion of the constitution, ubiquitous corruption and political instability, into a military dictatorship through a midnight coup planned in a dinner party at General Zulfikar's house.[9] By virtue of his being Zulfikar's relative, he helped 'active-metaphorically' (291) to change the fate of Pakistan. On the night of 7 October 1958, General Ayub announced his decision to end civilian rule and impose Martial Law in the country to top army officers present in the dinner party. Zulfikar demonstrated the manoeuvre of the army with the pepperpots on the dinner table and asked Saleem to assist him: 'General Zulfikar described troop movements; I moved pepperpots symbolically while he spoke.' (290) Together they made a revolution which not only overthrew the elected government but also, a few weeks later, consigned the President of the country, Iskander Mirza, to exile. Saleem earned the gratitude of his uncle (whose own son had publicly humiliated him by wetting his pants at the dinner table) and, thus, created a new father for himself: "Zulfikar became the latest in the line of men who have been willing to call me . . . 'my son.'" (290) Despite his disclaimer that he, at the age of eleven, made no political judgement, Saleem's disapproval of the topsy-turvy political scene in Pakistan is evident in the satirical treatment of the midnight coup which he calls 'revolution of the pepperpots.' (285) His censure of the coup-plotting army-generals, whom he sarcastically describes as 'gongs and pips,' (288) is implicit in his recognition of their intrigue as 'treason' (290) and in his trenchant remark: 'Midnight has many children; the offspring of Independence were not all human. Violence, corruption, poverty, generals, chaos, greed and pepperpots. . . . I had to go into exile to learn that the children of midnight were more varied than I . . . had dreamed.' (291) At the age of eleven Saleem was concerned not with the fate of a country where he stayed as a refugee but with his 'personal rehabilitation' (291) in the Zulfikar household. It was this parochial motive which inspired his 'most crucial foray into history.' (291) He stayed in Pakistan as a socially inferior relative of the Zulfikars and passively observed the deterioration of Indo-Pak relations, India's conquest of Goa and the Sino-Indian border skirmishes in Aksai Chin. During the four years of exile he grew into a teenager and helplessly watched the disintegration of his mother. He also witnessed the transformation of his sister from a wild and rebellious girl into a demure and submissive adolescent. It was during her Pakistanı sojourn Brass Monkey made the final break with the secular legacy of her grandfather by revealing a 'streak of puritan fanaticism' (292) and falling in love with God. On her fourteenth birthday, Saleem noticed her metamorphosis 'from monkey into singer.' (293) At the birthday party, she demonstrated her rare gift for song in a matured, unblemished voice and earned her name, 'Jamila Singer.' Her emergence as a singer put an end to Saleem's primacy for ever. After that evening he was forced to concede second place to her musical talent which would captivate the God-ridden country belong long.

Chapter XXI: Drainage and the desert

Soon after Brass Monkey's fourteenth birthday, Amina received a telegram from Alice Pereira in Bombay that Ahmed had suffered a massive heart-attack. The crisis in the Sinai family, which synchronized with a national catastrophe—the Chinese aggression on the Himalayan frontier, culminated in Saleem's eviction from his inner world. His magical gift of telepathy had set him apart, enabling him to live simultaneously in two worlds—the imaginative and the mundane. But Alice's telegram ended his flights of imagination and dragged him down to the earth to face a painful drainage and a silent, empty desert.

After the departure of his wife and children for Pakistan. Ahmed had steadily declined in his private world of abstraction and drunkenness with no human companion except his secretary, Alice. Consumed by resentment, self-pity and grief, he had ranted at his family and the injustices of his life. For four years, he had been besieged by loneliness, strange fears and telephonic blandishments of the Narlikar women to sell his house. Under the combined pressures of anger, grief, fear and coaxing his heart had bulged ('booted,' as Alice wrote in her message) and 'felled him like an ox.' (296) On receiving the news of his illness, Amina returned to Bombay with her children. The crisis brought about a remarkable change in her; it jerked her out of despondency and lassitude. She miraculously regained her youthful assiduity and set about the difficult task of Ahmed's physical rehabilitation. Under her unflagging care Ahmed not only made a speedy recovery but also returned to his former self which was 'filled with contrition and forgiveness and laughter and . . . the finest miracle of all . . . love.' (297) Having recovered from the fatal sickness by the loving attention of his much-maligned wife, Ahmed Sinai, at long last, fell in love with her. Meanwhile, the tension between India and China had turned into a full-fledged war. With the escalation of hostilities between the two countries, the crisis in Saleem's inner world intensified.[10] Glad to return to the cacophony and 'the rainbow riot' (297) of Bombay, he renewed his contact with the midnight's children. On 9 October, 1962, when the Indian soldiers marched towards the battle-field, Saleem convened the children's council, not knowing what was in store for him. The children returned to the forum of his mind and, like the Indian army which was ready for an 'all-out effort' (298) to resist the Chinese invasion, made an all-out attempt at re-union by burying their old differences. With China's unprovoked attack on India, on 15 October, Saleem found himself assailed by unprovoked questions about Shiva's absence from the conference and about the closing of a part of his mind. On 20 October, the Indian forces were severely beaten by the Chinese near Thag La ridge. The same night, Saleem's miraculous siblings launched a concerted assault on him; they accused him of 'secrecy, prevarication, highhandedness, egotism.' (298) The parliament of his mind turned into a battleground on which the children thrashed him. He was completely defenceless against their aggression since he could not bring himself to disclose the secret of his birth. The children lost their faith in him and in the parliament he had created for them. They began to flee from Saleem like the Indian troops running away from the advancing Chinese army. The Children's Conference, which represented the very essence of multiplicity and the true hope of freedom, thus, fell apart. It was destroyed by internal divisiveness and dissension, prejudice and selfishness. The possibility of renewal was closed by Saleem's denial of access to Shiva who continued to haunt him, first as an 'obsession' and, finally, as a kind of principle representing 'the vengefulness and violence and simultaneous-love-and-hate-of-Things in the world.' (299) Shiva continued to influence the course of history to which he was connected, like Saleem, by virtue of his birth on the stroke of midnight.

The debacle at Thag La ridge triggered off an unprecedented optimism in the country. It spread like an epidemic. At exactly the same time Saleem was afflicted by an excruciating sinusitis. While the nation, puffed up with optimism, convinced itself of the imminent end of the yellow peril, Saleem's sinuses swelled to block his nasal passages. While hopeful politicians promised the people to avenge Chinese perfidy, mobs attacked innocent Chinese businessmen and the Government arrested Indian citizens of Chinese origin as 'enemy aliens,' (299) Saleem suffered from 'asphyxiation' because the air, 'thickened by optimism, refused to enter [his] lungs.' (299) He felt suffocated in the buoyant atmosphere in which rights of humanity were denied and militant propaganda generated anti-human chauvinism and xenophobia. In the first week of November, when the Indian troops renewed their assault on the Chinese, Saleem's nose was in a state of severe crisis because his sinuses refused to respond to medication. While the Indians attacked under cover of artillery, Saleem's mother arranged the time and place of his nasal drainage under the pretext of telephoning a friend. The war brought about 'an emotional integration' (300) in the country just as the end of hostilities between Ahmed and Amina emotionally integrated their family. With the renewal of his love, Ahmed gave up boozing and returned to his jovial self. He began to call Saleem his 'son' again and smother him with his affection. Basking in the new glow of happiness which permeated their house, Saleem felt assured that his parents really loved him. Because they had never, since Mary's confession, attempted to find out 'the true son of their blood.' (301) Saleem had remained their son because 'they could not imagine [him] out of the role.' (301) And it was for their love, as narrator Saleem says with a bitter hindsight, that they planned his ruin under cover of a lie. The Indian soldiers were finally routed by the Chinese army on 20 November. The shameful defeat drained the public morale and ended the optimism disease. It was followed by a private drainage the next morning when the Chinese unilaterally declared a ceasefire. Ahmed and Amina took the children out in the family car on the pretext of a picnic to celebrate the heart-warming news. Saleem was forcibly admitted to a hospital where the doctors performed an operation to remove his inflamed sinuses and clear his nasal passages. The evacuation deprived him of his nose-given gift of telepathy and snapped his connections with the children of midnight. He no longer heard voices in his head which was now filled with the silence of a desert. Saleem Sinai, thus, became a victim of his name. Because 'Sinai' suggests not only 'the place of revelation,' Mount Sinai, but also 'the name of the desert—of barrenness, infertility, dust, the name of the end.' (305) After the war, Amina persuaded Ahmed to migrate to Pakistan and make a fresh start. They sold Buckingham Villa to the Narlikar women and, in February 1963—fifteen years after Independence-permanently left India for the 'Land of the Pure,' Before the departure from his 'Shangri-La,' (306) Saleem put the surviving relics of his past, Prime Minister Nehru's letter and the *Times of India* baby-snap with the caption 'Midnight's Child,' into a battered tin globe and buried it for posterity in a bed of cactai. Soon after their arrival in Karachi, Jamila was launched on her career and Saleem's loss of voices was compensated by his discovery of a powerful sense of smell.

Chapter XXII: Jamila Singer

The Sinais reached Karachi and accepted the hospitality of Alia Aziz. Spinster Alia, now the Principal of a college, lived alone in a large, old building across which there fell 'the long accusing shadow' (308) of a mosque every afternoon. After his arrival in Karachi, Saleem discovered that the drainage of his sinuses had endowed him with an enhanced sense of smell. He the beginning of his Karachi life, Saleem's olfactory organ gave him 'knowledge, but not power-over-events.' (307) He did not like Karachi because it lacked the exuberance and multiplicity of Bombay. Living in uniformly grotesque and windowless houses built on reclaimed desert land, Karachiites 'had only the slipperiest grasp on reality.' (308) They always turned to their political and spiritual leaders for advice and, thus, learnt submissiveness. This acquiescence appeared depressing to Saleem who had been brought up in the 'highly-spiced non-conformity of Bombay.' (308) But his parents accepted the country as their own and decided to build a new home. They bought a plot of land in the posh area of the city. At the foundation-laying ceremony, Saleem's umbilical cord was implanted in the earth amidst the blessings of a mullah and his parents' proclamation that they would be 'new people' and make a fresh beginning. Determined to put down roots in the country, Ahmed even purchased a towel factory and started producing a brand of towels named after his wife, Amina. With the newly found happiness of his late-flowering love, he declared his resolve to 'make the whole world clean' (311) with his product. Purity and cleanliness, thus, became the ideals of his parents in the Land of the Pure. But Saleem, 'tainted with Bombayness' (310) and the secularism of his grandfather, revealed a marked preference for impurity and remained a misfit in Pakistan. He could not identify himself with the country which was bereft of midnight's children and where the demand for 'a stricter, more Islamic society' (310) had already become strident. He reached adolescence in Karachi and began to study history in aunt Alia's college while Jamila launched her spectacular career as a singer.

The enormous success of Jamila Singer owed a great deal to a friend of General Zulfikar, Major Alauddin Latif (nicknamed 'uncle Puffs' by mischievous Brass Monkey). With a spherical head and a mouth filled with gold teeth, Major Latif was Pakistan's 'number-one impressario.' (311) The 'sublime magic' (312) of Jamila's angelic voice captivated him and he persuaded her parents to allow her to sing in public. By exploiting his contacts and organizing skills Alauddin, like his name-sake in the

Arabian Nights, performed magic and made Jamila a star overnight. Within months Jamila became the most popular singer in Pakistan and her records topped the sales chart. She came to be known as the 'Voice of the Nation' and the 'nightingale-of-the-faith.' (313) But with her growing popularity, she became the victim of her public image. To allay the fears of old-fashioned Ahmed, who was unwilling to put his daughter on a stage in front of strangers, Latif devised for her an all-concealing veil with a hole at the centre. Jamila was placed behind the perforated sheet during her public appearance and her voice was dissociated from her body. That was how the history of the Aziz family 'became the fate of a nation.' (313) Because when Jamila sang through the aperture, 'Pakistan fell in love' (313) with a partly visible beauty as Aadam Aziz had fallen years ago. She became 'the new daughter-of-the-nation' (314) and, thus, a captive to the nationalist rhetoric of Islamic Pakistan. The fanatical aspects of the national persona began to dominate her newly constructed stage personality. Jamila's transformation became complete when, after a recital in the President House, Ayub Khan—'the commander of the pepperpots' (315)—told her that her voice would be 'a sword for purity' with which Pakistan would 'cleanse men's souls.' (315) Through her perforated sheet, she dedicated herself to the cause of the nation.

While Jamila rose meteorically to stardom and learnt submission and cleanliness, Saleem tried to come to terms with himself amongst the 'barren certitudes of the land of the pure' (316) and, with his heightened sense of smell, discover the profane odours of the city. Amidst the news of his grandfather's death in Kashmir and deteriorating Indo-Pak relations, he mounted his Lambretta scooter, a parental gift on his sixteenth birthday, and 'explored the olfactory avenues' (316) of Karachi. The bewildering variety of amorphous smells left his head reeling until his 'desire for form asserted itself.' (317) Saleem classified the odours by colour and weight and shaped them, first into a 'general theory of smell' and then into a 'science of nasal ethics,' (317) thus giving the scents a moral dimension. He sharpened his skill so much that he could not only smell 'the perfumes of emotions' (317) but also distinguish between sacred and profane scents. But with his ingrained impurity Saleem found no interest in the sacred. While his sister sang of holiness and patriotism, he roamed the city in search of 'profanity and lust.' (318) It was during a visit to an inconceivably old whore named Tai Bibi, Saleem discovered the ultimate impurity of his love for his own sister. The 'oldest whore in the world,' (319) who could imitate any physical scent, sniffed out the malodorous secret of his incestuous sister-love.

The narrative breaks into a fairy tale to reveal the darkest secret in Saleem's heart and describe the political grotesquerie in Pakistan—the tyranny, corruption and self-aggrandizement of the ruling class which had turned the country into a theatre of the absurd. In 1964, Ayub Khan decreed an election amidst growing disenchantment of the people with the military rule and rumours of 'embezzled money and Swiss bank accounts.' (315) The opposition parties united under the leadership of Fatima Jinnah, the sister of Pakistan's founder, and threw a serious challenge to the Muslim League of President Ayub. The election coincided with the engagement of Zafar, General Zulfikar's embarrassingly enuretic son, to the daughter of the Nawab of Kif, a northern princedom. Jamila Singer was invited to Kif to sing at the engagement ceremony which was held on the evening before the election. At midnight, when the guests were fast asleep, Saleem secretly went to his sister's room in the zenana quarters of the palace and, abandoning 'all notions of purity,' (325) confessed his love to her. Consumed by an insane desire, he explained to awe-struck Jamila that 'they were not truly brother and sister' and that 'the blood in his veins was not the blood in hers.' (325) But his attempt to undo the ties which had been sanctified by time, failed. Jamila rejected his love and he left her room in shame. The election was rigged next morning. The supporters of the Combined Opposition Party were debarred from voting by the army. At the end of the day, the newspapers proclaimed an overwhelming victory for Ayub's Muslim League. This fantastic jugglery with facts and the divorce between news and reality did not, however, astonish Saleem. As he says in retrospect, 'in a country where the truth is what it is instructed to be, reality quite literally ceases to exist, so that everything becomes possible except what we are told is the case.' (326) This scathing remark offers an illuminating contrast between his Indian childhood and Pakistani adolescence and a valuable insight into the twin realities of the subcontinent. Saleem's account makes it clear that India was better than Pakistan—where truth was manufactured to distort reality—because of its superior political system. India beset Saleem with 'an infinity of alternative realities' but Pakistan left him disoriented 'amid an equally infinite number of falsenesses, unrealities and lies.' (326) Hence the Pakistani part of his story ends in fantasy.

Chapter XXIII: How Saleem achieved purity

The last chapter of Book Two begins with another countdown, not to a numinous beginning but to a calamitous end. There is a tonal shift in the narrating voice. With a feeling of weariness and a sense of fatalism Saleem recounts how the members of his deracinated family exhausted all possibilities of renewal shortly after their migration to Pakistan and waited with a 'general fatigue' (327) for their extermination. The end came at the midnight of September 22, 1965, in the form of a disaster which wiped them completely from the face of the earth and, ironically, cleansed Saleem of his impurity.

In the middle of 1964 Naseem Aziz came to Pakistan from India where a bitter struggle for power had started after Nehru's death. Aged politicians like Morarji Desai and Jagjivan Ram had united 'to prevent the establishment of a Nehru dynasty.' (327) They had denied leadership of the Congress Party to Indira Gandhi and helped Lal Bahadur Shastri to become the new Prime Minister. After her arrival in Pakistan Reverend Mother neither mentioned nor grieved over Aadam Aziz who had despised the God-ridden country all his life. She settled in Rawalpindi with her widowed daughter-in-law Pia and purchased a petrol pump which they ran very successfully. Naseem and Pia, who had never liked each other, turned out to be a 'magical combination.' (328) Pia attracted customers with the beacon of her beauty while Naseem invited them into her glass booth, offered cups of Kashmiri tea and lent her 'eternally patient' (328) ears to their personal and familial woes. Reverend Mother gradually lost interest in her family and became preoccupied with other people's lives. She turned her glass booth into a confessional and, in order to forget her own tragedy, began to solve the problems of the world. But in the process, she became 'the first victim of that spirit of detached fatigue' (328) which gradually afflicted the other members of the Aziz clan. Pia, too, followed her mother-in-law and retreated into a private world. Not content with selling gasoline to truck drivers, she began a series of liaisons with Pakistani cricketers and army officers. But her frenzied romancing soon exhausted her and she realized that her 'heart wasn't in it.' (329) Her hollowed promiscuity appeared to be a desperate attempt to resist the inevitable decline of her beauty and personality. Meanwhile, Saleem had started withdrawing into himself under the dislocating influence of his unrequited and impure sister-love and the 'diseased reality' (338) of his Pakistani life. He lapsed into long spells of gloomy silence and succumbed to a fatalism which led him to accept all that happened as inevitable. After the shameful experience at Kif, the brother and the sister avoided each other being unable, for the first time in their lives, to exchange any word. Jamila began to spend less and less time at home, touring the country instead to give her concerts. Saleem, on his part, receded into 'private despondency' (330) and helplessly watched the disintegration of his family which seemed to him to be a retribution for tearing up their roots in Bombay. They were still living in the mosque-shadowed mansion of Alia Aziz in Karachi because their own house had not been completed. Alia never forgave Ahmed for abandoning her and she hated her sister, Amina, for marrying her lover. Her hatred combined with the bitterness and frustration of spinsterhood and leaked into her college where she raised a tribe of religious fanatics and into her home which turned into an 'insane asylum' (331) fraught with dissension and discord. Under the vengeful impact of her age-old grievances, the autumnal love of Ahmed and Amina went sour. In early 1965, Amina became pregnant again. The fear and shame of bearing a child at an advanced age took a heavy toll on her. She became prematurely old and turned superstitious. Crushed under the weight of her new baby, she began to receive, like her father, 'visits from the spectres of her past.' (332) The rapid and alarming disintegration of his wife unnerved Ahmed—so much so that he neglected the management of his towel factory and it crumbled before his eyes. He took to boozing again and ultimately suffered a paralyzing stroke which 'restored him to the dribbles and giggles of his infancy.' (337) It was a bewildering time for Saleem who found life wrapped in a haze of unreality. The ruination of his family and their flight from reality made him fatalistic and careless about his future. The confusion in his private world was reflected in the public life of Pakistan where a similar divorce from reality was taking place. With the declining reputation of President Ayub Khan, rumours of electoral malpractice, nepotism and corruption spread very fast. But there was a rupture between government propaganda and reality. While the state-controlled newspapers proclaimed the nation's progress and the probity of the leaders, people cursed the 'so-called green revolution' and talked about 'Swiss bank accounts.' (334) As the pro-government press assured the world of the improvement of Indo-Pak relations, trouble broke out, in April 1965, between the two countries over the 'disputed territory' (335) of the Rann of Kutch. The Pakistani army was routed in the battle of Kutch and the ignominious debacle, which Saleem—mistrustful of the official account—records in a Rabelaisian grotesque style, was represented by the 'jelly-like breakdown' (336) of the Pakistani soldiers at the approach of the enemy and the incontinence of Zafar Zulfikar—now a Lieutenant—who voided his bladders with 'hysterical frequency' (336) for seven nights. The humiliating experience of defeat and the accidental discovery at Kutch that his father operated the largest network of smuggling in Pakistan maddened Zafar. On his return home, he murdered General Zulfikar and went to jail. The trouble in the Rann of Kutch triggered off a full-scale war between the two nations, this time over Kashmir.

The description of the catastrophic war evinces narrator Saleem's non-parochial and humanitarian attitude. He distrusts the official version, which conceals the truth in a miasma of make-believe and overlooks the human loss and pain, and presents a subjective—though somewhat fantastic—account. The passage that reports the war is riddled with questions reflecting the uncertainty and unreliability of the official view: 'Nothing was real; nothing certain.' (340) His alternative version exposes the contradictory claims of the governments of India and Pakistan as lies and denounces the anti-human chauvinism and the communal prejudice in both the countries. Since the truth is lost in the confusing maze of official statements, he offers a personal explanation of the motives of the war. 'The hidden purpose of the Indo-Pakistani war of 1965 was,' he says, 'the elimination of [his] benighted family' (338) and the purification of his unclean soul.

With the fragmentation of reality and his family, Saleem's fatalism assumed a terrible proportion. Distracted by the insanity of the war and of his private life, he 'sought out the oblivion of death' (341) which now seemed to him not only inevitable but desirable as well. On the night of 22 September, Indian air-raids took place over every major Pakistani city, annihilating one by one the members of Saleem's 'drained, hopeless family.' (342) Naseem, Pia, Emerald and Zafar died in Rawalpindi. In Karachi, a bomb was dropped on the mosque-shadowed house of Alia and it killed the embittered spinster, Ahmed, Amina and her unborn child. Saleem escaped death because he was outside the house at the moment of explosion. But he was hit at the back of his head by his mother's silver-spittoon which had been flung in the air by the blast. The blow thrust him on the ground to prostrate before his 'parents' funeral pyre.' (343) He bowed his head at long last and acquiesced in the necessity of the end. The accident (prophesied years ago by Ramram Seth) released Saleem from his historical role, his past and present, shame and love. He was cleansed of his iniquities and restored to the purity and innocence of childhood. He survived the war, like his sister Jamila and uncle Mustapha Aziz, but lost his memory.

Book Three

The last section of *Midnight's Children* deals with the Bangladesh war and the consequent dismemberment of Pakistan, the Emergency and its aftermath. In war of 1971 Saleem experienced the ultimate degradation of man to bestiality. The horror and trauma of the war prompted his flight into the Sundarbans where he reached a state of near insanity and recovered, through a snake-bite, his lost memory. He returned to India before the Emergency and got involved in politics. The authoritarian rule of Indira Gandhi ended in 1977 with the liquidation of the Midnight's Children and the drainage of the nation's hopes generated by Independence. This is a darker and more political book than the other two because it deals with the direct collision of Saleem with the forces of history leading to his marginalization, withdrawal into privacy and his ultimate fragmentation. The narrative in this section is less digressive and more straight-forward. The tone becomes grim and the political satire becomes devastating. The ending of the novel is bleak, indicating the defeat of the human spirit at the hands of unscrupulous and demoniac politicians. But it is not without a ray of hope. The last pages of the book suggest the emergence of a new, more pragmatic generation—represented by Saleem's son Aadam Sinai—who takes over from the Midnight's Children.

Chapter XXIV: The buddha

Saleem's story resumes, after a gap of five years, in 1970. The passage of time is conveyed by a cinematic technique: the close-up of 'a calendar ruffled by a breeze, its pages flying off in rapid succession' (346) on which the narrator superimposes select public events that had happened in the intervening period. The war of 1965 had left Saleem 'orphaned and purified' (345) to enter alone into a grotesque adulthood. The accident had robbed him of his memory and numbed his feeling. Drained of human emotions, family and history he had metamorphosed into a man-dog whose head contained nothing except smells: 'No memory, not interested in people, lives like a dog!' (349) But

Saleem's state of amnesia induced by the blow of the flying spittoon had effected a loss which was much more than a simple loss of memory. It signified a loss of his identity and his connection with a verifiable past which had situated him in the socio-historical context that outlined his individuality. After his release from the hospital, Jamila had wormed him into the army to get him out of her sight. He was enlisted in a CUTIA Unit (a she-dog unit) of the Pakistani Army in place of a tracker for his exceptionally powerful sense of smell which could 'follow any trail on earth.' (349) Since he had forgotten his name and grown prematurely old, he was called, in Urdu, 'buddha,' an old man. An air of antiquity hung around him and his face, like that of Gautama Buddha, wore an expression of calm and quietness. Like Buddha, the enlightened, he was both present in the world and absent from it since his spirit remained elsewhere. Cleansed of family, joys and sorrows, pleasure and pain, the mock-'buddha' moved around alone with a silver spittoon which was his only connection with the past and also the cause of its erasure. He did only what he was asked to do and followed orders uncomplainingly. Cut-off from history, Saleem the-buddha, thus, learnt the art of submission and became 'a citizen of Pakistan.' (351) Saleem's embrace of Pakistani citizenship was an act of submission, and his lack of consciousness when he became a tracker dog in the Pakistani army led to a split in him which reflected Pakistan's own rift to form Bangladesh. In a covert army camp, whose existence would be later denied by the Pak authority, the man-dog demonstrated his skill at following the 'faintest of trails' (351) while three newly recruited boy-soldiers of his Unit—Ayooba Baloch, Farooq Rashid and Shaheed Dar—turned into automatons. The young soldiers (so young that they 'had not had time to acquire the type of memories which give men a firm hold on reality' [349]) were subjected to rigorous training and religious programming. A 'high Islamic sense of self-discipline and responsibility' (348) was instilled in them. They were taught 'to obey unquestioningly; to seek unflaggingly; to arrest remorselessly.' (348) The purpose of the training was, the innocent child-soldiers learnt, to root out subversive elements and traitors who challenged the country's unity. The narrative picks up in the midst of a political crisis in Pakistan. The Indo-Pakistani war of 1965 had led to the downfall of Ayub Khan. General Yahya Khan had become the next President of the country and promised a free and fair election. The election was held in 1970 and Mujib-ur-Rahman's Awami League in East Pakistan won a crushing victory over the People's Party of Zulfikar Ali Bhutto in the West Wing.[11] But he was denied the right to form the new government by the West Pakistani leaders. The political stalemate plunged the country into a civil strife as Mujib-ur-Rahman "led the East Wing into secession and declared it independent as 'Bangladesh'." (351) The fratricidal war, which witnessed 'the biggest migration' (357) and one of the worst genocides in human history, ended in the disintegration of the two wings of Pakistan which had been held together, despite their linguistic and cultural differences, by the glue of religion. The political events leading to the dismemberment of Pakistan are presented in the novel as bare facts while the human experience is evoked through Saleem's peregrinations in war-ravaged East Pakistan as a man-dog. The war in Bangladesh filters through the experiences of Ayooba, Shaheed, Farooq and Saleem who witnessed the atrocities committed by the Pakistan forces.

On 25 March, 1971, when Mujib proclaimed the birth of the new nation, the Pakistani army made a foray into the East Wing to quench the rebellion. Sixty thousand crack troops, who had been previously air-borne to Dacca as civilians, swung into action at midnight. The dog-soldiers were unleashed to hunt down the secessionists—the supporters of Awami League and 'the volunteers of the Mukti Bahini [the liberation army of Bangladesh]. In the greatest adventure of the night, Saleem—the accredited tracker of the canine unit—sniffed out Mujib from his hideaway. The most popular East Wing leader was 'manacled, manhandled' (356) and flown to a West Pakistani jail. While driving through the streets of Dacca, the buddha and the three boy-soldiers watched the indescribable savagery of the Pak army. Women were dragged out of their hostels and raped; students and teachers, poets and journalists were arrested and killed.

Innocent people sleeping on the roadside were riddled with bullets; slums were gutted; newspaper and trade-union offices were ransacked and burnt. The ruthless 'dogs of war [cried] havoc in the city' as the 'soldiers for Allah' (357) tried to hold Pakistan together by perpetrating a dreadful outrage against humanity.[12] Saleem's state of amnesia prevented him from taking responsibility for the betrayal of his fellow countrymen. But the gruesome experience had a traumatic effect on the child-soldiers who had no such excuse for 'withdrawal from responsibility.' (351) They irrevocably lost their innocence, certainty and 'moral absolutes.' (358) Still, with unquestioning loyalty and adherence to the 'philosophy of acceptance,' (356) they followed orders while the mock-buddha followed the scent-trails of sedition. They tracked the enemies of national unity through 'the blackened streets' (358) into the blood-soaked heart of the city which the avenging soldiers of the West Wing had turned into hell. They remorselessly performed their duties even though their hearts went mad with the horror of the nightmarish scenes unfolding before their awe-struck eyes. They were sent on sinister assignments to the countryside which was littered with the traces of the Pakistani army's atrocious revenge: burnt-out villages, abandoned paddy-fields, uprooted railway tracks and endless processions of migrating villagers. Finally, their mission drew them through 'a darker heart of madness' (358) to the Gangetic delta in the south. Led by the buddha, the three soldiers of his unit relentlessly chased an elusive quarry down the river in a boat for days and nights until, 'hungry unslept exhausted,' (358) they entered the Sundarbans. The pre-historic rain-forest, where time and space disappeared, engulfed the traumatized boy-soldiers and the amnesiac man-dog.

Chapter XXV: In the Sundarbans

In this episode the narrative, completely free from jocularity and digression, slides into a dream. The tone becomes recognizably grim in keeping with the boys' loss of innocence and turbulent passage into adulthood that the chapter describes. Vivid, sumptuous details, which marked the earlier part of the book, are also missing because what the narrator describes here is not the real Sundarbans but a dream forest which seems to occupy the same geographical space and because what the jungle looks like is less important than what it says to the boys about themselves.

The pursuit of an elusive foe turned out to be a lie. Saleem, the man-dog, had deserted the army and fled to the safety of the primeval forest dragging the three boy-soldiers in his wake. The insanity of the war and the soul-racking sense of guilt, induced by his blind obedience and unquestioning performance of duty, had prompted him to run away from the nightmarish reality of East Pakistan into the 'historyless anonymity' (360) of the impenetrable jungle. But the flight exacted a high price from Saleem and his companions. The withdrawal into the Sundarbans proved to be a descent into hell, into the steamy jungle of the sub-conscious which the rainforest externalized, where the frenzied minds of the boys led them circuitously through shifting landscapes towards a recognition of their crime and an acceptance of its responsibility. The experience was painful but a chastening one. The infernal jungle not only tormented them for their sins but, at the same time, led them to a 'new adulthood.' (364)

Once the forest closed behind them 'like a tomb' and the boys realized that they had irretrievably lost their way in its 'sepulchral greenness,' (360) they broke down. Ayooba, the toughest of the three soldiers, started crying inconsolably like a baby and Farooq, unnerved by the sight, pounced upon the buddha and dealt blows on his numb body. Then rain came and intensified the mystery of the forest and the unreality of the trees. In the torrential downpour the magical jungle grew 'in size, power and ferocity.' (361) The huge roots of the ancient mangrove trees sneaked about thirstily to suck in the rain. The sundari trees and the nipa palms grew immensely in height to block out the possibility of the sun. The nipa fruits fell alarmingly on the water and exploded like bombs, threatening to capsize the boat. The boys rowed their craft to the shore, landed and, in a 'miasmatic state of mind,' (362) fell asleep. When they awoke, they found their bodies covered with colourless, blood-filled leeches and remembered their hunger and thirst. They set their feet on the hard soil crawling with translucent insects and blind snakes. They drank rainwater pouring off the leaves and 'fell deeper . . . into the thraldom of the livid green world.' (362) Since there was no respite from the incessant rain, the boys built a makeshift shelter with palm fronds and oilskins and lived on nipa fruits in the timeless jungle where days dissolved into each other 'under the force of the returning rain.' (363) Reduced to an elemental order of reality, they managed to stay alive in their primitive shelter, despite snakes, fevers and diarrhoea, and forgot the purpose of their journey. Gradually, they succumbed to the strange logic of the fantastic forest which now began to whisper unpleasant secrets in their ears and punish them by sending 'terrible phantasms' at night: 'the accusing eyes of the wives of men they had tracked down and seized, the screaming and monkey-gibbering of children left fatherless by their work.' (363) The nocturnal punishment continued, reducing the boys to shadows of their earlier selves until they started regressing towards childhood and were assailed by memories. Night after night Ayooba, Farooq and Shaheed were visited by 'wraithlike' (363) monkeys with the faces of their parents and ancestors. The regression to infancy and the onset of memory restored in them their lost sense of responsibility. The retribution of the jungle compelled the soldiers to own up the misdeeds they had committed and their disastrous consequences. The buddha was rejoined to his past not by any phantom of nostalgia but by a snake-bite. One afternoon, while he was sitting cross-legged under a sundari tree amidst torrents of rain, a blind, transparent serpent bit him in the leg and poured its venom. His insensitive body became rigid and his eyes crossed but he did not die. The snake-poison miraculously brought back his memory. Words came pouring out through the lips of the quiet buddha and he began to recount the stories of his life to the spellbound boys in an attempt to reclaim the past. He remembered everything except his name which escaped him. As the rain continued relentlessly and the water level rose dangerously high, they tied their boat to a tree and moved deeper into the dense jungle in search of higher ground. With the changing landscape, the forest renewed its punishment and filled their ears with the 'accusing, pain-filled voices' (365) of their victims and the lamentation of the bereaved families. The boys began to run wildly through the enigmatic jungle to escape from the insufferable voices and the unpleasant, shameful secrets whispered by the trees. Finally, unable to bear the torture of renewed accusations and 'the burden of shame' (365) which was magnified by their newly awakened sense of responsibility, the three boy-soldiers plugged their ears with mud and turned deaf. The buddha alone bore the punishment of the jungle and accepted the 'inevitability of his guilt.' (366) Then the voices stopped and the magical forest allowed the panic-stricken wanderers a vision which was overwhelming in its loveliness. In a glade filled with the soothing melodies of birds, they found an enormous Hindu temple with erotic pictures of men and women carved on its walls. Inside the temple they saw 'the towering statue of a black dancing goddess' (366) whom the buddha recognized as Kali. The exhausted travellers lay down at her feet and fell into a restful sleep. They awoke at midnight and found four identical girls of surpassing beauty smiling upon them. The young beauties undressed themselves silently and came towards the soldiers. As the boys abandoned themselves to the 'women of their most contented dreams' (367) below the statue of the black goddess, they realized that 'they were leaving infancy behind for ever.' (367) The dream-like experience, tinged with sexuality and religion, continued as the 'daughters of the forest' (366) returned night after night and silently brought the lost boys to an 'incredible united peak of delight.' (367) Having punished them for their misdeeds, the jungle eased out their pain and fulfilled their hearts' desire. At last, one day the wayfarers frightfully discovered that they had become translucent like glass and that it was possible to see through their bodies. Jolted out of their dream-life by the shock of transparency, they looked at the temple with disillusioned eyes and found, at one corner, four funeral pyres with heaps of uncrushed bones at their centre. They fled in panic from the temple and almost reached their boat when a tidal wave ejected them from the illusive forest to the world governed by time and history. They came out of the Sundarbans in October 1971 when the war was nearing an end. The Mukti Bahini had started terrorizing Pakistani troops with Indian help. Emerging from invisibility after seven months, the deserters made an attempt to rejoin their army. On the way, Ayooba was killed by a sniper's bullet. In early December, the buddha, Farooq and Shaheed reached a place near Dacca on stolen bi-cycles and witnessed a bizarre spectacle. In a large ground littered with the corpses of soldiers in Indian and Pakistani uniforms, a peasant was scavenging treasures. The man, who called himself a 'vendor of notions,' (372) informed the trio of the arrival of the Indian Army to liberate Bangladesh. As the crazy fellow, whose son had been killed in the war, described to them the daring exploits of a mighty Indian officer with lethal knees, Farooq was gunned down by a dying soldier. When the buddha stumbled across the field to his fallen comrade, he heard someone calling him from a pyramid of mutilated bodies and found Eyeslice and Hairoil Sabarmati and Sonny Ibrahim. The grotesque re-union with his childhood friends in the strangest of places convinced him that the purpose of the insane war, which saw the ultimate degradation of man, had been to re-unite him with his old life.

Chapter XXVI: Sam and the Tiger

After his emergence from a state of near-insanity in the Sundarbans, the buddha returned to the devastated city of Dacca with his sole companion Shaheed and got re-united with his old life. The war had ended with the defeat of the Pakistani forces at the hands of the Indian Army. The migration of ten million refugees into her territory had put tremendous economic and political pressures on India to intervene in the Bangladesh dispute and send her troops to liberate the country from Pakistani occupation. (The Indian Communists, however, suggested different reasons for the Indian intervention. [376]) The war of 1971, which signalled India's most decisive military victory since Independence and shattered the myth of a nation founded solely on religion, was over in three weeks. The heavy losses Pakistan suffered during the war, together with her isolation in international politics (because no country except America had supported her misadventure in the East Wing), obliged her to capitulate to India. On 15 December 1971, Lt. General Tiger Niazi, the officer responsible for Dacca, surrendered with ninety-three thousand troops to his Indian counterpart, Jagjit Singh Aurora (not to Sam Manekshaw, the then chief of Indian Army, as Saleem erroneously writes). The buddha and Shaheed secretly entered the beleaguered city on the night of 14 December and witnessed the last vengeful atrocities committed by the desperate Pakistani troops. They saw carnage of innocent civilians, mass graves, massacre of the city's intelligentsia and beastly torture on women, which were, however, officially denied by Pak authority. The hideous sights of monstrous violence agonized them and the buddha became apprehensive of their personal safety. He entered an abandoned house and found a loose hooded cloak lying on a small landing. Without a second thought he changed his tattered uniform including the she-dog badge and became 'anonymous' (376) in the unfamiliar city. Shaheed remained in the street and watched, with unbelieving eyes, 'soldiers scurrying away from what-had-not-been-done.' (376) Suddenly a grenade was thrown in his direction and the explosion blew away his legs. At the request of the dying boy, the buddha carried his bisected body to the minaret of a nearby mosque and began to wait for day-break. Shocked by the unexpected turn of events, he contemplated the unfairness of life and the misfortune that had befallen his young companion, while Shaheed 'screamed out the terrible agony of war' (377) through the accidentally activated loudspeaker of the minaret and, ironically, earned his name. He became a martyr in an 'unfair,' irrational and insane war which had killed innocence and relegated man to the level of beast. Fearing detection, the buddha left the mosque and joined the procession of people moving towards the centre of the city to see the ignominious surrender of Tiger Niazi and the victory parade of the Indian troops. Amidst jubilation of the Bangladeshi citizens, the Indian Army marched into the capital of the newly liberated country with its war-heroes, including Major Shiva who had earned great fame by destroying the enemies with his knees, and a large group of magicians and entertainers who relieved the pain of the city by a wonderful display of their arts. Among the entertainers who delighted the people most were Picture Singh, a gigantic snake-charmer known as the 'Most Charming Man in the World,' (378) and Parvati-the-Witch, the midnight's child born with the gift of sorcery. Parvati recognized Saleem in the crowd and gave him back his forgotten name. Evidently pleased with the re-union, she did not let Saleem go. Thus, as Niazi and his troops surrendered to the Indian Army and became prisoners of war, Saleem 'became the willing captive' (379) of Parvati and her fellow magicians. She took him along with her back to India, secretly hidden in a magic basket which enabled her to make men disappear until she willed them to return. It was a 'basket of invisibility' where he was preserved in a state of limbo. But the invisibility, which enabled Saleem to escape from Bangladesh without any passport, threatened to enervate him and rob him of his very essence. He feared that the magic basket would send him into oblivion. In the grip of Parvati's sorcery Saleem lost his hold on reality, and his pride in a 'prophesied historical role' (382) began to fade. But he was saved from complete enervation by the silver spittoon, which crystallized Saleem's sense of his personal history and reminded him of the outside world, and by a sudden anger. In the 'disembodied loneliness' (382) of his invisible condition, Saleem discovered within himself a seething fury which he directed at 'everything . . . [he] had, until then, blindly accepted.' (382) He raged against the accident of his birth which had inextricably linked him with his nation through multiple modes of connection and made him responsible for all the events of historical significance in the sub-continent. It was a self-righteous anger which compelled him to question the inevitability of his victimhood: 'Why, alone of all the more-than-five-hundred-million, should I have to bear the burden of history?' (382) It was this wrath that helped Saleem endure, and finally overcome, the lures of invisibility and made him 'determined . . . to choose [his] own, undestined future.' (383)[13] His rebellion had another salutary effect on him; it rescued him from numbness.

When he was released from Parvati's wicker basket in the magicians' ghetto near Delhi's Friday Mosque, Saleem discovered that he could feel again.

Chapter XXVII: The shadow of the Mosque

Saleem accelerates his narrative pace as his disintegration becomes quicker and the cracks in his memory widen. Five empty jars on the shelf in his room at the pickle factory remind him of his incomplete task. So he ignores Padma's 'dream of an alternative future' and her pleas for marriage, which will give her relationship with him a social legitimacy, and dashes for the 'finishing line.' (384)

Saleem had tumbled out of Parvati's magic basket in the ghetto of magicians near Delhi's Friday Mosque with a resolve to choose a better future, an overwhelming sympathy for the country and an exalted sense of mission. The time was December 1971, when Indira Gandhi was at the acme of her fame and her New Congress Party held a comfortable majority in the Parliament. But the signs of her abnormal craze for power and dynastic aspiration were becoming evident. Rumours of corruption being institutionalized by her government and her growing obsession with astrology and the occult spread very fast. In short, there was a switch-over from Nehru's India and the country's politics had begun to rot. Saleem's first sojourn in the slum was short-lived. He soon left his saviours and went to his only surviving uncle Mustapha Aziz in New Delhi. Because he was in the clutches of a fantastic dream, that of saving the nation from her fate. He hoped that his uncle, an influential bureaucrat, would encourage him to fulfil his 'Messianic ambitions' (388) and that with his help he would 'find the keys of national salvation.' (389) There was also a second, and more personal, reason for abandoning his friends. During his brief stay in the ghetto, Parvati confessed to Saleem that he was not the only midnight's child to have crossed her path. She had encountered Shiva in Dacca and the war-hero had not only presented her a lock of his hair but also promised to meet her in future. The confession reminded Saleem of unpleasant things he had tried hard to forget.

The fear of a possible re-union with his alter-ego whom he had banished from the Parliament of his mind, forced him to leave the colony and go to the house of 'Mr. Mustapha Aziz and Fly.' (390) 'Fly' was a truncated form of the highly emotive term 'family' and within a few days Saleem realized that it was an appropriate description of the grotesque family of his uncle which was 'as crushed, as insect-like, as insignificant as that mythically truncated Fly.' (390) Mustapha accepted his orphaned nephew but his half-Irani wife Sonia resented his presence. Saleem put up with the insults of his aunt and the ignominy of living in that savage and riotous family, 'beside which a tribe of gibbering cannibals would have seemed calm and civilized,' (394) because of his hope of finding a place in the world with his uncle's help. A senior Civil Servant with unflinching loyalty to the successive Prime Ministers, Mustapha had never been promoted to the top post of his department. He ascribed it to the anti-Muslim prejudice of the rulers and sought consolation for his inadequacies in trouncing his children and in an 'obsession with genealogies.' (391) He spent his spare time researching into the lineages of the greatest families in the country, a bizarre hobby which he would soon place at the service of a Prime Minister who was 'falling increasingly beneath the twin spells of power and astrology.' (392) Sonia Aziz had been driven to near-insanity by a life of frustrated ambitions. Her husband's inefficiency had obliged her to suffer the humiliation of being perpetually the wife of number-two and the condescending behaviour of the wives of his successive bosses. Her bitterness found expression in noisy quarrels with her husband and harrowing violence towards her children which turned the house into a lunatic asylum. The joint thrashing of Aziz and Sonia had thoroughly destroyed the personalities of their children who 'lived in daily expectation of murder.' (392) The presence of this terrible family in Delhi, where young Ahmed and Amina had spent a valuable part of their lives, seemed to Saleem to be a 'desecration' (392) of his past. It was at Mustapha's house he learnt about the annihilation of his family in the Indo-Pak war of 1965 and the mysterious disappearance of his sister, Jamila, in Pakistan. Jamila had heard about Saleem's desertion from the army during the Bangladesh war. Driven mad by the news, the famous singer had publicly reviled the Pakistani rulers. But a few days later she had vanished from the face of the earth. Saleem spent the next four hundred and twenty days in belated mourning for the dead and pleaded with his uncle for preferment in public service. But his dream was shattered as Mustapha, with his canine devotion to Indira Gandhi and absolute faith in her statesmanship, declined to help him. His uncle's rejection of his pleas and adulation of Indira only intensified Saleem's hatred for the lady.[14] Two days before the end of the mourning period, Sanjay Gandhi, the youngest son of the Prime Minister, came to dinner in Mustapha's House. As the 'labia-lipped youth' (398) entered his uncle's study, Saleem sneaked a look and found a 'top-secret' folder titled 'PROJECT M.C.C.' (395) lying on the table. The Civil Servant's attitude towards his nephew changed overnight. He began to look at Saleem with fear and loathing. To avoid that inexplicable gaze Saleem went out of the house and found Parvati squatting on the pavement with her magic basket. She was piqued to discover Saleem in that luxurious bungalow and reproached him for abandoning her. That night she secretly entered his bedroom and as Saleem kissed her in the dark, he found her face strangely changing into the face of Jamila filled with 'the dreadful . . . cankers of forbidden love.' (396) He jerked away with a cry which reached the ears of his insane aunt. The faux pas deprived Saleem of his last respectable shelter in the world. He left Mustapha's house and returned to 'that true inheritance of poverty and destitution' (396) of which Mary Pereira's crime had cheated him for so long. Saleem settled into the magicians' colony situated in the comforting shadow of the Friday Mosque, which offered relief from the heat of the sun. Despite his affluent background, he felt comfortably at home in the slum and found himself capable of enduring cold, hunger and thirst. A solidarity grew between him and the magicians, who were communists to a man, and under their influence he began to turn red. Saleem shared the shack of Picture Singh, the communist snake-charmer, and fell under his spell. He soon realized that were communists to a man, and under their influence he began to turn red. Saleem shared the shack of Picture Singh, the communist snake-charmer, and fell under his spell. He soon realized that the magicians were artists with absolute hold on reality which they could bend in whatever way they liked without forgetting for a moment what it was. Their presence tended to give the city of Delhi a carnivalesque atmosphere and reflected the intermingling of languages and social practices that included high and low culture. In spite of acute poverty and daily troubles, their ghetto was free from 'religious and regionalist bigotry.' (399) But it was racked by the 'divisions and dissensions' (399) which marked the communist movement in India. Picture Singh, the unquestioned patriarch of the colony, was above such differences. He always carried with him an umbrella 'whose shade could restore harmony to the squabbling factions' and he 'spoke of a socialism which owed nothing to foreign influences.' (399) His company infected Saleem with an optimism and he began to believe that the snake charmer would one day leave the ghetto like the legendary Hummingbird and shape the future of the country by the force of his indomitable will. It was Picture Singh who told Saleem about the corruption in the government and explained to him the black and white economy in the country with the analogy of the Prime Minister's hair-style. (Her centrally parted hair was white on the one side and black on the other.) While Picture Singh initiated him into politics, Parvati revealed to him 'the secret of her midnight-given gifts.' (401) Under the power of her sorcery, hair began to grow on his bald head and the disfiguring birth-marks on his face vanished. But, in return, Saleem, who was still under the bewitching spell of Jamila, could not give her the only thing she desired: his love and company in bed. Her thwarted love drove Parvati into a state of mournfulness and her face developed an alarming pout which the combined efforts of the magicians could not remove. Picture Singh, who loved the fatherless girl like his own daughter, felt distressed to see her plight and began to search a husband for her. Many eligible young men of the ghetto were produced before Parvati but she rejected them all. In desperation, Picture

Singh approached Saleem and requested him to marry his saviour and friend. But Saleem, distracted by the nocturnal transformation of Parvati's face, turned down the proposal with a blatant lie. He told his mentor that he could not marry Parvati because he was cursed with impotence.

Chapter XXVIII: A wedding

Parvati was one of an endless series of women who had influenced the course of Saleem's life. From Naseem Aziz to the Widow—he had always been at the mercy of women who both 'made' and 'unmade' (406) him and whom he, in a brief but wild flight of fancy, associates with the 'multiple faces' of Mother India and even with the 'dynamic aspect of maya' which is called 'Shakti.' (406) Padma is impressed by the list of women in his life and his puranic wisdom but, with her interest only in what-happens-next, she checks his flight and brings him down to earth. Remembering the need for speed, he abandons his cosmological reflections and resumes his story which describes, in this episode, Parvati's marriage and the birth of her child.

Saleem's lie drove Parvati to the arms of his arch-rival Shiva whom he had pushed into the background throughout his narrative. Spurned by the man whom she had saved, she remembered his enemy and summoned him to her hovel by the powers of her sorcery. Saleem pieced together and reconstructed Shiva's story from Parvati's account. The transformation of his fellow changeling, whom Mary's crime had doomed to a life of destitution, from the leader of a gang of hooligans in a Bombay slum to India's 'most decorated war-hero' (407) was fraught with ironies. Because he had risen to 'commanding heights' (407) as Saleem fell and became a penniless slum-dweller. The war of 1971 reinvented Shiva's life and turned him into a national idol. The legends of his awe-inspiring exploits during the war spread throughout the country and he was elevated both in military rank and social status. He was invited to innumerable social gatherings 'to be applauded and monopolized by the noblest and the fairest' (407) in the country. They saw the rat-faced youth 'through the magical film of his myth.' (407) The beautiful wives of the rich and the powerful were attracted to the charismatic army-officer, who openly expressed his admiration for Indira Gandhi, and fell into his arms. In the exciting days after the war, Shiva earned a dubious reputation which grew rapidly with his official fame. He became a 'notorious seducer' (408) and proudly fathered thousands of bastards on the lovely wives of his influential admirers across the country. But he had a peculiar habit of losing interest in the women and deserting them once they became pregnant. One such abandoned mother, the wife of a steel-magnate in Bombay, deflated the pride of the promiscuous hero. The vengeful lady told him that the upper class women laughed at him behind his back for his clumsiness and boorish manners and that they looked upon him only as a 'pet ape . . . very useful, but basically a clown.' (409) The shattering revelation forced Shiva to look at his world with demystified eyes and reinterpret the gestures of the beautiful ladies. He was seized by a hatred for the noble and the powerful and by a 'desire to be done with the rich bitches of Indian high society.' (410) It was at that time he suddenly remembered Parvati, whom he had met in Dacca, and went to see her in the ghetto of magicians on 18 May 1974, when the desert of Pokhran was rocked by India's first nuclear explosion. Saleem was preoccupied at that time with politics and his dream of saving the country. He was attending a secret meeting of a communist group to discuss the national railway strike when Parvati left the colony and went with Shiva to the army quarters. For four months the war-hero remained infatuated with the saucer-eyed girl and devoted his undistracted attention to her. But things changed when she revealed to him that she was carrying his child. Overnight their liaison turned into a stormy affair. Fights and quarrels clouded their extra-marital relationship, reflecting the storm-clouds which were gathering in the country's political sky. While Shiva seethed in anger at Parvati's disclosure and began to drink and whore, people all over the country were getting angry with the corrupt government of Indira Gandhi. By the end of 1974, the aged socialist Jaya Prakash Narayan and the elderly Gandhian leader Morarji Desai formed a coalition of opposition parties known as the Janata Morcha to put an end to the mis-rule and corruption of the ruling Indira Congress. While Indira Gandhi reeled under the mounting pressures of the combined opposition and the hostile media, Shiva whirled from whore to whore, strewing the capital with an 'army of street-urchins' (411) which mirrored the legions of bastards he had reproduced in the boudoirs of the rich ladies. Parvati at last released him from her magic spell and the disenchanted hero found before him a 'balloon-fronted slum-girl' (412) who reminded him of all the horrors and miseries of slum-life from which he had been rescued by the war. On a cold morning in January 1975, when the Railway Minister, L.N. Mishra, was killed by an explosion at Samastipur, Shiva dragged Parvati by the hair and left her in the mosque-shadowed slum. In the meantime, Saleem, too, had been disillusioned with communist politics. He had accompanied Picture Singh during his political lectures which invariably followed his serpentine performances in the poorest quarters of Delhi. But he had found people unconvinced of the snake-charmer's dream of a revolution which would remove poverty and inequities from the country. They had heckled him and ridiculed his grandiose promises. Saleem himself could not accept his mentor's portrayal of the unrelenting viciousness of the rich and the unalloyed nobility of the poor. He realized that he could never fully share Picture Singh's world-view, and that his own dream of 'national salvation' was 'insubstantial, the maunderings of a fool.' (413) Picture Singh was disturbed by the condition of Parvati who disintegrated under the weight of her child and the vehemence of insults which the women of the slum hurled at her after her return. He requested Saleem once again to marry the hapless girl and save her honour. Saleem could not refuse this time because Parvati's pregnancy had invalidated his defence. On the Republic Day, 1975, he married the girl who bore his enemy's child. Parvati was converted to Islam and she took a new name, Laylah.[15] She was, thus, 'caught up in the repetitive cycles' of Saleem's life which had always been governed by 'inevitability, the anti-thesis of choice.' (415) Like his mother Amina, Parvati changed her name in order to have a child who would be born to a father not his own. But, ironically, the baby would be 'the true grandchild of his father's parents.' (415) The birth of her child mirrored Saleem's own as the countdown to the Independence found a farcical echo in the events leading to the declaration of Emergency on the midnight of 25 June, 1975.

Parvati went into labour on 12 June when the Allahabad High Court found Indira Gandhi guilty of 'campaign malpractice' (417) and disqualified her from holding public office for six years. The labour, which lasted for thirteen days, coincided with the thirteen days of political turmoil and uncertainty in the country when Indira refused to resign after the verdict of the High Court. The parallel between Parvati's travail and Indira's was horribly precise. While the midwives urged Parvati to push, the opposition leaders, like Jaya Prakash and Morarji, goaded Indira to resign and exhorted the Army to defy the illegal orders of a disqualified Prime Minister, thus forcing her to deliver a child of her own. On the stroke of midnight, 25 June, Indira Gandhi proclaimed 'Emergency' and suspended all civil rights. Dissent of any kind was proscribed and it brought the democratic process to a grinding halt. Her police cracked down on the political leaders and the journalists throughout the country. At that 'precise instant of the birth of the new India,' (419) Saleem's son—Aadam Sinai—was born. He was a perfectly formed baby except for his enormous, flapping ears, like those of an elephant (a grotesque joke which was not lost on elephant-nosed Saleem), and his refusal to cry or utter any sound. By virtue of his birth at that dismal hour which marked the end of the Independence era and the country's arrival at Emergency, the mute baby became, like his adoptive father, 'handcuffed to history.' (420) He, too, was a child of his time when a widowed Prime Minister, in her lust for power and centrality, spawned a terrible monster and distorted reality beyond repair.

Chapter XXIX: Midnight

As Saleem's narrative approaches the climactic moment, the rift within him widens. He finds it difficult to embrace and recreate the nightmarish experience which had cut him off from his past as well as his future. But left with no choice but to finish what he has begun, the story of his battered life and benighted times, he jerks towards the climax 'like a puppet with broken wings.' (426) With scraps of memory and newspaper headlines he builds up the reality at the time of the Emergency. He presents the two-year-long despotic regime of Indira Gandhi-the-Widow, metaphorically as a continuous midnight when all human rights and civil freedoms were suspended and Indian democracy, based on the Nehruvian ideals of secularism, multiplicity and liberal freedom, was damaged irremediably. It symptomatized the collapse of the dream of new India and released dictatorial and communal tendencies in the body-politic. Characterized by repressive laws, censorship of the press, midnight knocks by the police, detention of opposition leaders and untold brutalities on the people, it was a time when India had almost turned into a totalitarian state. Saleem dramatically recreates the country's brush with dictatorship and the overwhelming feeling of impotence and despair it had generated. He wields his pen like a scintillating scimitar and ruthlessly exposes the attempts of the murderous widow to aggrandize herself and retain power through self-mythification and her ambition to rewrite Indian history with herself at the centre. Rushdie, who considers himself to be 'radio-active with history and politics' and opposes the position of political quietism recommended for writers by George Orwell in 'Inside the Whale' (*IM*, 95,100), mercilessly criticizes the political injustice of his time in this chapter, significantly titled 'Midnight.' The Emergency had two parts, like the 'parti-coloured hair' (432) of the Prime Minister: a 'white' or visible and documented part, and a 'black' i.e. secret and unrecorded part. It is this untold part which Saleem chronicles in terms of devastating political satire. He challenges the official version of the Emergency which passes over the excesses committed by Sanjay Gandhi and his henchmen as fiction and baseless opposition propaganda.

In the winter of 1975, Aadam Sinai was infected with tuberculosis which did not respond to either the medication or the magic of his mother, Parvati. Saleem found something 'darkly metaphorical' (422) in the disease which was not cured while the Emergency lasted. The ailment of the child, who did not speak, signified to him the sickness of the country under the Emergency with its lack of the freedom of speech. Aadam thwarted Parvati's desperate attempts to make him cry or utter a sound with an implacable will. While Saleem, the child of Independence, had succumbed to the 'joint tyrannies of family and fate,' Aadam, the offspring of Emergency, 'fought ferociously, refusing to yield.' (425) He was tougher and stronger than his adoptive father. But unlike Saleem, who, as a child, had developed at a dizzying speed, his son showed signs of stunted growth. Parvati, too, suffered from a gnawing despair because of her unconsummated marriage. Saleem could not bring himself to share her bed for fear of the nightly transformation of her face into that of his sister. But he had no solace to offer to his inconsolable wife. Reduced to penury, he scraped a living by his olfactory gift which enabled him to entertain tourists by smelling out their simple secrets. When the government changed the constitution to give the Prime Minister 'absolute powers' (424) and an opportunity to establish a dynasty, Saleem sniffed 'the ghosts of ancient empires in the air' and 'the sharp aroma of despotism' (424) and worried about personal safety. But he did not run away from the city because he knew, from his experience in the Sundarbans, the uselessness of flight. He threw in his lot with the poor magicians and remained in the ghetto out of loyalty and gratitude to Picture Singh whom he regarded as his father like Ahmed, Hanif and General Zulfikar, and as an incarnation of the Hummingbird. In the wake of the Emergency a gloomy silence had descended on the slum. Despite his phenomenal hold on reality, Picture Singh became depressed in that atmosphere of fear and gloom and forgot to lecture his audience about the inevitability of a revolution. The illusionists also neglected their shows because they had arrived at a time 'beyond illusions.' (426) Incredible things happened in the country which amazed even the famous magicians and conjurers in the slum. People vanished inexplicably; shantytowns and slums mysteriously disappeared from the face of the earth. The state-controlled media, which deified Indira Gandhi and equated her with the nation through a fascist slogan: 'Indira is India and India is Indira,' (427) foisted the myth of development on the people but it remained silent about the atrocities of the government. No one knew for certain how many people lost their freedom during the Emergency—'either thirty thousand or a quarter of a million' (434)—because the truth was lost in the doctored news catered by the censored press. The forces of tyranny were let loose to discipline the people and crush all opposition to the Prime Minister who began to look upon herself as an embodiment of 'Bharat Mata.' Major Shiva, who hated the powerful, found in the dictatorial regime an opportunity to grab some power for himself; he became Indira's henchman and a 'warlord of tyranny.' (430) The Emergency tried to create a world of startling uniformity and people were forced to conform to bureaucratic models of personality and conduct. Those who were different—such as the midnight's children—constituted a threat to the unitary world-view on which the dictator based her claim for unchallenged authority. It was no wonder, therefore, that Indira Gandhi should find a rival in Saleem whose self-delusion of being India parallels that of the Prime Minister and upon whom her father had bestowed 'the role of the mirror of the nation' through a letter in which 'her own, sloganized centrality was denied.' (427) The star-obsessed Widow had learnt from her astrologers about the 'secret potential' (427) of the midnight's children and asked an obsequious Civil Servant and genealogy expert to trace their origin. Saleem was convinced that the purpose behind the declaration of Emergency was the liquidation of the miraculous children who stood for an alternative reality and before whom 'the astrology-ridden Prime Minister trembled in fear.' (434) On a dismal morning in winter, a group of volunteers of Sanjay Gandhi's Youth Congress arrived at the slum with medical vans and bulldozers to implement their leader's 'civic beautification' and forced sterilization programmes. The well-dressed young men and women looked identical and resembled the son of the Prime Minister and his ex-model wife. Picture Singh rallied the magicians to his side and led an attack on the invaders. But their resistance was broken by Major Shiva and his troops who opened fire on the slum-dwellers and bulldozed their hovels. In the ensuing turmoil Parvati was killed. Saleem started running away from the fury of the guns leaving behind him his son and his last link with a 'historically verifiable past,' (432) the silver spittoon. But he was pursued, captured and betrayed by his arch-rival and destructive alter-ego. Shiva had come to the colony, upon the instructions of the Widow, to arrest the only man on earth 'who held the key to the location of every single one of the children of midnight.' (432) Saleem was taken to a home for bereaved women in Benaras, symbolically one of the holiest places of Shiva worship in India, and forced to betray his midnight siblings. A massive hunt was conducted throughout the country to round them up. Some of them escaped; four hundred and twenty were caught. When they were brought to the 'Widows' Hostel' and tortured, Saleem 'gave way to his grief.' (434) In an emotionally charged address to the children he confessed his shameful betrayal and announced his verdict on politics which had sucked them into its vortex, stripped them of illusions and, finally, crushed their spirits:

> Politics, children: at the best of times a bad dirty business. We should have avoided it . . . I am coming to the conclusion that privacy, the small individual lives of men, are preferable to all this inflated macrocosmic activity. (435)

This assertion of the primacy of individual and non-political action is defeatist. It signifies the ultimate defeat of the human spirit by the demoniac forces of politics in contemporary society.

On the New Year's Day, 1977, Saleem was visited by a lady who was in charge of the Prime Minister's sterilization programme. 'The Widow's Hand' (437) told Saleem, who had been brought up in Bombay which epitomized the multiplicity of India and the plurality of her faiths, that Indians were 'only capable of worshipping one God' and to them the Widow was 'a manifestation of the OM.' (438) She also told him that 'those who would be gods fear[ed] no one so much as other potential deities.' (438) Indira Gandhi, who had elevated herself to the status of a goddess, feared the magical children and planned their undoing because she found in their existence a challenge to her claim for omnipotent power. In her new incarnation, she represented the most abhorrent and fearful aspects of a despot who exploited religion to mythologize her personal rule.[16] The Widow's minion, thus, provided Saleem with an answer to the question of his meaning which had plagued him all his life: 'Who am I? Who were we? We were are shall be the gods you never had.' (438) For the next eighteen days, they were taken to underground chambers and irreversibly 'vas-and-tubectomized' by doctors, and thus disconnected from their linkage with the country's history. To ensure that the prodigious children, who embodied the nation's hope generated at the moment of Independence, would have neither progeny nor future, their 'ectomized parts' (440) were fried and fed to the pie-dogs. The 'sperectomy' or 'the draining-out of hope' (437) was the cruellest joke of the avenging goddess. Saleem understood the purpose of the children, who represented the originally 'one-thousand-and-one marvellous promises of a numinous midnight,' only after their destruction: 'Who were we? Broken promises; made to be broken.' (439) The Emergency was lifted in the middle of January and in the following election Indira Gandhi and her party were routed. The Janata Party came to power and the nation placed its 'tattered hopes' (441) at the hands of an ancient urine-drinker. In March, the children were released from captivity like other political prisoners. The traumatic experience had brought about a profound change in Saleem. It had left him dazed and unenthusiastic. He was disillusioned with politics and the party of old, faddish leaders did not seem to him to be a harbinger of 'a new dawn.' (441) Bereft of hope and his connections with history, Saleem returned to Delhi with a painful feeling that an age, which had begun on a glorious midnight amidst promises of plenitude and fulfilment, had come to an end. After a brief search he found Picture Singh and was reunited with his son.

Chapter XXX: Abracadabra

As Saleem enters the final chapter of his pickled memories, he rushes to touch the finishing line. Because his disintegration has reached an explosive stage and it will not be long before he splinters into a myriad of fragments. His tone becomes pessimistic and he concludes his narrative by offering a bleak, disconsolate vision of the country.

After the fall of the Widow in the general election of 1977, Saleem returned to Delhi. The nightmarish experience of direct confrontation with political forces had led to his marginalization. He had been reduced from a protagonist at the centre-stage to a victim at the periphery. Battered by fate and castrated by a Prime Minister, he was now a prematurely old and dwarfish creature 'to whom history could do no more.' (447) But he was dismayed not so much at his own plight as at the change he noticed in the people around him. They had started forgetting a historical disaster like the Emergency. Even the communist magicians, the worst victims of the authoritarian regime, seemed to have lost their memories. Plagued by daily troubles and economic ills, they were unwilling to look behind them: 'Emergency was rapidly being consigned to the oblivion of the past, and the magicians concentrated upon the present with the monomania of snails.' (444) To Saleem, who had survived amnesia and experienced its terrible consequences, the change in his old friends seemed immoral, even 'obscene.' (445) In his mind the past grew vivid with every passing day while the present appeared dreary and inconsequential. His son, Aadam, had been cured of tuberculosis with the end of the Emergency. Through his sickness he had been looked after by Picture Singh and wet-nursed by a washerwoman named Durga who was 'full of gossip and . . . milk' (445) and whom the snake-charmer loved and intended to marry. Picture Singh had fallen into a decline. He looked 'old and forlorn' (446) and his magical powers appeared to have waned. Communism had seeped out of him and he no longer talked about social change and revolution. Left adrift in a world which he could not understand, he, like Saleem, clung to baby Aadam 'as if the child were a torch in a long dark tunnel.' (448) The constant attention the child demanded was one reason why Saleem managed to stay alive after his return from captivity. Less than two years old, Aadam was a tough and strong-willed kid who exerted tyrannies upon the adults. The 'mute autocracy' of the child reminded Saleem that he 'was a member of a second generation of magical children who would grow far tougher than the first' and forge their fate 'in the implacable furnaces of their wills.' (447) The Emergency had destroyed the promises of Independence but his silent, strong-willed son, like a thousand other potent kids—Shiva's bastards—growing up in the country, represented to Saleem the nation's hope for regeneration. He was symbolically born of the most powerful of the traditional gods, Shiva and Parvati who represent the mythical cycle of destruction and regeneration. His name, Aadam, signified the progress and optimism symbolized by Aadam Aziz. But he would need magical powers to cope with the fractured world Saleem was leaving for him. Significantly, the first word that Aadam uttered was 'abracadabra,' a magic formula which indicated the inheritance of his mother, Parvati-the-Witch. Saleem stayed with Picture Singh in his ragged hovel under a railway bridge and assisted him in snake-charming. Then, one day, the taunt of a mischievous paan-wallah in Connaught Place—that Picture Singh was not the best snake-charmer and that he had seen a better performer at a nightclub in Bombay—provoked the old man into travelling to that city to challenge his rival and prove his superiority. He requested Saleem to accompany him in the worst battle of his life. Thus, like a 'magic spell,' (450) the paan-seller's taunts opened a door for Saleem through which he returned to the city of his birth with his son. But he was shocked to find that Bombay had been changed beyond recognition. All the familiar landmarks of his childhood paradise, including Methwold's Estate, had vanished. On the two-storey hillock now stood a huge, pink mansion, proclaiming the power and competence of the Narlikar women. Following the directions of the paan-wallah, they reached an underground den of licentiousness named, in a grotesque parody of Saleem's own M.C.C., the 'Midnite—Confidential Club.' It was a place of 'Stygian darkness, black as hell' (453) where the westernized youth of the city, devoid of memories and past, gathered to drink imported wine and enjoy 'illicit sexuality.' (454) With his infant son in his arms, Saleem descended into that 'place outside time, that negation of history' (454) where Picture Singh challenged his opponent, a handsome youth named, ironically, the Maharaja of Cooch Nahin. In a hair-raising battle for supremacy, the old snake-charmer, who might have been a second Hummingbird, defeated the grandson of Mian Abdullah's benefactress by putting on the show of his life and retained the title of 'The Most Charming Man in the World.' The winner and his companions were treated to a celebratory meal of rice, dal, puris and chutney. The unforgettable taste of the green chutney carried Saleem through memory lane back to his childhood and he was seized by a determination to find out its maker. He collected the address of the pickle factory from a blind waitress and, like an 'open sesame,' (456) it unlocked the last door of his life through which he reached his journey's end. He took leave of Picture Singh and went with his son to Braganza Pickles Ltd., which was run by his former ayah and foster mother, Mary Pereira.

At the end of the framed narrative (the account of the public and private events which bring him to the verge of fragmentation), Saleem returns to the framing story, his present plight that compels him to write down his experience. The protagonist, thus, catches up with the narrator and Saleem, the autobiographer; completes a circular journey from himself to himself. His involvement with history and with the personages central to it leaves him impotent, both physically and politically. No longer interested in politics, Saleem—at thirty—withdraws into the privacy of a retired life. He manages the pickle factory for old Mary who now lives in the pink mansion on Methwold's Estate and raises his son. He even accepts the proposal of Padma, his co-worker in the factory and faithful narratee, to marry her despite his impotence and fear of imminent disintegration. With the drying out of the hopes and possibilities of Independence, Saleem, whose life mirrored the vicissitudes of his country's, has started cracking up at an alarming rate. Since he fears the absurdity of his condition—that of not belonging to the country—re-embodies and apprehends his end, he hastens to recollect and record his experience. The act of recollection becomes a desperate effort on his part to resist fragmentation and retain his control. He tries to impose an order of meaning on his meaningless existence through his writing. Memory helps him to put together the fragments of the past some of which have been irretrievably lost. It is his safeguard against fragmentation and loss of touch with reality. By day he supervises the production of Mary's legendary pickles and by night he chronicles the events of his life and times. He pickles his memory and gives it 'shape and form—that is to say, meaning.' (461) The taste of the pickles may be 'strong' and, in some cases, 'overpowering' (461) but they will hopefully preserve the authentic taste of truth. Thirty jars, containing the pickled version of the thirty years of history—his own and the country's—stand on a shelf above his writing desk, 'waiting to be unleashed upon the amnesiac nation.' (460) (One jar remains empty because the future cannot be pickled and preserved.) Completely alienated from the world outside the factory, he watches the people preparing to celebrate the coming Independence Day which will coincide with his thirty-first birthday. The euphoria and optimism that marked the country's emancipation from colonial rule, have been replaced by cynicism, despair and a general sense of waste. The myth of the nation, born thirty years ago, has decayed in the wake of its postcolonial history. Saleem realizes that the country needs new myths to inspire her people. But, drained of his powers, he leaves the task to a new generation. He writes, instead, his own epitaph and articulates the unenviable condition of his own generation—the generation of the midnight's children—who have been privileged and cursed 'to be both masters and victims of their times . . . and . . . sucked into the annihilating whirlpool of the multitudes . . . to be unable to live or die in peace.' (463) Saleem Sinai, who began his life at the moment of independence with unlimited potential, is now a broken creature waiting, amidst another countdown to a midnight, to explode into voiceless particles of dust. The child of midnight ends his story with a midnight cry of mutant freedom. The wheel comes full circle.

NOTES

1. This chapter is inspired by a real-life incident which is described by Rushdie in his latest book entitled *Step across this Line*. The famous Urdu poet Faiz Ahmed Faiz (1911-1984)—who was not only a communist but also an outspoken believer—survived the riots that followed Partition with the help of one of Rushdie's aunts who lived in Karachi and was a close friend of the poet. Fleeing from the fury of an angry mob looking for him, Faiz took shelter in the aunt's house. There was, under the carpet in the sitting room, a trap door, which led down into an underground cellar. The panicky poet descended into the cellar, the trap door was closed and the carpet was rolled back by the aunt. When the murderous mob came for the poet, they did not find him. And Rushdie writes: "Many years later I used the memory of the incident at my aunt's house as the inspiration for a chapter in *Midnight's Children*, but it's the real-life story of the real-life poet, or at any rate the story in the form it reached to me by the not-entirely-reliable route of family legend, that has left the deep impression on me." (*Step across this Line: Collected Fiction 1992-2002* [London: Jonathan Cape, 2002], p. 433.)
2. But, ironically, Ramram's prediction would come true. Because Saleem with the gargantuan nose would be actually Shiva with the knobbly knees. He would have thus two heads but his parents would see one. He would be born at the midnight hour of Independence and, therefore, no older than his country. Like the newly born nation, he would have multiple parents because he would also be fathered by history.
3. Indian readers would remember the slogan of the communist party at the time of Independence: 'Ye Azadi Jhutha Hai, Bhulo Mat, Bhulo Mat.'
4. In an essay entitled 'In God We Trust' (1990) Rushdie refers to Anderson's seminal study *Imagined Communities: Reflections on the Origin and Spread of Nationalism* (1991) which supports the view (implicit in Saleem's narrative) that 'the idea of sequence, of narrative, of society as a story, is essential to the creation of nations.' (*IH*, 382) Saleem reinforces this idea of a nation as an 'imagined community' when he speaks of India variously as a 'mass fantasy,' a 'collective fiction' and a myth dreamed into existence by a 'phenomenal collective will.' (112) In another essay,

'A Fantasy called India,' he writes: "The narrator of *Midnight's Children* describes [India] as a kind of collective fantasy. I suppose what he—or I, through him—was saying was that there never had been a political entity called India until 1947. The thing that became independent had never previously existed, except that there had been an area, a zone called India. So it struck me that what was coming into being, this idea of a nation-state, was an invention. It was an invention of the nationalist movement. And very successful invention." (*India Today*, 18 August 1997, p. 58)

5. Narlikar died under the weight of his favourite obsession, the concrete tetrapod, which he climbed while fleeing for life from the mob of irate language marchers whose cause he had denigrated, and which succumbed to the force of their numbers and fell into the sea.
6. This dream-sequence is directly influenced by the children's film *The Wizard of Oz*, which Rushdie had watched in Bombay's Metro Cinema as a ten-year-old boy. As he writes in an essay entitled 'Out of Kansas': "Years afterwards, I gave these dreams to the narrator of *Midnight's Children*, having completely forgotten their source: "No colours except green and black the walls are green the sky is black . . . the Widow is green but her hair is black." In this stream-of-consciousness dream-sequence, a nightmare of Indira Gandhi is fused with the equally nightmarish figure of Margaret Hamilton: a coming together of the wicked Witches of the East and West." (*Step across this Line*, p. 18)
7. Hanif's aesthetic position is symptomatic of a larger debate about the conflicting demands of fantasy and realism as a narrative mode which runs through the entire fictional oeuvre of Rushdie. He settles the issue in favour of fabulism which alone, he believes, can reflect the multi-dimensional reality of the sub-continent.
8. The Lord will reappear in *The Moor's Last Sigh* to give the freakish Moor a valuable piece of advice at a critical moment of his life.
9. Rushdie reduces the coup of 1958, which made General Ayub Khan the first dictator of Pakistan, to a parody of military operation by farcically describing its inner fictional story and turning the sinister political game into an absurd after-dinner exercise.
10. Obsessed with the 'national longing for form' and correspondence 'between apparently unconnected things,' (300) Saleem draws continuous parallels between private events and public occurrences in this chapter as throughout the book.

11. Around the same time a general election was also held in India in which the Indira Gandhi-led faction of the split Congress Party, known as Naba Congress or the New Congress, won an overwhelming majority with a popular slogan: 'Garibi Hatao.' While Pakistan prepared for war, India celebrated Indira's electoral victory.
12. Pakistan's 'state truth' about the 1971 war is that no atrocities were committed by her army in the East Wing. The Pak authorities proclaimed that the horrible things, which happened on the fateful night of 25 March, 'weren't-couldn't—have-been true.' (356) But Saleem's alternative account, which evokes the ineffable human tragedy, disclaims the officially sanctified version.
13. In retrospect, Saleem realizes the futility of his anger and revolt against inevitability. Because he has learnt from experience that there is no escape from historical destiny or inevitability. Drained of rebellion and hope and apprehensive of his fragmentation into million specks of invisible dust, he no longer wants to be anything except what he is. He is one of the millions of Indians who contains within himself a multitude of intertwined lives and events, one whose life influences, and is influenced by, the course of history. As he says: 'I am the sum total of everything that went before me, of all I have been seen done, of everything done-to-me. I am everyone everything whose being-in-the-world affected was affected by mine.' (383) To understand him, one has, thus, to 'swallow a world.' (383) Saleem contains a world within himself; he is history encapsulated in human frame.
14. This episode contains some passages of scathing political satire. Saleem's derisive remarks about Indira Gandhi, her son Sanjay who enjoyed extra-constitutional power, and about the hollowness of her populist slogans like 'Abolish Poverty' (which is mercilessly lampooned by Picture Singh when he harasses a congress worker campaigning for his leader [398]) stick in the mind. His social and political comments as well as imputations of corruption reveal his hatred for unscrupulous politicians and provide a stringent critique of the politics in India after Nehru.
15. This voluntary change of identity through the adoption of a new name is a trait Parvati shares with some other characters in the novel. Mumtaz became Amina while Nadir Khan, the rhymeless poet, became Lal Qasim. This reinvention of identity through change of name suggests, in the wider context of postcolonial lit-

erature, that an individual's fate cannot be determined once and forever. (See Catherine Cundy, pp. 41-42)

16. The intrusion of Hindu religious thinking into the country's politics was the biggest damage done to Indian democracy during Indira Gandhi's Emergency rule. The reason why Rushdie was so outraged by the Emergency was that it opened the 'Pandora's box' of communal discord. '. . . many of the evils besetting India today—notably the resurgence of religious extremism—can be traced back to those days of dictatorship and State violence,' he writes in an essay on Indira Gandhi entitled 'Dynasty.' (*IH*, 52)

Autobiography as History: A Study of *Midnight's Children*

SATYA BRAT SINGH
Bhagalpur University

Singh's exploration of the history-fiction interface in Midnight's Children *leads him to assert that Rushdie has attempted a different kind of historical novel that imaginatively links the fictive autobiography of an individual to the history of a nation. It is a creative re-writing of history which denies any opposition between history and fiction and supplants official records with a comprehensive account of the historical process.*

Editor

The observations of Lukacs on the historical novel, even on a novel dealing with remote Biblical history such as Thomas Mann's *Joseph and His Brothers* concentrate in a typically modern manner on the business of the novelist to recreate the past and make it contemporary. One might think of such an attitude as a revolution in the concept of the historical novel. It involves the paradox of turning the fluid nature of fiction into clear outlines of history. Written history has a pattern of certainty, whereas the pressure of innumerable details which has yielded such a pattern in course of time is the ground of all fiction. Fiction as history is a concept of the historical novel which designates the actual process of taking on the full challenge of events and turning them into the kind of significance that history has instead of dismissing them as peripheral and dealing with the essential drift underneath. This latter process might easily lead to subjective or philosophical distortion of history. As Collingwood observes about the writing of history: "This conception of 'turning into' the conception of becoming is . . . the fundamental idea of all history."[1]

Fiction as history at its best is turning events into history just as it is turning the historical material into art. What G.M. Trevelyan defines as the requisites of a historian are equally applicable to the novelist treating fiction as history: "He will give the best interpretation, who, having discovered and weighed all the important evidence available, has the largest grasp of intellect, the warmest human sympathy, the highest imaginative powers."[2] The paradox of freedom of fiction and the form of history yields an insight into the nature of events and what they mean in relation to history.

Writing fiction as history involves an effort which is similar to Collingwood's reflections on the nature of event and history: "For history, the object to be discovered is not the mere event, but the thought expressed in it. To discover that thought is already to understand it."[3]

Reading history is more or less like reading a story, living and writing history is like finding a plot or a pattern of significance. Fiction as history, therefore, is extra-ordinarily rich in potentials both fictional and historical. It is the ultimate truth, realism and awareness of a particular time of which the novel is capable. One would as such agree with Georg Lukacs: "True great realism depicts man and society as complete entities, instead of showing merely one or the other of their aspects."[4] At the same time it is the deepest and broadest foundation that history can acquire in the unresolved variety of facts and events at any time.

History and fiction do not blend easily. It is an act of great genius enjoying great liberties particularly in matters of imaginatively interpreting history in order to suit the purpose of the creative writer. Both these forms are dominant forms capable of overshadowing each other without letting either know that they are being overshadowed. However, there have been great masters of this form who have taken great liberties with history and have successfully managed to maintain a perfect balance to contribute in their own ways towards the development and enrichment of this literary form. They have known their histories intimately and moved among scenes of past as if natural and have reconstructed the atmosphere, the habits, the prevailing psychology of a generation or a race. The versions of history proliferate endlessly, every version being a provisional reconstruction, that "it is never possible to know all the facts about anything even the smallest act. The things done vanish with their doing."

Salman Rushdie may not be knowing all the facts of whatever he has written in historical terms in *Midnight's Children*. So, he is finding new angles at which to enter reality with the aim of re-interpreting to read significance, into events according to a selected frame of reference. The story narrated herein is the story of a national history aiming to give a comprehensive and comprehensible form to documentary history. Historical events and documentary evidences are used for its framework operating on margins of referentiality introducing other stories—concocted, fantastic, even private stories which put the official records in question. It does not deny official historical records, but by offering so many different stories they refuse any claim to absolute truth in the official version. As a reader and interpreter of history Rushdie is writing about and recreating a crisis point in a nation's history, of the history of the Indian sub-continent from August 15, 1947 to the subsequent evolution of Bangladesh. But he is recreating the past of a nation after having been distanced. Although he is born an Indian, he is writing after he has left India and settled in North England.

Writing history as autobiography is another way of connecting the individual component of society with the collective stream of history. This is the most pervasive in Saleem's own religious frictions, mixed ancestries, loss of identity etc. to the extent that in him we might notice Rushdie with his English father, Indian mother, Mission schooling and cared by a Catholic ayah. The symbols used to link the autobiography of an individual to the history of a nation are obvious, sometimes heavy handed. Salman Rushdie's *Midnight's Children* is an autobiographical fiction where the narrator is mysteriously "handcuffed to history."

Saleem Sinai, the narrator, is at the centre of a vast web of stories which constitutes postcolonial Indian history, which is also his own life story. In his quest for individual identity, Saleem weaves together the stories of his family through several generations of India's independence and partition, of the State of Emergency in 1975, of Indian myths both Hindu and Muslim, of the thousand and one children born in the first hour of India's Independence etc. In this attempt he is forced to rewrite the whole of Indian history experientially—with himself at its centre, draws correspondences between national events and his personal life, dissolving referentiality into fantasy, forging connections in order to confer meaning on chaos:

> And am I so far gone, in my desperate need for meaning, that I'm prepared to distort everything to re-write the whole history of my times purely in order to place myself in a central role? Today in my confession, I can't judge I'll have to leave it to others. For me there can be no going back. (166)

The theme of the partition is dealt with by Khushwant Singh in *A Train to Pakistan*. B. Rajan in the *Dark Dancer* Manohar Malgonkar in *Distant Drum*, Attia Hosain in *Sunlight on a Broken Column* and Collins and Lapierre in *Freedom at Midnight*, Paul Scott in *The Raj Quartet* etc. But to Rushdie these attempts are anaemic and dull. The freedom movement in India was not merely a political struggle, but an all-pervasive experience that became a part of the life of almost all the sensitive and enlightened Indians. *Midnight's Children* is Rushdie's interpretation of a period of about seventy years in India's modern history dealing with the events leading to the partition and beyond.

In *Midnight's Children* Rushdie encapsulates the experiences of three generations of the Sinai family, living in Srinagar, Amritsar and Agra and then in Bombay and, finally, migrating to Karachi. Saleem Sinai, the narrator engaged in the actual writing of the story, works at a pickle factory during day time and records his experiences by night, hoping that

> One day, perhaps, the world may taste the pickles of history. They may be too strong for some palates, their smell may be overpowering, tears may rise to eyes; I hope nevertheless that it will be pos-

> sible to say of them that they possess the authentic taste of truth. (550)

Saleem's personal history depicts the collective experience of a people and the history of a nation. There is in the novel virtually all the twentieth century Indian history; the Jallianwalla Bagh tragedy, Quit India Movement, Cabinet Mission, Freedom Movement, Muslim League and its role, riots and bloodshed subsequent to the independence, Five Year Plans, reorganization of Indian states and language riots, Chinese aggression, the theft of the sacred relic from the Hazratbal Mosque, Pakistan war, liberation of Bangladesh, the Emergency and various other historically important events. Portrayed as well are the divisions and dissents, chaos and disillusions, communal tensions, religious fanaticism besides traditional values and modernizing efforts of India. These evoke the truth of India and Saleem and make the novel an extraordinary record of epic dimensions and reverberations.

Right from the beginning Saleem is conscious of his destiny being chained to his country and so he says:

> And there are so many stories to tell, too many, such an excess of intertwined lives events miracles places rumours, so dense a commingling of the improbable and the mundane! . . . I must commence the business of remaking my life from the point at which it really began, some thirty-two years before anything as obvious, as present, as my clock-ridden, crime-stained birth. (4)

Saleem is conscious of destiny, historical role, (and) numen. The historical forces prove so powerful against him that he feels overburdened by "too much history" and begins to show symptoms of "falling apart". His life is shaped meaningfully by his family history and traditions. What he can never shake off, however, is national history, which he claims to be influencing at critical junctures. "My vengeful irruption into the history of my age, was certainly no trivial affair." (317) His coming to the world, according to him, was nothing less than a historical necessity:

> At the end of that January (1948), history had finally, by a series of shoves, brought itself to the point at which it was almost ready for me to make my entrance. There were mysteries that could not be cleared up until I stepped on to the scene. (103)

Even as child, he adds, he started exerting an appreciable influence on incidents and people around him. He ruminates: "Already my very presence is having an effect on history; already Baby Saleem is working changes on the people around him." (152) His involvement with mighty events and public lives was to continue almost throughout his whole life, through his entry into the public affairs of India. Even in Pakistan, this connection-to-history refused to abandon him. Only later, emptied of history he learned the art of submission, and did only what was required of him. Finally, during the Emergency in India he was drained of his history, "past present future."

In his over-enthusiasm, Saleem becomes the self-styled convenor of the conference of the thousand and one midnight's children, born in the fatal hour of Indian Independence. The children of midnight were also the children of the time: "fathered . . . by history." This can happen only in a country like India "a country which is itself a sort of dream." (137) These children, including Saleem, possessed various miraculous and magical talents:

> as though history, arriving at a point of the highest significance and promise, had chosen to sow, in that instant, the seeds of a future which would genuinely differ from anything the world had seen up to that time. (234-35)

Probing about himself he tries to find out:

> Who what am I? My answer: I am the sum total of everything that went before me, of all I have been seen done, of everything done to me. I am everyone everything whose being . . . in the world affected was affected by mine. I am anything that happens after I've gone which would not have happened if I had not come. . . . I repeat for the last time: to understand me, you'll have to swallow a world. (457-58)

About the shooting of Indians by the orders of Brigadier-General Dyer, he resorts to understatement rather than melodramatic rhetoric:

> Brigadier Dyer's fifty men put down their machine-guns and go away. They have fired a total of one thousand six hundred and fifty rounds into the unarmed crowd. Of these, one thousand five hundred and sixteen have found their mark, killing or wounding some person. "Good shooting," Dyer tells his men, "We have done a jolly 'good thing.'" (36)

This seemingly unemotional statement of facts is more powerfully affecting than any verbose description by the narrator of the intensity of his emotions would have been. The statement attributed to Dyer, however, brings out his inhumanity in particular and that of the whole phenomenon of colonial rule in general. The narrator reports it without comment but the description of the innocent people, the deliberateness of the killing evokes the emotion and sympathy for the victims and indignation against the British in the average reader. Paul Scott in the *Raj Quartet* similarly affirms the story that Dyerism was wrong and proves a historical truth that if Plassey laid the foundation of the Raj, Amritsar had shaken it off.

Similarly he is concerned with the pain caused to human beings irrespective of the side they happen to be on in the 1965 and the 1971 wars between India and Pakistan. The descriptions of these wars, indeed, are supreme examples of his non-partisan attitude and the ability to write the truth. The claims of the then governments of India and Pakistan are exposed as lies. To him war's first victim is Truth. The tone is apparently descriptive, but the narrator rather condemns the claim of the Pakistanis about being militarily superior, points out their arrogance, as well as their communal arrogance, and snobbery rampant in Pakistan.

The 1971 war sees the ultimate degradation of man. Saleem Sinai, who suffers from amnesia and emotional numbness as a consequence of the death of his parents is enrolled in a *cutia* unit (a she dog unit) in place of a tracker-dog. Having preternaturally developed olfactory capabilities, he has been chosen to function as a dog. But this symbolic relegation of the human to the bestial is a measure of the bestiality of the 1971 War itself. However, the human condition is evoked through the narrator's existence in East Bengal as a man-dog. On the orders of the Pakistan Army, the man-dog helps in getting Mujibur Rahman, the popular leader of Bangla Desh, arrested: "it was I who sniffed him out. (They had provided me with one of his old shirts; it's easy when you've got the smell)." (335) When the war is over and the narrator finds himself in India, he finds the doings of unscrupulous politicians just as inimical for humanity as the war had been. Now he takes up Mrs. Indira Gandhi's alteration in the Indian Constitution to give the Prime Minister well-nigh-absolute powers as the specific issue in question. A state of 'emergency' is declared and people are forcibly castrated. For Saleem this is a stupendous event and he re-discovers the use of his emotions. When all the children born with him at midnight on 15 August 1947 are also caught and tortured, he gave way to his grief. In the following address to the midnight's children, he gives his verdict on politics:

> Politics, Children: at the best of times a bad dirty business. We should have avoided it, I should never have dreamed of purpose, I am coming to the conclusion that privacy, the small individual lives of men, are preferable to all this inflated macrocosmic activity. But too late. Can't be helped. (435)

This final assertion of the primacy of individual non-political actions, is of course, defeatist. It is the ultimate defeat of the human spirit by the cruel and dehumanizing forces of the politics of India and Pakistan.

Saleem's reading of history yields an artificial product, for colouring and spicing are important in giving immortality to the raw materials. Rushdie uses numerous narrative devices to connect Saleem's personal story with the story of India between 1947 and 1977. The main structural devices are:

a) use of birth images and metaphors to mark turning points in history and symbolize their long-term significance.

b) use of Padma as a character, functional at both narrative and symbolic levels.
c) links political and historical events, starting with the Jallianwala Bagh massacre of 1919 with Saleem's circle of friends and family.
d) use of irony as a technical device.
e) periodic previews of events to come.

added with the most pervasive element in his narrative-humour.

To link autobiography with an interpretation of India's recent history, Saleem uses birth images which refer to the coincidence of his mother experiencing her labour pains exactly 24 hrs. earlier, when Pakistan came into existence and of his birth with the birth of independent India on the stroke of midnight August 14-15, 1947. Saleem and the other one thousand infants born in that numinous hour of Independence are representative of the post-Independence generation born to promises of plentitude and fulfilment and later chutneyfied by circumstances and the Widow. Saleem's son is born at midnight of the day when Indira Gandhi clamped down Emergency Rule on India. Parvati's 13-day labour coincides with the 13 days of political tumult when Indira refused to resign after the verdict of the Allahabad High Court. On the contrary she proclaimed Emergency. The parallel between Parvati and Saleem's travail and India's is precise and almost nightmarish:

> come on Parvati push, push, push and while Parvati pushed in the ghetto, J.P. Narayan and Morarji Desai . . . were forcing Mrs. Gandhi to push . . . the Prime Minister was giving birth to a child of her own . . . suspension of civil rights, and censorship of the press, and armoured-units-on-special-alert, and arrest of subversive elements. (419)

Rushdie thus creates in Saleem a chronicler who provokes much of the history he records and who enshrines in his personal heritage the identity of India itself. The interplay of the personal and national histories is what makes *Midnight's Children* a significantly different type of fiction neither 'anaemic nor dull.'

Rushdie's style of galloping through current newspapers and its headlines, sticking it on the caps of family friends and relatives so that the history of India reads like a family album. Saleem's uncle Zulfikar is a Pakistani General who helps Gen. Ayub plan a military takeover in 1958. Through satire he shows that some of history's violent events have their source in trivial accidents as with the language demonstrations (language riots in Bombay) or the theft of the Prophet's Hair. However, he takes liberties with dates, and takes refuge of an excuse in memory in recording events. His novel spoofs traditional histories for often being no more than biographies of kings and generals, but it says that the autobiography of a common man contains and participates in the making of history as well.

As a historical fiction linking a nation's history with an individual's autobiography, *Midnight's Children* has certain rare qualities which may be listed as follows:

1. It has epic aspirations, though expressed in different images.
2. It has multiplicity and duplicity of history which contain so many histories and so many silences.
3. It seeks to make visible/audible and audible/visible what has been pushed to the margins and forcibly silenced.
4. It seeks to deconstruct the opposition between fiction and history, to make available what has been suppressed and by so doing to reveal the official interests at stake in this suppression.
5. It is revisionist history which subverts the official view and offers a critique of authority.

On the whole *Midnight's Children* rewrites history as protest. It is a creative reworking of history which supplements historical facts in order to give a more comprehensive account of historical process and of the continuum between lived experience and recorded history, history as well as his story or fictive autobiography, above all such an account is neither anaemic nor dull. In course of reading this work, one should not forget that autobiography linked with history is to be read intelligently, involving two kinds of judgement. One, the judgement of the author's idea in writing and the other, the formal principle upon which it was composed., To find the idea and the formal principle of the work one can not rely solely on what the author may have said about it. However, there is only one fina one can not rely solely on what the author may have said about it. However, there is only one final court of appeal—the work itself and the self, that lives a life in a point or period of history that give one an experience of truth particularly a historical truth:

> The process of living seems to consist in coming to realize truths so ancient and simple, that, if stated, they sound like barren platitudes. They cannot sound otherwise to those who have not had the relevant experience, that it why there is no real teaching of such truths possible and each generation starts from scratch.[6]

NOTES

1. R.G. Collingwod, *Essays in the Philosophy of History*, p. 74.
2. Quoted Richard Langhorne, "Historiography," *The Twentieth Century Mind* , p. 107.
3. R.C. Collingwood, p. 214.
4. Georg Lukacs, *Studies in European Realism*, p. 6.
5. Ruby Wiebe, "A Novelist's Personal Notes on Frederick Philip Grove," *A Voice in the Land*, p. 219.
6. C.S. Lewis, *Letters*, ed. W.H. Lewis, 196: To Bede Griffiths, 8 May, 1939.

Rushdie the Pathbreaker: Unique Use of History and Myth in *Midnight's Children*

TAPAN JYOTI BANERJEE
Vidyasagar University

Tapan Jyoti Banerjee considers Midnight's Children *as a pioneering work that makes innovative use of history and myth, and traces the secret of the book's success to the 'in-between' position of cosmopolitan Rushdie. He analyses the uniqueness of Rushdie's treatment of history as well as its difference from western historiography, and the function that myth serves in the novel.*

Editor

Salman Rushdie has been described by Timothy Brennan (in his well-written book, *Salman Rushdie and the Third World*) as a "Third World Cosmopolitan." By "Cosmopolitan" Brennan means a writer whom the western reviewers would choose as an interpreter and authentic voice of the Third World.

One would perhaps not hesitate much to accept Brennan's thesis that no one in the remarkable history of Indo-Anglian had anything like Rushdie's success in popularizing the subcontinent for a Western public. Even such illustrious exponents of Indian English prose as Jawaharlal Nehru, M.K Gandhi, Mulk Raj Anand, Raja Rao and Kamala Markandaya had failed in their endeavour. The "inbetweenness" of the cosmopolitan is not only quite clearly discernible in Rushdie's person but also theoretically accounted for on every page of his work. And that is the secret of his success.

Rushdie appears as a wonderful interpreter of the relationship which 'Empire' essentially means. It is in his Britain that the effects of that relationship on the First World are most striking. The post-Second World War British novel, in spite of William Golding, John Berger, Pat Barker, Doris Lessing, etc. produced almost nothing to suggest the seething energies of a specifically post-imperial England. Also, the experience of the black communities in England—their importance, their endurance and their divided sense of place has not been seriously documented. Thirdly, no other writer before Rushdie had tried to evolve an English stylistic equivalent of 'magical realism' of Gabriel Garcia Marquez and Alejo Carpenter. Rushdie has not only made the seething energies of the post-imperial England an important ingredient of his fiction, but has helped bring the black communities into public view (in an ambiguous cosmopolitan way) and definitely created the English equivalent, in terms of style, of magical realism. On top of this, Rushdie has also successfully used the modernist style as a vehicle for news extravaganza, popular uprisings, populist rant and forced migrations. The totality of neo-colonialism as a world system has been recorded by him.

Rushdie's *Midnight's Children (*as also most of his other works) is a path-breaking novel in many respects. The typical post-Independence Indian English novel has been basically the illusion of a bustling world of India with its teeming diversity of peoples and locales—in some cases, the picture of sociological stability. Quite a few of the modern Indian novels in English (Vikram Seth's A *Suitable Boy* is a very good example) evoke an "imagined community" of disparate peoples, recognized by readers as the nation. They certainly serve to ideologically secure the idea of India as a single nation. By largely using the conventions of realism, rather than acknowledging its genealogy within cultural forms, these novels go for the creation of a transparent picture of postcolonial conditions. Rushdie's *Midnight's Children* is a refreshing exception in this regard. This novel traces the genealogy of India-qua-nation from the moment of its inception in 1947. For mapping the social formation of the Indian subcontinent in multiple stories, Rushdie takes to a non-mimetic mode of storytelling and depends quite heavily on the indigenous, oral narrative styles.

Kum Kum Sangari wrote: "Saleem Sinai is to be at once the voice of the individual and of a collectivity, to be spectator and participant." The mock-allegorical structure is quite effectively employed—the narrator as both a child and a representative of the fate of independent India. A neat, logical and linear ordering or psychological coherence of the realist fiction is not available in the world of *Midnight's Children.* What both intrigues and enlightens us is the fragmented terrain of the narrator's inner and outer worlds. The fragmentary mode of story telling activates multiple conceptions of India and Indianness. Saleem's inability to locate any "truth" about the nation or to distinguish between the "real" and imagined India is shared by the readers. Rushdie shows that the category of the nation is not a stable entity, but something that emerges within multiple and even competing "realities."

"Postmodernism problematizes not only fiction but also history," writes D.C.R.A. Goonetilleke. While discussing Rushdie's handling of history in *Midnight's Children*, Goonetilleke writes the following: "Saleem's—and Rushdie's—version of history is different from the traditional, which is logical, imposes patterns, a chain of cause and effect, is seemingly objective, definitive, unitary, repressive and closed. History in *Midnight's Children* is, in a postmodern way, fragmented, provisional, openly subjective, plural, unrepressive, a construct, a reading. It is different from European master . . . narratives."

A migrant writer's position has an interesting advantage. It provides him with resistance to cultural authoritarianism and its claim to speak the absolute truth, and thus, unmake a discourse that claims absolute forms of knowledge—the discourse of western historiography. As suggested in the above paragraph, Rushdie in *Midnight 's Children* is into a consideration of the notion of history as a field of diverse human and cultural possibility. His situatedness and his use of Indo-Anglian novel—itself a hybrid textual form—qualifies him to undertake this project. An Indo-Anglian work like *Midnight's Children* does not have a homogeneous audience, but has a diverse, diffuse and class divided relationship with colonial culture and the English language. Many western readers having preconceived notions about the sub-continent also form a part of the audience. Kum Kum Sangari has rightly pointed out that such a narrative has to bear the strains of "double-coding for different audiences." Rushdie himself says this in his essay, 'Outside the Whale': "The various films and T.V. shows and books . . . propagate notions about history which must be quarrelled with as loudly and as embarrassingly as possible." He does just that in his *Midnight's Children.* The indigenous people of the sub-continent in this book are not allowed just "walk-ons," but parts in the British history, as in the novels of Paul Scott and M.M. Kaye.

It is also possible to say that Rushdie in *Midnight's Children* treats of history from the 'underside,' exposing the differential impact of events on different sections of the population. In this respect he can be equated with Fernand Brandel whose 'longue duree' view of history (discussed in *French Studies in History*) was in favour of a historical study that should move from surface to the depth, from event to structure and move back to the event—a view contrary to the position that concentration on 'the most capricious and delusive . . . short time span' dealing only with major events and front-line actors is good enough for a historical study. The projection of the Indian hour of Independence in *Midnight's Children* is a good example of the application of the 'longue duree' view.

Myth has been used by quite a few of Rushdie's predecessors for interpreting history and reality, but what he does in *Midnight's Children* is to defuse and debunk myth itself since by itself myth is ultimately no solution and never can replace history. Use of myth by a 'colonized' writer for purposes of 'liberation' (when one thinks in terms of the ideology of containment as discussed in Frederick Jameson's *The Political Unconscious: Narrative as a Socially Symbolic Act*) may sometimes lead to historical petrification. Franz Fanon says that when the colonized writer wants to 'belong' to his people by choosing a system of 'black' values and constructing an alternative ideology, he is in danger of renouncing the present and the future in the name of a mythical past. Rushdie's mythification in *Midnight's Children* can be viewed both as a "strategy of liberation" and as an ideological form that avoids historical petrification. For one thing, the epic form of the novel (Rushdie indicated during an interview with Michael Kaufman of the *New York Times* that he was in favour of using the form of Comic Epic for "that part of the world") tries to describe or 'contain' an India of innumerable stories. Through the entire book, stories develop out of other stories in a never-ending cycle. But even an epic is not large enough to 'contain' all the stories that need to be told. So, the use of the epic form, in the final analysis, turns out to be an ironical device, since the 'reality' of India is 'uncontainable' in any form. Also, the tragedy is nicely masked by the 'comic' since its intensity and extreme painfulness can hardly be expressed otherwise. Making the Indian people full of 'holes' (metaphorically speaking), Rushdie implies that in a land like India no 'whole' relationship can emerge.

In fact, in Rushdie's handling of the Comic, the Tragic, the Real, the Surreal and the Mythic there seems to be a deliberate attempt at negating the theory of a unified whole that India has been made to stand for. This 'de-fusing' of genres, actually, is the strategy of liberation, rather than of containment. In the presentation of Tai, the boatman, there is a combination of the realist and the mythic modes. And Saleem is made to receive knowledge of his magical powers while hidden in a washing-chest ("a hole in the world, a place which civilization has put outside itself.") But the mythic retreat being what it is, a washing-chest, the ludicrousness of the presentation becomes obvious. To take another example. The readers are led to expect a mythical, magical re-union of all the 'Midnight's Children.' But they are told by the narrator that the way in which he is able to contact the other 'magical' children of Independence is by becoming a sort of All India Radio. Myth is, thus, used to debunk myth in *Midnight's Children.* The novel demonstrates in a unique way Rushdie's ultimate faith in history, whose burden, he believes, has to be accepted and borne. Myth, at his hands, serves to liberate his people from the hegemonic "strategy of containment," but, by debunking itself, it also helps him avoid historical petrification.

Works Cited

Fernand Brandel, *French Studies in History,* Vol. 1, *The Inheritance,* ed. M. Aymard and H. Mukhia (Delhi: Orient Longman, 1988).

Timothy Brennan, *Salman Rushdie and the Third World* (Macmillan, 1989).

Franz Fanon, *Black Skin, White Masks* (New York: Grove Press, 1967).

D.C.R.A. Goonetilleke, *Salman Rushdie* (Modern Novelists Series, Houndmills: Macmillan, 1998).

Frederick Jameson, *The Political Unconscious: Narrative as a Socially Symbolic Act* (Ithaca: Cornell University Press, 1981).

Kum Kum Sangari, "The Politics of the Possible," *Cultural Critique*, 7, 1987.

A Tryst with Fate and History: A Study of *Midnight's Children*

MARÍA ELENA MARTOS HUESO
Italy

María Elena Hueso's paper identifies Rushdie's aim in the novel as accentuating the value of personal history which, despite its inaccuracies, can be as valid as painstaking historiographic recording. It reveals how the inexorable forces of fate and history intervene in Saleem Sinai's life, favouring and deserting him—like Karna in the Mahabharata*—at crucial moments and making him simultaneously an emblem of India and a homeless wanderer.*

Editor

If there should be a reason for commenting on such a topic as fate and history in the novel *Midnight's Children*, the explanation can be found when reading the novel throughout. The first impression that approaches the readers is a pervading sense of nostalgic recalling, passing in front of our very eyes in the guise of a family album, a recollection of remembrances put into a whole. But Saleem Sinai's memories are not simply that, a bunch of loosely connected images carried in his mind: these constitute the very essence of his self; these recallings seem to be like different rivers that pour their waters into the river of his own life.

Considered variously as a historical novel, a magical realist tale, or as a postmodern parody, Salman Rushdie's *Midnight's Children* is one of the most complex and complete novels of the past century, not only as far as its stylistic brilliance is concerned, but also due to its intimate interconnection with the postmodern conception of history. Quite significantly, Rushdie himself made it clear that his target when writing this magnificent work were very far from rigorous historiographic recording, that his real aim was highlighting the immense value of personal history as opposed to the official versions of it that pervade scientific studies in the very name of truth. According to Rushdie, one's own recollections of our personal story, though inaccurate, can be as valid as any official records of history, embellished with a veneer of scientificism. In his famous article entitled "'Errata': or, Unreliable Narration in *Midnight's Children*," he outspokenly states his using the strategy of parody and antihistorical inaccuracy for this precise purpose:

> When I began the novel (as I've written elsewhere) my purpose was somewhat Proustian. Time and migration had placed a double filter between me and my subject, and I hoped that if I could only imagine vividly enough it might be possible to see beyond those filters, to write as if the years had not passed, as if I had never left India for the West. But as I worked I found that what interested me was the process of filtration itself. So my subject changed, was no longer a search for lost time, had become the way in which we remake the past to suit our present purposes, using memory as our tool. Saleem's greatest desire is for what he calls meaning, and near the end of his broken life he sets out to *write himself*, in the hope that by doing so he may achieve the significance that the events of his adulthood have drained from him. (*IH*, 23-24)

As Srivastava (70) has rightly pointed out, the Rushdiean approach to history is not so much Proustian as it is Foucaultian, for genealogy plays a fundamental role in the reconstruction of Saleem Sinai's history. Definitely, the genealogical approach to personal as well as to political history pervades the narration, revealing as well the intervention of two irresistible forces at play within this game of fragmentation and redefinition that takes place inside Saleem's mind: fate and history, like two powerful fairies, shape his life in a capricious fashion, favouring and deserting him in various central moments of his existence.

In spite of the apparently chaotic juxtaposition of images that collide in Saleem's story, his narration has also a definite purpose: he is trying to recompose himself again through that painful exercise of recollection, opening the forgotten bottles of pickled history in order to find out the truth about his own essence. He knows that his life is a continuation of other past lives, and that is precisely why he feels the need to deepen in that past: he tries to find the meaning of his existence by searching for the meanings of other existences before his. That is the only way to succeed in his quest, and the importance of genealogies is therefore highlighted.

The impact of genealogies in Saleem's life cannot be easily denied, and his interest seems to be derived from the strong influence of other members of the family who also reveal an eager affection for this alternative form of history: "As for genealogies: Uncle Mustapha spent all his spare time filling giant logbooks . . . researching into and immortalizing the bizarre lineages of the greatest families in the land." (468) But genealogies are also deceiving and Rushdie's approach to them is openly farcical, taken, the same as history, as an object of parody and mockery.

Saleem, deserted by his true parents, cannot even rely on genealogy as an accurate scientific tool for recomposing the fragmented images of his life. His wretched fate, like Karna's in the *Mahabharata*, deprives him of living and growing beside his true family, and makes him unaware of his real origins, even though the subsequent effects of Mary Pereira's crucial action play in a reverse direction as compared to the twisted fate of Karna: Saleem's humble origins are changed for the luxury life of Shiva's, while Karna lives unaware of his noble blood and leads an ordinary life until Duryodhana names him King of Anga. Mary Pereira's betrayal is parallel to that of Kunti's, although the selfishness of the latter can in no way be likened to the good will of the former. In any case, the only result, the sad common fate shared by Saleem and Karna is a dismembering of identities, that only results in profound unhappiness, a sense of an authentic self which has been inevitably lost and cannot be retrieved.

Saleem instinctively feels responsible for his own fate, and thus he will always be haunted by a feeling of guiltiness for taking the place of Shiva in life's design. He often resorts to blaming Mary Pereira for his destiny, as he had no control over Shiva's twist of fate. Notwithstanding, his parents still accept him, even if they know that Saleem is not their real son. When Padma finally discovers the real Anglo-Indian origins of Saleem, she feels cheated, and once again Sinai shows his obsession with appearing as an innocent victim:

> No, I'm no monster. Nor have I been guilty of trickery. I provided clues . . . but there's something more important than that. It's this: when we eventually discovered the crime of Mary Pereira, we all found that it *made no difference!* I was still their son: they remained my parents. (136)

Thus, fate and history conspire against Saleem Sinai's life from the very first minute of his existence, making an emblem of India out of him and simultaneously tearing him apart from his real roots. This situation makes the readers aware of a plain and simple fact to which everyone of us is bound: no one can choose the place and circumstances, not even the historical atmosphere in which we come into life. This may seem a truism, but it really affects the most essential right of any human being: the right to enjoy one's own freedom. Freedom is proclaimed, vindicated and highly valuable for everyone, but, to a certain extent, freedom seems to be a mere illusion in the light of Saleem's narration. No matter how unbound and free we may feel, all of us have our freedom restricted by a common tie whose name is fate:

> I, Saleem Sinai . . . had become heavily embroiled in Fate—at the best of times a dangerous sort of involvement. And I couldn't even wipe my own nose at the time. (3)

Saleem calls the readers' attention to the fact that he was not conscious of such a restriction at the time of his birth: he could not do anything to stop the pressure of fate upon him. This represents a terrible injustice, a violation of his personal right to be free. That is why he sorely complains about the burden that fate has put on him. His identity was put on him by history, like a mark put on the skin of a slave. He is not really satisfied with his role of embodying India, and he wonders: "Why, alone of all the more-than-five-hundred-million, should I have to bear the burden of history?" (457)

But Saleem is not precisely an innocently forgetful narrator, logically prone to mild confusions in his recollections of history. He also selects those episodes that he is most interested in recording, becoming in a way a "conscious manipulator of history." (cf. Santaolalla, 168) Thus, Saleem's challenges to history and fate are nothing but deceitful, for he can never be strong enough to confront them. Thus, when Saleem Sinai becomes invisible inside Parvati-the-witch's basket, he feels free from all restraint; he feels angry about the burden that he is obliged to carry, and this anger makes him feel a freer being: "Anger made me determined . . . to begin, from that moment forth, to choose my own, undestined future." (457) But this is nothing but a temporal delusion, for when he returns to the mosque and recovers his mortal visibility, he awakes from his dreams of fleeing fate and bumps into Aadam Aziz's silver spittoon once again, the symbol of his family and, therefore, of his inescapable history. He bitterly recalls this episode as follows:

> When I tumbled out of the basket of invisibility into the shadow of the mosque, I had been rescued by rebellion from the abstraction of numbness; as I bumped out on the dirt of the magicians' ghetto, silver spittoon in hand, I realized that I had begun, once again, to feel. (458)

Amnesia also looms into Saleem's horizon as an additional threat to his act of (hi)storical recording. Curiously enough, the same silver spittoon that he fondly refers to as a token of his familial (genealogical) origins had provoked long ago the amnesia, the numbness of his identity as Saleem Sinai. But this accident had also saved his life, thus making possible his actual recollection of facts until his last minutes of life at the early age of thirty-one:

> Spittoon-brained, Saleem suffered a merely partial erasure, and was only wiped clean whilst others, less fortunate, were wiped out; unconscious in the night-shadow of a mosque, I was saved by the exhaustion of ammunition dumps. (413)

His amnesia as the Buddha had constituted his numbness: he had forgotten all about his origin, which nevertheless was a false one, being wrongly considered as the son of Ahmed Sinai after Mary Pereira's shifting of identities. Fortunately, after becoming a trail-dog for the CUTIA unit, he eventually finds Parvati, another "midnight child": "Then Parvati-the-witch saw me, and gave me back my name." (453)

In addition, the presence of colours plays a highly central role in Saleem Sinai's story. As a newborn, wrapped in India's national colours at midnight on that glorious 15th of August, 1947, Saleem's fate is inevitably associated with that of his country. Summoned by *The Times of India* and by Jawaharlal Nehru as a "child of midnight," (138) Saleem cannot escape their demands, and he reluctantly complies with the central role assigned to him. From that moment on, he will be woefully tied to India's history and will suffer India's evolutions in his own body and person, marked again by the colour combination that aborts his efforts to escape by revealing his presence at the time of Bangladesh's birth:

> How the buddha regained his name. Once long ago, on another independence day, the world had been saffron and green. This morning, the colours were green, red and gold. And in the cities, cries of "Jai Bangla!" And voices of women singing "Our Golden Bengal!," maddening their hearts with delight . . . in the centre of the city, on the podium of his defeat, General Tiger Niazi awaited General Manekshaw. . . . And amid green and red and gold, the buddha in his shapeless anonymous garment was jostled by crowds; and then India came. India, with Sam at her head. (451)

For Saleem Sinai, then, the personal is truly political, to such an extent that both elements could be perfectly combined into a powerful equation. His personal story is appropriated by official history, and, according to Alison Lee, "Saleem does become, in a sense, the text upon which India's history is written." (47) Inevitably linked and "handcuffed to history," (3) Saleem's private life is invaded by his other Mother's life, "Bharat Mata," Mother India. This historical link opens the way to another genealogy, quite different from the one understood in a strictly familial sense. But these are not distinct and disjointed genealogies, for Saleem Sinai's double origin, political and personal, will pour down into a common stream with the birth of his own son, Aadam Sinai. At the same time, even though he was also born under the vigilant eye of history, Aadam also represents a liberation from the handcuffs of the historical past, as he is symbolically cured from tuberculosis at the precise moment of the fall of the Widow, whose repressive government had made a victim out of his father, Saleem. (531)

On the level of genealogies, as well as that of history, Aadam Sinai emerges as a new promise through which everything falls into place again. Being the real son of Shiva, Aadam Sinai reconstructs the broken patriarchal line opened by Doctor Aadam Aziz: Shiva is the real grandson of Doctor Aziz, and Aadam Sinai is therefore his real great-grandson. Consequently, Aziz's dynasty is restored again. But Saleem, as always, offers his own interpretation to the facts, seeing little Aadam as a "synthesis" of both Shiva and himself, a new "midnight child" who comes out of both: "Saleem-and-Shiva, nose-and-knees . . . we shared . . . our son, Aadam, our synthesis, unsmiling, grave, with omni-audient ears." (507)

Rushdie is, undoubtedly, a masterly parodist. The powerful role of parody and satire in the preservation of collective history has been noted by Ansgar Nünning, who states:

> by conducting a double-coded dialogue between the present and the cultural past, postmodern parody can also serve as a means of highlighting the complex language and inventory of cultural memory . . . central to the formation and maintenance of collective identities. (130)

In this sense, Rushdie's use of parody in his tackling official history cannot be more accomplished. One of the most outstandingly farcical moments of the novel is perhaps Saleem's accidental involvement in the language march in Mumbadevi (225-39) that resulted in the partition of the state of Bombay and the creation of those of Gujarat and Maharashtra. Saleem, barely a child, was far more interested in developing his private life, trying to impress his friend Evie Burns, when yet another crucial episode of history comes his way and blocks his path once again.

The tragic and the comic flourish together when Saleem is thrown into the Marathi demonstration, and his innocent rhyme in Gujarati becomes a chant of war for the Marathi vindicators, causing death and destruction; but Saleem's childish conclusion replicates the farcical for he "at least . . . was on the winning side." (229)

No matter how involved Saleem is in India's history, he will always be a wanderer, for he never gets to find his place inside his country. This circumstance constitutes, as María Luz González significantly notes, a reflection of Rushdie's own situation as an expatriate writer. (45) It cannot be forgotten that *Midnight's Children* was Rushdie's second novel, and it opened a long way of narrative creation throughout which the writer has strived to portray the situation of the writer of the diaspora by telling "migrant tales." (cf. Dingwaney, 366) Significantly enough, Cropley-González inscribes *Midnight's Children* within a tradition of "revolt," (198) a clear act of apolitical writing through a self-contained story with a distinguishable beginning and end, whose kernel is the birth and death of Saleem Sinai. But, at the same time she considers it revolutionary as it provides a useful guide to its audience, and operates a clear transformation in its readers, for "its aim is not to shut us in, but to let us out, to free us through change." (199)

To conclude, it should be pointed out that Saleem is a victim as well as a perpetrator of (hi)stories, as he—often unconsciously—uses the role imposed on him as a weapon to model India's history and his own personal story. His exercise of reconstitution through memory is neither aimed directly at an imaginary audience nor intended to answer the big questions of history. It is addressed to his own self, in a desperate attempt to get meaning out of him, to "achieve self-consummation." (cf. Swain, 152) That is why in everyday life, the same as in Rushdie's universe, history should not be considered as an oracle of truth, a reliable source of facts and statistical accuracy. History should be a guide to other alternative stories, seen as commingling and colliding into a meaningful whole, as the only key to our personal truths.

Bibliography

Cropley-Gonzalez, Madelena (1994). "The Birth of Revolt through Historiographic Metafiction in Salman Rushdie's *Midnight's Children* and *The Satanic Verses*," in Max Duperray, ed., *Historicité et Metafiction dans le roman contemporain des Îles Britaniques: Historicity and Metafiction in the Contemporary British and Irish Novel*. Provence: Publications de l'Université de Provence, pp. 196-206.

Dingwaney, Anuradha (1993). "Salman Rushdie," in Emmanuel S. Nelson, ed., *Writers of the Indian Diaspora* (Westport, Connecticut: Greenwood Press), pp. 363-83.

González, María Luz (1994). "Subversion of History and the Creation of Alternative Realities in Salman Rushdie," *Revista Canaria de Estudios Ingleses*, 28, pp. 41-51.

Lee, Alison (1990). *Realism and Power. Postmodern British Fiction*. London and New York: Routledge.

Narayan, R.K. (1978). *The Mahabharata*. London: Penguin.

Nuning, Ansgar (1999). "The Creative Role of Parody in Transforming Literature and Culture: An Outline of a Functionalist Approach to Postmodern Parody," *European Journal of English Studies*, 3:2, pp. 123-37.

Rushdie, Salman (1991). *Midnight's Children*. London: Penguin, 1981.

Rushdie, Salman (1992). "'Errata': or, Unreliable Narration in *Midnight's* Children," in *Imaginary Homelands: Essays and Criticism (1981-1991)*. London: Penguin, pp. 22-25.

Santaolalla, Isabel, ed. (1994). "A Fictitious Return to the Past: Saleem Sinai's Autobiographical Journey in *Midnight's Children*," in Vera Mihailovich-Dickman, ed., *"Return" in Post-Colonial Writing: A Cultural Labyrinth*. Amsterdam: Rodopi, pp. 163-70.

Srivastava, Aruna (1991). "'The Empire Writes Back': Language and History in *Shame* and *Midnight's Children*," in Ian Aadamand Helen Tiffin, ed., *Past the Last Post: Theorizing Post-Colonialism and Post-Modernism*. New York and London: Harvester Wheatsheaf, pp. 65-78.

Swain, S.P. (1999). "Theme of Fragmentation: Rushdie's *Midnight's Children*," in M.K. Bhatnagar, ed., *Commonwealth English Literature*, pp. 147-55.

History as a Mode of Literature: A Study of *Midnight's Children*

REENA MITRA
Christ Church College, Kanpur

Reena Mitra's paper offers an absorbing analysis of Midnight's Children, *highlighting some important aspects of Rushdie's use of history in the novel like the search for identity, the fusion of autobiography and fictional narrative, and the breach in chronology. It also examines some key metaphors, the blend of realism and fantasy and the role that fantasy plays in the book.*

Editor

In *Midnight's Children*, Salman Rushdie makes Indian history a co-ordinate in his fictional art—his presentation of historical facts covers a vast span, from the pro-Independence Jalianwala Bagh incident of 1919 to the period of Emergency in 1977, and adopts a variant mode of portrayal. The facts themselves are of little interest as they have been repeatedly given to us by several novelists as well as historians. What is significant is how Rushdie has fantasized his depiction of historical reality. The introduction of the element of the magical and the supernatural has lent the work a dimension that makes it characteristically Rushdie's own, for he has his typical way of concocting a blend of art and life.

"Art," as Kakutani observes, "does have a way of imitating life and writers have always been skeptical or incapable of unilaterally separating the two."[1] Salman Rushdie, too, in writing *Midnight's Children*, seems unable, by nature and by intention, to dissever the two. He had started, as Zola believed every literary artist did, "from the true facts, which are our indestructible basis, but to show "the mechanism of these facts,"[2] he had to modify them and it is in this specific orientation given to facts that his distinctive genius lies. By his own admission it is in *Midnight's Children* that he finds his "true voice."[3]

Nancy E. Batty, in her comparative study of the narrative techniques of *Midnight's Children* and *A Thousand and One Nights*[4] draws careful attention to the dramatization of "the problematical relationship of life to art, art to life"[5] in *Midnight's Children*. This dramatization, she argues, is the effect of the deliberate juxtaposition of "the oriental tale, the eighteenth century Shandean novel and the modern historical 'realities' of India."[6]

In an article in defence of his novel, *The Satanic Verses*, Rushdie has made his aesthetic predilections very clear when he says: "do not ask your writers to create 'typical' or 'representative' fictions. Such books are almost invariably dead books."[7] The novels that he really cares for are "those which attempt radical reformulation of language, form and ideas, those that attempt to do what the 'novel' seems to insist upon: to see the world new."[8] And, this novel worldview, if it provides implications that are worth thinking about, fulfils one of the important functions of literature.

Midnight's Children is a literary response to a series of real life situations that have been cleverly fictionalized through allusions disguised as well as direct, to the country's recent as well as not so recent past. The novel has an epic sweep[9] covering about six decades in the history of the Indian subcontinent. Book One covers the time from the Jallianwala Bagh incident in April 1919 to the birth of the protagonist, Saleem, on August 15,1947; Book Two extends upto the end of the Indo-Pakistan war in September 1965, and Book Three envelops the period upto the end of the Emergency in March, 1977, and includes the Bangladesh war as well.

At the fictional level, *Midnight's Children* depicts the events and experiences in the lives of three generations of the Sinai family. The account begins with their days in Srinagar and follows their passage through Amritsar, Agra and Bombay to Karachi from where Saleem alone returns hidden in the basket of Parvati, the witch,[10] only to experience the tremors of the Emergency that had been clamped in India. At the semantic level, it is far more complex and has intriguing social and political connotations.

A careful analysis of *Midnight's Children* reveals three major aspects of Rushdie's use of history in his novel that deserve study: (i) the commingling of autobiography and narrative, (ii) the striking breach of chronology and (iii) the search for identity and the meaning of life. The opening page of the novel gives us a decipherable clue to them. Characteristically, Rushdie begins:

> I was born in the city of Bombay. . . . once upon a time. No, that won't do there's no getting away from the date: I was born in Dr. Narlikar's Nursing Home on August 15, 1947. And the time? . . . On the stroke of midnight, as a matter of fact . . . at the precise instant of India's arrival at independence, I tumbled forth into the world. . . . I had been mysteriously handcuffed to history, my destinies indissolubly chained to those of my country. For the next three decades, there was to be no escape. . . . I, Saleem Sinai, . . . had become heavily embroiled in Fate—at the best of times, a dangerous sort of involvement.
>
> Now, however, time (having no further use for me) is running out. I will soon be thirty-one years old. . . . I must work fast . . . if I am to end up meaning— yes, meaning—something.
>
> And there are so many stories to tell, too many, such an excess of intertwined lives events miracles places rumours, so dense a commingling of the improbable and the mundane! I must commence the business of remaking my life from the point at which it really began, some thirty-two years before anything as obvious, as present, as my clock-ridden, crime-stained birth.[11] (1-2)

The very first sentence of the work is illustrative of the hybrid art of the novelist. The tale is meant to be at once an autobiography and a narrative, an account of facts and a yarn spun out of imagination, a blend of truth and fiction. "I was born in the city of Bombay" clearly sets the tone for an autobiography but the latter half of the sentence shifts the reader's attention and focus, and leaves him baffled as he makes a futile attempt to approximate fiction while facts call for their share of attention. He is mystified as to how "once upon a time" can be a natural sequel to what goes before. And yet, the two are confidently set against each other as a revelatory beginning to "so dense a commingling of the improbable and the mundane!"

That the novelist is not punctilious regarding the observance of chronology is also evident on the very first page of the book. There is a frequent forward or backward shift in time that makes it to trace the proper sequence of events in the life of the protagonist. What the publisher's blurb[12] says of Rushdie's book *The Satanic Verses*, we can say of his *Midnight's Children*, too "the past and the future chase each other furiously." At the very outset, after having given the date of his birth, the narrator somersaults to his thirty-first birthday. He then dives deep into the past only to return to the present, and then to embark upon the future. He feels that it is incumbent upon him "to write the future as I have written the past." (462)

This marked break in chronology in the novel reveals the author's intention of giving not a record of events in the order of their occurrence but of projecting the basic historical truth as interacting with and affecting the life of the individual, that is, chiefly, the author himself as represented by the protagonist. On the one side we have Saleem's personal life, and, on the other, corresponding to this is the life and history of the nation. The story traces the various events in the life of the central character that synchronize with major happenings in the recent history of India. The parallel that is worked out, though strained at times, is designed to allow an understanding of the individual's life in terms of historical forces.

Also, one cannot but note that all through the novel Rushdie is preoccupied with a quest for identity and is impatient to gain an insight into the "meaning" of life. He has definitely launched out to search for ine purpose of existence. "I must work faster," his protagonist tells us," if I am to end up meaning—yes meaning—something." (9) And again, "Am I so far gone in my desperate need for meaning, that I am prepared to distort everything?" (166) Later in the novel, there is a reference to "Saleem, with his desperation for meaning." (356) Such indicators in the narrative leave us in no doubt as to what the writer, consciously or unconsciously, has set out to accomplish in his work. And, if we are to take D.H. Lawrence's advice, we would, instead of trusting the artist, "trust the tale,"[13] and construe timings in the light of whatever evidence there is in the work itself.

Returning, then, to the first of the significant aspects of the novel, there is no gainsaying the fact that Rushdie has ingeniously coupled the autobiographical with the fictional narrative. The narrator-protagonist, Saleem Sinai, prepares us at the very outset for just such a fusion when he writes of this "excess of intertwined lives events miracles places rumours." (9) The element of fantasy in the novel is introduced in such a matter-of-fact way that the reader swallows it almost unquestioningly through he knows quite well that this is one of those extra-historical factors in the novel that lend it interest rather than authenticity. In fact, the juxtaposition of the two contrastive elements of fantasy[14] and reality[15] has been so skilfully effected in the narrative that one is left not with a sense of incongruity but with the consciousness of a comprehensive general design in which the magical and real shade off into each other very naturally, the former bringing into relief the historical truth the writer sets out to explore and fix.

Rushdie's protagonist talks about "the mind's divisions between fantasy and reality" (167) but in the novel itself no such divisions seem to exist for both these constituents jointly contribute towards the aesthetic realization of the author's as well as his narrator's "urge to encapsulate the whole of reality." (75) We have the symbolic Lifafa Das, the peep show man, who tries to capture "the whole of reality" in his box. Thus, the fantastic here is not merely "the occult, the inexplicable telepathy, people disappearing in baskets, and so on"[16] it is essentially strategic in nature in the sense that it becomes a fictional mode of projecting reality and offers the real in terms of the fanciful and the bizarre.

Certain observations made in the course of the novel reveal Rushdie's attitude to reality, and bring home the message that the novelist's truth is different from that of the historian. "Sometimes legends make reality and become more useful than the facts,"(47) says Rushdie's narrator in trying to bring out the nature of fictional reality. And, again: "Reality can have metaphorical content; that does not make it less real." (200) It is clear that Rushdie's treatment of history is in conformity with his idea of "illusory fictional reality,"[17] which while recording historical truth does not insist upon a total transcription of reality.

Midnight's Children themselves are metaphorically conceived in that they can be made to represent many things. The author himself suggests this:

> They can be seen as the last throw of everything antiquated and retrogressive in our myth-ridden nation, whose defeat was entirely desirable in the context of a modernizing twentieth century economy; or as the true hope of freedom which is now forever extinguished ; but what they must not become is the bizarre creation of a rambling diseased mind. (200)

It is this "quality of visionary insight"[18] created by Rushdie's use of metaphors and symbols that lends distinction to his work.

Apart from the metaphorical value that the midnight's children have, each one of them has also been endowed with certain magical traits:

> What made the events noteworthy was the nature of these children every one of whom was, through some freak of biology, or perhaps owing to some preternatural power of the moment or just conceivably by sheer coincidence, endowed with features, talents and faculties which can only be described as miraculous. (195)

The supernatural qualities ascribed to these children are the author's means of lending validity to his protagonist's omniscience. Saleem's power of telepathy and the voices speaking inside his head enable him to provide the missing links in the narrative and to maintain the continuity of the story for "most of what matters in our lives takes place in our absence." (19) Besides, even "memory cracks beyond hope of reassembly." (384) There are "fadings" and "gaps" and hence it is "necessary to improvise on occasion" (384)—"the trick is to fill in the gaps." (427)

The providing of miraculous powers to the children born on the midnight of Independence also enables the novelist to expatiate upon the superhuman traits of the mythic Hindu heroes by comparing his "midnight's children" with these prodigies:

> So among the Midnight's Children were infants with powers of transmutation, flight, prophecy and wizardry . . . but two of us were born on thc stroke of midnight. Saleem and Shiva . . . to Shiva the hour had given the gifts of war (of Ram who could draw the undrawable bow; of Arjuna and Bhima, the ancient prowess of Kurus and Pandava united unstoppably in him!). (200)

Saleem himself refers to his "miraculous nature, which involved me beyond all mitigation in the myth life of India." (244)

Rushdie's sense of fantasy seen in his prolific inventiveness[19] and comic approach pervades his entire art of novel writing but it is never allowed to exist without the surer base of realism which lends the world of the book a truth of its own. It is his "bivision of fact and fantasy,"[20] then, that strikes the balance. Rushdie's defence of his use of fantasy in *The Satanic Verses* is equally applicable to *Midnight's Children*: "I genuinely believed that my overt use of fabulation would make it clear to any reader that I was not attempting to falsify history, but to allow a fiction to take off from history."[21] Elsewhere in the same article, Rushdie explains: "Fiction uses facts as the starting place and then spirals away to explore its concerns, which are only tangentially historical." (92)

In *Midnight's Children* Rushdie has ingeniously demonstrated his ability to historify myth and fictionalize history. His most potent message in the novel, as Nancy E. Batty points out, is that "if history is composed of fictions, then fiction can be composed of history."

In this regard it is noteworthy that in *Midnight's Children* the degree of fantasy introduced varies with the extent of his acquaintance with facts. He indulges in fantasy when he is ignorant or unsure of facts—to fill in the "gaps," as the narrator tells us. His Pakistan is more of a fantasy[22] than reality and he himself admits it with characteristic casualness: "Anyway, it was not 'my' country" (291) he makes his protagonist in the novel say. It is, however, not true that he did not know enough about Pakistan for he does give us in a nutshell a fairly authentic history of that nation and he also tries to establish "connections" with that country; for example, we hear Saleem say, "I helped to change the fate of the land of the Pure" (287) and "with the Fate of the nation in my hand." (290) But, he certainly knew much more about India, the country of his birth, and, at certain unguarded moments, his emotional ties clearly reveal themselves. In one of his interviews, Rushdie tells us about *Midnight's Children*:

> Well, I suppose, it began by being a novel of memory. The original motivation was to write about my childhood home, Bombay at the time when I was growing up there.[23]

This original motivation, however, took on larger implications and the work came to be a literary exploration of "the memory of a society in political and social decline."[24]

Rushdie's blending of fiction and fact we see also in the especial way in which he portrays imaginary people—though some of his characters are clearly identifiable—reacting to real events. The result again is the desired one: a kind of mythicized history, a work that conveys more the feeling than the facts of the period, though the basic limits imposed by history are never entirely violated.

The "real" events that Rushdie depicts are not mere concrete incidents tracing the political history of India from the pre-independence days to the present times; they comprise the complex of events and situations that is certainly not quantifiable.[25] *Midnight's Children* does not reveal the movement of history in vividly realized concrete occurrences given in their chronological order, nor does it depend on meticulous details. In fact, as we have already seen, there is a marked break in chronology and this is significant in revealing the novelist's intention and design. The novel is not meant to be a bald chronological account of the period portrayed. It concentrates on projecting the kind of fuller historical truth that incorporates the social and historical reality of the times as interacting with, and affecting, the life of the individual, that is chiefly the protagonist himself who undoubtedly represents the author.

On the other band, the imaginary characters portrayed are indicative of the novelist's indulgence in fantasy and imagination. All the "midnight's children" have been endowed with certain magical powers and it is through them that we learn to accept the fantastic in the novel. The other characters, too, range from the absolutely human to the strikingly superhuman, from man in general to witches and wizards. Interestingly, while Rushdie's men are not without the power to crystallize the drops of blood coming out of their nostrils into rubies, the inmates of the magicians' ghetto are not devoid of human feelings and sentiments.

So. Rushdie in *Midnight's Children* has made of history "an amazing pot-pourri of clever tricks."[26] He has framed his own "literary aesthetic truth telling"[27] which skilfully incorporates factual as well experiential truth.[28] He has availed himself of the artist's license to take certain imaginative liberties in his work with the intention of giving narrative shape to recorded facts. He re-enacts the past in terms of recognizable constructs and configurations and in doing so, he "allows himself the freedom to weed out pure facts or events, to twist facts, as long as the final view of history does not contradict what happened in the larger scheme."[29]

Rushdie, clearly represented by Saleem the narrator of his novel, makes of his childhood memories a powerful creative force[30] and in writing about his own life and that of his nation, he chooses the vantage point of the present and his mind delves deep into the past giving the tale a historical perspective.

Waghmare, in assessing Chinua Achebe's vision of the past, discusses the novelist's assumption of the part of a biographer:

> When a novelist deals with the past of his own people or community, he has to assume the role of a biographer. A biographer, as Andre Maurois points out, has two duties: he must be a portrait painter and a historian (Maurois, 1960: 30), As an historian he should discover the cultural heritage of his people and chronicle all the important events that might have changed the destiny and moulded the social pattern of his people. . . . Soon he realizes that the past of his people or community is his own past in a way.[31]

Rushdie, too, in chronicling his own past and that of his people takes on the mantle of a biographer and performs his "duties" effectively, that is the duty of a portrait painter as well as that of an historian. The work, however, becomes easier when he reminds himself of the parallel drawn by Henry James between the art of the painter and that of the novelist—"as the picture is reality, so the novel is history."[32] It is not enough to offer the reader a mere journalistic reproduction. As Howell puts its, "when realism becomes false to itself, when it heaps up fact merely, and maps life instead of picturing it, realism will perish, too."[33] Rushdie is well aware of this aspect of the art of the novelist as historian. He avoids piling up facts and making his work only a mirror of the times. His is not a mere conventional chronological narration of history but there certainly is a forward linear movement in the account that traces the history of the protagonist and his "twin," the nation, from the pre-Independence days, through the attainment of Independence to the recent times. The telescoping of time and the condensation of space is noteworthy. Also, the novel certainly does have an irreversible linear progression which K. Raghavendra Rao fails to identify. When Rao ventures to say, "Indeed the novel can be read backward without any essential loss of direction or location," obviously, he has failed to appreciate the informing principle underlying the narrative structure. Besides, history, irrespective of how much of it is given to us through the novel, can never be traced backward for it is characterized by an irreversible forward movement. Linked to history, the growth of the protagonist as well as that of the nation is seen as a process. There is no going back. That the novel is autobiographical in content is evident from what Salman-Saleem says in the course of the story telling: "I reach the end of my long-winded autobiography; in words and pickles, I have immortalized my memories." (459)[34] Saleem, at the time of narration, is working in a pickle factory and in writing this saga hopes that

> one day, perhaps, the world may taste the pickles of history. They may be too strong for some palates, their smell may be overpowering, tears may rise to the eyes; I hope nevertheless that it will

> be possible to say of them that they possess the authentic taste of truth. (461)

He clarifies his stand further and warns us against unsuspecting faith in his version of factuality—"distortions are inevitable in both methods (i.e. words and pickles). We must live, I am afraid, with the shadows of imperfection."(459)[35] Elsewhere he writes, "I remain conscious that errors have already been made . . . the risk of unreliability grows" (270) but "in autobiography, as in all literature, what actually happened is less important than what the author can manage to persuade his audience to believe." (270) So, autobiography is not totally reliable, authentic history, yet it is made convincing by a parallel narration of the biography of the members of Saleem's family and of the concomitant reconstruction of the history of the nation. Saleem himself refers to the probability of his being "only the first historian to write the story of my undeniably exceptional life and times." (295)

Regarding the break in chronology in *Midnight's Children*, it is evident from very beginning that the author never had in mind a sustained biographical account of the life of the protagonist or a record of historical events in order of time. As he himself tells us, his purpose in writing the novel was to focus on "the connection between public affairs and private lives." As he elaborates, "You cannot separate the two. They interpenetrate and that is how the writer needs to examine them, the tint in the context of the other."[36] It is with this objective of examining "one in the context of the other" in view that Rushdie concentrates on the junctural events in the life of Saleem as well as that of the nation. In the novel, on the one side we have Saleem's personal life, and on the other corresponding to this, is the life of the nation. Yet, in the lives of both, only those events which demonstrate the interaction of the two have been selected. The story traces the various crises in the life of the protagonist that synchronize with the major events and movements in the history of modern India— the Jallianwala Bagh tragedy, the Quit India Movement, the Cabinet Mission, the struggle for Independence, the role of the Muslim League, the post-Independence riots, The Five year plans, the re-organization of the states in India, the language agitation, the Chinese aggression, the theft of the sacred relic from Hazratbal mosque, the war with Pakistan, the Independence of Bangla Desh, the Emergency and other historical landmarks. This varied experience including the ordeal of the freedom movement, became, as Shyam M. Asnani puts it, "a part of the life of almost ail the sensitive and enlightened Indians."[37]

Saleem, from the very beginning, as he himself tells us, is conscious of his "centrality' in giving direction to the major events in the history of the nation. At one point in time, much later in life, he even considers himself a "competitor for centrality" (420) along with Indira Gandhi, who was perhaps unaware of the role of the mirror-of-the-nation bestowed on Saleem by her father, Jawahar Lal Nehru, in his letter to Baby Saleem. (122)[38] In fact, in the novel, Saleem's life is the microcosm that reflects and affects the macrocosmic life of the state and reverberates with the impact of the happenings that plague the latter. Saleem is born at midnight on August 15, 1947, the very moment at which India attained her Independence. He is one of the thousand and one midnight's children who are also "the children of the time; fathered . . . by history." (118) The child and the nation go through parallel experiences of the pangs of birth, the caprices of childhood, the traumas of adolescence and the uncertainties of adulthood. As a consequence of the coincidence of his birth and the consistency of this synchrony between his life and the nation's, Saleem becomes "heavily embroiled in Fate" and is "mysteriously handcuffed to history," his destinies "indissolubly chained" to those of his country. (9) He is conscious throughout of his "historical role" (86) for on his shoulders is placed the mantle of being "the newest bearer of that ancient face of India which is also eternally young" (122) and of mirroring the life of the nation. But his historical role does not merely mark him out as the recipient of the impact of historical events; his own personal realities in life often direct the course of history[39]: "already my very presence is having an effect on history, already Baby Saleem is working changes on people around him." (130) And, this continues consistently enough to make one acquiesce in

Saleem's observation at the close of the novel: "It is the privilege and the curse of midnight's children to be both masters and victims of their times." (463)

At a critical time in the history of the "child-nation" (172) when, Five-year plans are being charted and elections are in the offing, when language marchers are vociferously demanding the division of Bombay according to linguistic boundaries, the nine-year old Saleem acquires the miraculous gift of telepathy by which he can enter into the minds of people, "tune" (168) his inner ear to their inside-voices to learn their secrets. This "eavesdropping" (173) on people he knew is Saleem's first entry into the public affairs of India:

> I paradoxically took my first tentative steps towards that involvement with mighty events and public lives from which I would never again be free . . . never, until the Widow . . . (173)

And, henceforth, every event in Saleem's life is linked with some incident in the life of the nation. The elections of 1957 take place before his tenth birthday. A little after his eleventh birthday, "at the end of the year of accelerated history," (241) Saleem attains his full adult height and then, in the elections of 1962, just as 'status quo' is maintained in India, so nothing changes in Saleem's life, too. On December 16, 1971, when Saleem, after his period of exile in Pakistan, returns to India, concealed in Parvati's wicker-basket, Mrs. Gandhi is celebrating her fresh lease of life in Indian politics, for her new Congress party now holds more than two-thirds majority in the National Assembly. In a fit of rage, Saleem resolves to give the nation as he had given himself, the right to choose a better future, for he looks upon the country as "not only my twin-in-birth but also joined to me (so to speak) at the hip, so that what happened to either of us, happened to us both." (385)

At this juncture in the life of both Saleem and the nation, the pace of history accelerates and there are a number of synchronous events on either side. Shiva's "explosion" (410) into the life of Saleem at the magician's ghetto coincides with India's surprising nuclear capability demonstrated with the first nuclear explosions in the deserts of Rajasthan on 18 May 1974. The wedding celebrations of Saleem and Parvati synchronize with the Republic Day festivities in the country and from then onward, the parallels drawn between the life of the protagonist and that of the nation continue through Parvati alias Laylah Sinai; at the time that Lylah enters labour, Indira Gandhi is found guilty of malpractices in the previous elections; Laylah's son, Aadam Sinai, is born on 15 June 1975, the day the Emergency was imposed in India; he, too, like Saleem, is "mysteriously handcuffed to history" (420) and his fortunes are inseparably linked with those of his country; his distress caused by tuberculosis is suspected of having "something darkly metaphorical" in it; it seems to be a manifestation of his "connection-to-history." (422)

> . . . believing that, in those midnight months when the age of my connection-to-history overlapped with his, our private emergency was not unconnected with the larger macrocosmic disease, under whose influence the sun had become as pallid and diseased as our son. (422)

And then, history narrowed down to this final full point!" (436)—Saleem is arrested and imprisoned, he loses his freedom and significantly enough he loses with it his silver spittoon swallowed by bulldozers to sever him from "the last object connecting me to my more tangible, historically verifiable past." (432) Saleem is given no reason for his incarceration, for "Who of all thirty thousand or quarter of a million was told why or wherefore? Who needed to be told?" (434) The culmination, however, comes with Saleem's forced sterilization so that now he is "no longer connected to history, drained above and drained below." (442) Irrevocable harm has been done but, finally, appeasement comes with the fall of the Widow with which also vanished the ailment of Aadam Sinai.

The consistent equation drawn between the principal character in the novel and the nation is a measure to make explicit the empathy experienced by the former (and his creator) with his twin-in-birth." (385) This is how Rushdie projects his concept of history as interacting with the individual and we are introduced to his idea of the interplay of the two on the very first page. Rushdie himself declares that everything in his two novels, *Midnight's Children* and *Shame*, "has had to do with politics and with the relationship of the individual with history."[40] In particular, Book Three of *Midnight's Children*, he feels, has "more to do with the direct collision of the individual with history,"[41] it deals with Emergency and its consequences. History in the novel is mediated through the narrator's consciousness and hence the apology for whatever distortions there may be. Born of history, the narrator gives birth (as creator) to history and this reciprocal creative activity knows no end till he is "sucked into the annihilating whirlpool of the multitudes," (463) and ceases to exist as an individual. Rushdie creates in his protagonist a chronicler who registers in his life the interplay of the public and the private spheres. Keith Wilson refers to Saleem as "a narrator who, quite literally, is the history that he records," and, elaborating further, he says: "He subsumes most matter of public record within himself."[42]

Rushdie's vision is clearly historical rather than personal in the sense that he is inclined to see the individual in relation to the larger social and historical forces that condition his life. In *Midnight's Children*, Rushdie's purpose, as B.K. Joshi points out, is "to relate private lives to public events and to explore the limits of individuality in a country as big, as populous and culturally variegated as India."[43] Rushdie is temperamentally averse to brooding. He does not withdraw inwards for his unhappy meditations. He avoids solipsistic reflections. His is not the imagination of escape, but of confrontation. He would rather grapple with intransigent reality and expose it than buy his peace by shutting his eyes to it. Consequently, some of this tendency rubs off on his characters, chiefly his protagonist. This results in an interesting insight which is revealed in Rushdie's realization that while great events take place around human beings, the truly significant developments occur within them, and that to understand life in its totality, one must recognize their interrelatedness. Just as the powerful tide of history cannot be stemmed by an individual, so too the latter's will or vision cannot be entirely paralyzed by history and his personal life is of interest in itself. It is this belief that makes Rushdie observe that "the small individual lives of men are preferable to all this inflated macrocosmic activity." (435)

Rushdie has, perhaps, carried this parallel between the life of the protagonist with the life of the nation a little too far, but then the matrix of events embroiling both the individual and the state has been so designed as to allow an understanding of the individual primarily in terms of the historical forces that operate in his life.[44] In his efforts to discover the "modes-of-connection," the writer may have stretched his imagination to excess but we may forgive him this as his attempt at understanding the history of the nation is only a strategy for a comprehension of the self.[45] He declares: "I am what I am only in relation to those about me." and his "those" together comprise "the other"[46] in relation to whom we see ourselves. One can have a sense of continuity on the wide map of history which is not easy to perceive in one's life because a nation's history encompasses far more space and time and can be studied on a much larger scale than an individual's. Moreover, the far greater range of history and its multiple perspectives afford a more complete understanding of the challenges an individual has to face and his capabilities to cope with them.

There is yet another advantage of implicating history in one's fate. As we know, proximity to an event tends to cause a loss of perspective. So Rushdie's use of history in an attempt to understand his own life may be seen as an appropriate distancing device. As he explains in the novel:

> Reality is a question of perspective; the further you get from the past, the more concrete and plausible it seems—but as you approach the present, it inevitably seems more and more incredible. (165)

And when we are too close to what is happening, "perspective is impossible . . . we're too close to the cinema screen, the picture is breaking up into dots." So, in the absence of a proper perspective "only subjective judgements are possible." (435) One delves into the past, therefore, to understand the present in terms of the bygones and through indirections to find directions.

It needs to be admitted that even when the past is evoked, it is punctuated by intermittent references to the present to remind us where we are in point of time and to maintain the proper perspective. Padma's presence as "narratee" and as Saleem's "necessary ear" (149) in any recountal of the past is indication enough of the point of view of the narrator. This point of view undergoes several shifts in the course of the novel. Chronology thus remains sacrificed to perspective.

Rushdie's treatment of history is probably a matter of scale. This may have decided his choice of setting one up against the other—the narrowly individual against the broadly public. Besides, the consistent parallel drawn between the individual and the sub-continent is also a deliberate aesthetic choice that helps the writer set the parameters of the plot structure of the novel and give it form. Form is important; nay, inevitable. As Rushdie observes: "Everything has a shape if you look for it. There is no escape from form." (226)

Walter Allen speaks of contemporary novels as "the mirror of the age," a special kind of mirror reflecting "not merely the external features of the age but also its innerface, its nervous system, coursing of its blood and the unconscious prompting and conflicts which sway it."[47] *Midnight's Children*, too, is a mirror reflecting "the deeper stirrings" (18) of the life of the times. Saleem's life, which *is* the novel, is sketched in metaphoric relation to the life of the nation. Aroused into analysis by the contents of the Prime Minister's letter, written to him at the time of his birth—"Your life will be, in a sense, the mirror of our own" (238)—Saleem is set thinking as to "How, in what terms, may the career of a single individual be said to impinge on the fate of a nation?" (238) And then, after strained thought comes the enlightenment, and the "modes-of-connection" are established:

> I must answer in adverbs and hyphens: I was linked to history both literally and metaphorically, both actively and passively, in what our (admirably modern) scientists might term 'modes-of-connection' composed of dualistically combined configurations of

> the two pairs of opposed adverbs given above. This is why hyphens are necessary: actively-literally, passively-metaphorically, actively-metaphorically and passively-literally, I was inextricably entwined with my world. (238)

Saleem explains further: "By the combination of 'active' and 'literal' I mean, of course, all actions of mine which directly—literally—affected, or altered the course of seminal historical events." (238) And, he goes on to relate how he provided the language marchers demanding the creation of the linguistic state of Gujarat and Maharashtra with their battle cry and thus became actively involved in public events. The second mode "the union of 'passive' and 'metaphorical" (238) included all sociopolitical trends and events which merely by their existence affected Saleem metaphorically, for example, in the reference to "The Fisherman's Pointing Finger" lay the latent connection between the child-nation's efforts to acquire adulthood and Saleem's own gigantic at tempts at growing up. Here the public affected the private in a rather extensive manner. The third 'mode of connection'—the active-metaphorical—encompassed all those occasions on which "things done by or to me were mirrored in the macrocosm of public affairs" (238) and Saleem's individual existence was symbolical of the nation's state. The mutilation of Saleem's little finger had let out spurts of blood; history, too, was marked by a similar maiming and bloody violence had erupted. Lastly, the 'passive-literal' covered all moments at which "national events had a direct bearing upon the lives of myself and my family." (238) Saleem includes under this head the freezing of his father's property and the explosion at Walkeshwar Reservoir.

The various 'modes-of-connection' established between the protagonist and the nation dearly demonstrate the individual's shaping of history and, in turn, being shaped by it.

This correspondence, though drawn too far, enables the novelist to blend the autobiographical, biographical and historical into an organic narrative which carries with it not only credibility and the "solidity of specification"[48] but also a sharpened consciousness of reality that convincingly relates the past to the present and "involves a perception, not only of the past, but of its presence."[49]

Metaphors in *Midnight's Children*, if rightly interpreted, often provide a key to an understanding of the novel and the reality it projects. A prominent and sustained metaphor in the work used in relation to the similar lives of Saleem and the nation is that of the "chutnification of history" (459)—the pickling of time. The symbolic significance of the pickling process is that it preserves time and experience—private as well as public—and makes them available to the generations to come. The taste of the pickles may be "too strong" for some and their smell "overpowering" (461) for others, but they do, hopefully, preserve the taste of truth.

The requirements for "chutnification" are obviously raw materials—fruits, vegetables, fish, vinegar, and spices. But also, clear, penetrating eyes which can gauge the true quality of the vegetables, and a "discerning" nose that can decide "what-must-be-pickled, its humours and messages and emotions." (460) At Braganza pickles are prepared not only by Mary's recipes but also Saleem's special blends which include "memories, dreams, ideas" and which are for mass consumption: "Thirty jars stand upon a shelf, waiting to be unleashed upon the amnesiac nation." In other words, the past is re-interpreted and articulated for those who wish to taste "the pickles' version of history." (460)

> There are, of course, because of "the spice bases," the inevitable distortions of the pickling process. To pickle is to give immortality, after all . . . a certain alteration, a slight intensification of taste, is a small matter, surely? The art is to change the flavour in degree, but not in kind; and above all . . . to give it shape and form—that is to say, meaning. (461)

This is Rushdie's aesthetic credo expressed in an easily understandable domestic image. The externals are no consequence; what matters is the spirit of the thing.

Saleem refers to his tale as "memory's truth," (211)[50] and what differentiates this truth from any other kind of truth is that:

> memory has its own special kind. It selects, eliminates, alters, exaggerates, minimizes, glorifies, and vilifies also; but in the end it creates its own reality, its heterogeneous but usually coherent version of events; and no sane human being ever trusts someone else's version more than his own. (211)

"Memory's truth" is highly selective and sets the limits of its own reality. Rushdie's "chutnification" may be seen as an attempt to blend and mix ideas and events, individual life and public life in such a way as to give life a sense of continuity in the future that he has a longing for, and that he probably feared as lost on the memorable midnight. This explains his reference to his son and his son's son carrying on the process begun by him. We normally look back for a sense of continuity but he has brought the past into the present in order to extend his desire for a sense of continuity into the future. For him the past is not over but continues to make itself felt through its impact. So, it becomes a function of his life in the present. No wonder the boundaries are blurred not only between past and present but also between fact and fiction, imagination and reality. Rushdie dreams his desire into reality—the reality which consists of his life and his country's. The desire for immortality as well as that for continuity are parallel desires, both of which Rushdie cherishes and expresses forcefully.[51]

Another important metaphor in the novel is that of the perforated cloth through which Saleem's grandfather, Dr. Aadam Aziz, once examined as a patient his grandmother Naseem, before he married her. The implication is that narrative is a perforated sheet which conceals the whole, revealing only parts which appear in the nature of "trailers"[52] to arouse our curiosity.

We come now to the third major aspect of the use of history in the novel, viz., the search for identity. *Midnight's Children*, like *The Satanic Verses*, is written from "the experience of uprooting"[53] that comes from the migrant condition. Rushdie himself, in an interview by the B.B.C., refers to the "aspects of personal history"[54] contained in *Midnight's Children*, "A man from too many places"[55] he calls himself. Born in India and living in

Britain, he is "a product of biethnicity" which according to Suryanarayana Murti is "the creative matrix of his fiction." (71)

Alistair Niven, referring to Rushdie and all those Indian writers, who live in England but write about their own subcontinent, describes what they would term "detachment" in their works as "a deracinated loss of identity. . . it is hard to see where they belong." Rushdie himself confirms this "sense of deracination"[56] experienced by him while studying at Rugby School, where racial prejudice was so pronounced that for the first time he realized that he belonged to "a race" and "suddenly in England I became Indian."[57] The irony, however, lay in the fact that while in England he felt like an Indian, in India his family felt discriminated against and moved to Pakistan. But even that move failed. So, when he settled down in England, he began to reach for his roots, and *Midnight's Children* became the medium of the quest of one who could never really "belong" anywhere.

Ashutosh Banerjee refers to Saleem in *Midnight's Children* as "Rushdie's fictional alter ego."[58] Saleem, having been born at the precise moment at which India attained her Independence, establishes a kinship with his creator in that the latter, too, was born about that time, that is, two months before the Indian Independence, in June, 1947, in Bombay. Rushdie has deliberately fictionalized his date of birth in his novel for narrative purposes, for it the time of Saleem's birth that subjects him to a more difficult fate by giving his identity a larger dimension. It is as "midnight's child" born on 15 August, 1947, that Saleem, is "mysteriously handcuffed to history." (9) He becomes, as M.K. Naik observes, conscious of his "larger identity"[59] rather early in life. Naik draws attention to "the protagonist's identity crisis," (52) and comes to the conclusion that *Midnight's Children* "illustrates the permanent plight of individual identity in the hostile modern world which makes it impossible for any one to remain an island but compels every one to be part of a continent, with the result that the individual is inevitably "handcuffed to history." (54) Thus, the central theme of the novel, according to Naik, is the fate of individual identity in a hostile world, which causes it to suffer fragmentation and sterility.

Saleem is the central consciousness in the novel whose ordeals and tribulations are closely followed and analyzed. He is an extremely sensitive and self-conscious narrator (like his creator), and, in spite of all other weakness, is confident of his competence as a storyteller. He knows that Padma, who, as Nancy Batty points out, is the "index for reader-response to the framed narrative," (53) will not be able to resist the charm of his narration: "No doubt about it my story has her by the throat." (38) Padma as narratee does offer attention in exchange for information but seems well aware of the "constructedness"[60] of Saleem's narration for she can seldom comprehend any connection between Saleem's stories and his "real" existence. "There is reason to believe," says Nancy Batty, "that even Saleem's explicit audience, Padma, regards Saleem's autobiography as a fiction." (60) Thus Saleem like his maker, is a "creator rather than recorder of his own history,"[61] and suggests that by filling in the gaps where . . . memory cracks" (384) he presents a narrative that is, in the ultimate analysis, tentative rather than unalterable and final—tentative because it deals in "broken mirrors, some of whose fragments have been irretrievably lost."[62]

Despite the tentative nature of the narrative that Saleem weaves out of his fractured *human* perception he never, during the course of the narrative, abandons his pursuit of the meaning of life, though "meaning he knows [as his creator does] is a shaky edifice that we build out of scraps, dogmas, childhood injuries, newspaper articles, chance remarks, people you love, people you hate, old films, small victories."[63]

Saleem is conscious of the whirling speed with which time is passing and in his search for identity and "meaning," he races against time which is "running out." (9) He never gives up the quest for meaning, though he has to maintain all along a certain degree of caution, for, in his desire to place himself in a central role, he is inclined to misrepresent things; this apprehension is revealed in his self-analysis later:

> Am I so far gone in my desperate need for meaning, that I'm prepared to distort everything—to rewrite the whole history of my

> times purely in order to place myself in a central role? Today, in my confusion I can't judge. I'll have to leave it to others. (166)

But soon, "after years of yearning for importance," (350) Saleem, the budha, who had abandoned consciousness and deliberately severed himself from history, comes to the realization that any determination to espouse a historical role was futile for every individual is nothing but a drop in the river of human life, and yet, human life is what it is merely because of the presence of that one drop and many other such drops:

> Who what am I? My answer: I am the sum total of everything that went before me, of all I have been seen done, of everything done to me. I am every one, everything of whose being-in-the-world affected was affected by mine. I am anything that happens after I have gone which would not have happened if I had not come. Nor am I particularly exceptional in this matter; each, 'I', everyone of the now-six-hundred-million-plus of us, contains a similar multitude. I report for the last time, to understand me, you will have to swallow a world. (383)

Thus, each individual, can claim an identity of his own, and yet, he has to submit to a final merger with the milling myriads who make their respective contributions and then pass into anonymity.

Saleem, like his creator, believes firmly in the ultimate merging in of the individual with the multitudes so that he is no longer a separate entity but an inseparable part of the "many." This faith is harboured with unflagging conviction from the first to the last page of the novel. In the beginning, Saleem tells us:

> I have been a swallower of lives; and to know me just the one of me, you'll have to swallow the lot as well. Consumed multitudes are jostling and shoving inside me. (9)

At the end, too, his faith remains unchanged and he reaffirms his belief: "I have been so-many too-many persons." (463) And he visualizes himself being "sucked into the annihilating whirlpool of the multitudes." (463)

Attributing Rushdie's protagonist's problems of identity to the writer himself, one would be inclined to think that throughout the novel, Rushdie is preoccupied with a searh for identity.[64] There is, I feel, justification enough for this though Rushdie himself would have us believe that he is engaged in no such quest: "I know who I am and I don't have a sense of having an identiy crisis. But people telling me I should."[65]

But, an assertion is no proof. We cannot always take the writer's word as the ultimate authority to arrive at our conclusions for he may be either deliberately misleading us in our attempt at interpretation, or he may himself be unconsciously trying to establish his identity. This will become clear presently. Such close parallels and correspondences between the life of the protagonist and that of the nation can be drawn only by one who himself is deeply involved, and thus finds it difficult to maintain objectivity and distance in his art[66] in spite of every distancing device adopted. Saleem clearly filters for us the author's own experiences.

The central query in *Midnight's Children*, then, is: what is the compulsion—aesthetic or personal—that makes the novelist assiduously weave such a complex web of parallels between the life of the protagonist (who may very well be identified with the novelist himself) and that of the nation? Could it be the artist's own way of reconstructing meaning out of the chaos of the times, of discovering his identity in the context of a large perspective? In spite of the novelist's denial one has little doubt that the work is a verbalization of the writer's quest for identity, his desire to "belong" somewhere and to discover where he belongs; an expression of his urge to know how he came to be what he is and how he came to be where he is. To Keats "what the imagination seizes as beauty must be the truth"; to Rushdie, what the fancy apprehends as content must be the meaningful truth. The apparently fanciful images and constructs must merge into a significant whole. Thus, what Rushdie embarks upon is an exploration of his life, which he identifies with the life of the state, and more specifically, with the life of the particular community to which he belongs, viz., the Muslims.

One admires in Rushdie, as one does in Dickens, the intellectual audacity to adopt fantasy as a means of depicting truth, for verisimilitude[67] and historical precision alone do not seem to serve his desire to project the kind of reality he wishes to. Fantasy allows a free play to the mind that realism would restrain, and hence a balance has to be struck between the fantastic and the real, for "this elusive and profound relationship between history and private fantasy is repeatedly the key to a whole fictional world."[68]

Rushdie's fantasizing mixed with first-person narrative is a kind of modernistic device to stress the fictive nature of his fiction as also to accommodate fantasy to fact to represent or reenact better those aspects of reality that have been poignantly experienced by him and would not be easily captured in words which never fail in a realistic novel.

As Tom Wolfe asserts, "fantasy is a part of reality"[69] but for Rushdie, it is so much more; it helps him rise above reality and "assert seeming independence of creativity as the distinctive quality of art."[70] It not only stresses the fictive element in the narrative but is, indeed, revelatory—revelatory of the mind behind the work. In other words, it is self-reflexive fiction in which fiction is nothing but a mode of reality, the reality of the author's self caught in a complex interplay with historical reality.

Fantasy in *Midnight's Children*, besides being a form of reality, also serves to add spice to the narrative and to provide relief from the strain of trying to comprehend the truth in terms of the factual. It energetically exploits the comic in character, situation and language providing the novel a strikingly fresh and absorbing dimension. Rushdie, in *Midnight's Children*, devises what Kundera visualizes as "a new art of novelistic counterpoint" (which can blend philosophy, narrative and dream into one music).[71]

NOTES

1. Michiko Kakutani "Do facts and Fiction Mix?" *New York Times Book Review*, Jan. 27, 1980.
2. Emile Zola, *Du Roman Experimental*, Chapter 1 Le Roman Experimental (1880), trans. Belle M. Sherman (New York, 1893); qtd.

Miriam Allott, "The Novel as a Portrait of Life," *Novelists on the Novel* (London: Routledge and Kegan Paul, 1965), p. 70.

3. "Raj Reversal," *Sunday*, 4-10 Dec. 1988, p. 30.
4. Richard F. Button, trans., *The Arabian Night's Entertainment or The Book of a Thousand and One Nights* (New York: Random, 1932).
5. Nancy E. Batty, "The Art of Suspense: Rushdie's 1001 (Midnights)," *Ariel*, Vol. 18, Number 3, July 1987, p. 94.
6. "In Good Faith," *Sunday*, 25 Feb.-3 March, 1990, p. 90. Rushdie's defence of *The Satanic Verses*.
7. Salman Rushdie, "Not Guilty!" *Sunday*, 18-24 Feb., 1990, p. 27.
8. Alistair Niven, "Indian Writing in English: Past and Present," Sahitya Akademi International Seminar, Indian Literature in English and English Translation, Feb. 25-28,1986, India International Centre, New Delhi. "He [Rushdie] has brought back Into English fiction a sense of the panoramic."
9. In an interview, Rushdie tells us that he is convinced of the existence of the supernatural world. 'Network East,' BBC 2, Sept. 24, 1998.
10. Rushdie, as he himself tells us, was actually born in June, 1947—Interview with Rushdie, *The Sunday Observer*, Sept. 6, 1987. In the novel Rushdie changes the date for narrative expediency. This is an instance of "fictionalizing fact."
11. Salman Rushdie, *Midnight's Children* (London: Picador, 1982), pp. 1-2.
12. Mentioned on the blurb of *The Satanic Verses* (London: Viking. 1988)
13. D.H. Lawrence, *Studies in Classical American Literature*, Chapter 1: "Never trust the artist. Trust the tale. The proper function of the critic is to save the tale from the artist who created it."
14. C.S. Lewis, *An Experiment in Criticism* (London: Cambridge University Press, 1961, p. 50. "As a literary term fantasy means any narrative that deals with impossible and preternatural."
15. *Ibid.* p. 59; Lewis refers to the "realism of content" and the "realism of presentation." The two, according to him, are independent of each other. Rushdie's, one would feel, is more the "realism of presentation" than the "realism of content" though the contents, too, may be interpreted at a different level of psychological realism.

16. P. Syal, "*Midnight's Children*," *New Quest*, Nov.-Dec. 1982. p. 349.
17. R.S. Pathak, "History and the Individual in the Novels of Rushdie," *Three Contemporary Novelists*, ed. R.K. Dhawan (New Delhi: Classical, 1985), p. 217.
18. Rita Joshi, "Fantasy as Reality: The Art of Salman Rushdie," *The Sunday Observer,* April 12, 1987.
19. C.D. Narasimhaiah in "Spurious Reputations: Vikram Seth, Rushdie and Tharoor," *Essays in Commonwealth Literature* (Delhi: Pencraft' International, 1995, p. 125) refers to Rushdie as "a juggler of words."
20. V.K. Suryanarayan Murti, "Secular Fantasy: Salman Rushdie's Fiction," *Kohinoor in the Crown: Critical Studies in Indian English Literature* (New Delhi: Sterling, 1987), p. 177.
21. Salman Rushdie "In Good Faith," *Sunday*, 25 Feb-3 March, 1990, p. 91.
22. K Raghavendra Rao, "The Novel as History as 'Chutney': Unriddling Salman Rushdie's *Midnight's Children*," *Perspectives of Indian Fiction in English*, ed. M.K. Naik (New Delhi: Abhinav, 1985), p.157.
23. "*Midnight's Children*—Memory's Recesses," *Northern India Patrika*, Sunday, 16 Jan. 1933, pp.1, 3.
24. "Raj Reversal," *Sunday*, p. 29.
25. Graham Hough, "The Novel and history," *An Essay on Criticism* (London: Duckworth, 1966), p. 114—"We should be wrong, however to judge a novel by the amount of social and historical reality that it incorporates. It is not a quantitative matter."
26. P. Syal, p. 349.
27. David Lodge, "The Novelist at the Cross Roads," *The Novel Today*, ed. Malcolm Bradbury (Great Britain: Pontana, 1977), p. 85.
28. Damian Grant, *Realism, The Critical Idiom Series* (London Methuen, 1970), p. 9. Compare Grant's theory of correspondence and coherence: "the correspondence theory refers automatically to the fact, and requires that truth be verified by reference to it. . . . In the coherence theory . . . truth is not earned by the labour of documentation and analysis but coined, a ready synthesis."
29. William Styron's interpretations on history: quoted in Michiko Kakutain's "Do Facts and Fiction Mix?" *The New York Times Book Review*, Jan. 27, 1960, p. 28.

30. Salman Rushdie, *Imaginary Homelands* (London: Granta Books 1991). p. 10 Rushdie writes of his "urge to reclaim" his childhood years in *Midnight's Children.*
31. J.M. Waghmare, "Chinua Achebe's Vision of the Crumbling Past," *Indian Reading in Commonwealth Literature*, Amur et al, p. 117
32. Henry James, "The Art of Fiction," *The Theory of the American Novel*, ed. George Perkins (U.S.A.: Holt, Rhinehart and Winston, 1970), p.178.
33. Qtd. *Ibid.*, p. xxxi. Compare Graham Hough, p. 111—"veridical imitation of objects in the real world is not the purport of literature."
34. The novel, however, is not to be taken as a sacrosanct version of the life of the novelist for Rushdie himself guides our interpretation of the novel. In an interview (*Northern India Patrika*, 16 Jan. 1983), he voices his opinion regarding the autobiographical element in the book: "It is entirely possible for a novel to be autobiographical and also to be completely fictional. That's what my book is. It is entirely closely and directly out of the city and the places I remembered but there are only one or two characters in that book I would admit as portraits. Probably the most direct portrait is of a street singer whom I remember from my childhood, but even he, in the book, becomes the parent of Saleem's alter-ego, Shiva, and certainly nothing of that nature happened in real life."
35. Cf. George Watson, "Tense and Time," *The Story of the Novel* (London: Macmillan, 1979), p. 73. Watson refers to a "Wordsworthian intuition that memory is imperfect."
36 Book Review of *Midnight's Children, The Sunday Standard*, 14 June, 1981, p. 6.
37. Shyam M. Asnani, "The Socio-Political Scene of the I930s: Its Impact on thc Indo-English Novel," *Commonwealth Quarterly*, Vol. 6, No. 21, Dec. 1981, p.15.
38. Jawahar Lal Nehru, in his letter to Baby Saleem, wrote: "We shall be watching over your life with the closest attention: it will be, in a sense, the mirror of our own."
39. Shirly Toulson in *Contemporary Novelists*, ed. James Vinson (London: St. James Press, 1972), p. 118, while referring to John Berger's novel, *G*, speaks of the novelist's objective of "depicting how each one of us is history in that we are both monumentally shaped by events, and in small measure, by the mere act of inhabiting our skins, influence their course."

40. Gordon Wise, Interview with Salman Rushdie, *Gentleman*, February 1984, p. 59.
41. *Ibid.*, p. 57.
42. Keith Wilson, "*Midnight's Children* and Reader Responsibility," *Central Quarterly*, Vol. 26, No. 3, Autumn, 1984, p. 23.
43. B.K. Joshi, "It May be Long, but it's Not Overwritten," *The Times of India*, 1 Nov. 1981, p. 8.
44. T.S. Eliot, *Selected Prose*, S. John Hayward (Harmondsworth: Penguin 1963), pp. 22-23: An individual with a consciousness of history is also "conscious of his place in time, of his own contemporaneity." However, an individual is an entity in his own right and should avoid "purpose" or aspirations regarding political life for as Rushdie in *Midnight's* Children observes, politics is a "bad dirty business." (p. 435)
45. Levi Strauss: "self, knowledge may only be achieved after establishing a critical distance on one's reality." Cited by Flora Gojnzales, "El Recuurse Del Metodo'," *The Centennial Review*, Vol. XXX, No. 2, Spring 1986, p. 251.
46. Carl R. Mentley, "The Hermeneutic project of Octavio Paz," *The Centennial Review*, Vol. XXX, No. 2, Spring 1986, pp. 156-57. "We all encounter our own self, our own being in the community of the other." Compare Marxism: The individual is seen in close relation to historical and socio-political events.
47. Walter Allen, *Reading a Novel* (Great Britain: Penguin, 1971), pp. 18-19.
48. Henry James, "The Art of Fiction," *The Theory of the American Novel*, p. 185. "I may therefore venture to say that the air of reality (solidity of specification) seems to me the supreme virtue of a novel—the merit on which all its other merits (including that conscious moral purpose of which Mr. Besant speaks) helplessly and submissively depend."
49. T.S. Eliot, p. 22
50. Rushdie, when interviewed by the B.B.C, referred to *Midnight's Children* as "a novel of memory," Network East; B.C. 2, 24 September, 1988. Again in "*Midnight's Children*: Memory's Recesses," his interview published in the *Northern India Patrika*, 16 January, 1983, p. 103, Rushdie speaks of the novel as being "about memory as well as being a novel of memory." He further explains: "It is about the way memory operates when you recall your life."

51. Cf. Carlos Fuentes, "Modern Literature Conference: The Politics of Experience," *The Centennial Review*, Vol. XXX, no. 2, Spring 86, p. 135. "It is important to realize that we remember in the present, that memory is a celebration of the present. It is in the present that we remember and we desire which are two things that come together in writing—memory and yearning. Wanting. Trying to identify with something."
52. Nancy E. Batty, p. 61.
53. Salman Rushdie, "Not guilty," *Sunday*, Feb, 90, p.27.
54. Salman Rushdie, Interview, B.B.C., 2 Sept. 1988.
55. *Ibid.*
56. Bryan Appleyard, "Portrait of the Novelist as a Hot Property," *The Sunday Times Magazine*, Sept. 11, 1998, p. 31.
57. *Ibid.*, p.28.
58. Ashutosh Banerjee, "Narrative Technique in Midnight's Children', *Three Contemporary Novelists*, ed. R.K. Dhawan, p. 196.
59. M.K. Naik, "A Life of Fragments: The Fate of Identity in *Midnight's Children*," *Studies in Indian English Literature* (New Delhi: Sterling, 1987), p. 51.
60. Gerard Genette, *Narrative Discourse: An Essay in Method* 1972, trans. Jane E. Lewin (New York: Cornell Press, 1980); there is an implication regarding the "constructedness" of all narrative.
61. Nancy E. Batty, p. 59
62. Salman Rushdie, "*Midnight's Children*: Memory's Recesses," *Northern India Patrika*, 16 January 1983, p. 3.
63. *Ibid.*
64. The novel clearly appears to be a sublimation of Rushdie's sense of a loss of identity and we have in it 'the constant transformation of what would be "suffering" into works of art . . . for the possibly higher experience of being "transparent"—that is an artist. *John Updike*, ed. David Thoburn and Howard Eiland (New Jersey: Prentice Hall, 1979).
65. Salman Rushdie, Interview, *Northern India Patrika*, 16 January 1983.
66. Cf. Flaubert: "I have always forbidden myself to put anything of myself into my work, and yet I have put in a great deal." Cited Robert Lidell, *A Treatise on the Novel* (1947; London: Jonathan Cape, 1953), p. 104.

67. Vassily Novikow, *Artistic Truth and Dialectics of Creative Work* (Moscow: Progress, 1981). Mark the difference between "verisimilitude" and "truthfulness."
68. Robert Alter, "History, and the New American Novel."
69. Tom Wolfe, "'The New Fiction: Interview with Innovative American Writers," ed. David Bellamy, *The American Review*, Summer, 1976.
70. Vassily Novikov, p. 18. Cf. Lenin "Art does not require the recognition of its works as reality." Lenin, *Collected Works*, Vol. 38, p. 73.
71. Milan Kundera, *The Art of the Novel* (trans. Linder Asher Faber) qtd. *Times Literary Supplement*, June 24-30.

Midnight's Children: A Blend of Autobiography, History and Fantasy

SATISH BARBUDDHE
B.S.P. College, Paratwada

Satish Barbuddhe's paper considers Midnight's Children *as an experimental work that achieves a successful fusion of history, autobiography and fantasy. It shows how episodes from Indian history are ingeniously linked to Saleem Sinai's autobiographical story which is presented in the mode of (postmodernist) fantasy.*

Editor

Part I of *Midnight Children* covers the major events that took place in India from 1915 to 1947 i.e. pre-Independence era of India. Part II narrates the childhood of Saleem Sinai, the chief character of the novel, and the last part deals with the emergency period and the related incidents in India in those days. The novel presents the three generations of the Sinai family. It is the story of Saleem Sinai, born with 1001 other Indian children in the hour of midnight, 15 August, 1947. Of the 1001 children, who were born in various parts of the country, only 581 have survived by 1957. Each of these children possesses a superb magical power. The most powerful among these children are Saleem and Shiva who are the arch-rivals for leadership. Saleem calls a conference of the midnight children. These children are not free from the faults that the adults have: "Children are the vessels into which adults pour their poison, and it was the poison of grown-ups which did for us."[1] (256)

Saleem blames the grown-ups for poisoning the minds of these midnight children. India's elite Muslim, Parsee and Hindu live happily here in Bombay:

> These were the people amongst whom I spent my childhood: Mr. Homi Catrack, film magnate and racehorse-owner . . . also old man

> Ibrahim with his goatee and sisal, his sons Ismail and Ishaq and Ismail's tiny flustery hapless wife Nussie. . . . On the ground floor lived the Dubashes, a physicist who would become a leading light at the Trombay nuclear research base, . . . And, finally, on the top floor, were Commander Sabarmati and Lila—Sabarmati who was one of the highest flyers in the Navy, and his wife with her expensive tastes. . . . Selected by William Methwold, these people who would form the centre of my world moved in the Estate and tolerated the curious whims of the Englishman—because the price, after all, was right.[2]

The Methwold estate in Bombay where Saleem lives is described as "three-story homes of gods standing on two-story Olympus, a stunted Kailash!" (108)

In Part One, Saleem, the protagonist, narrates the story of his grandfather, Aadam Aziz, a young doctor who returned from Germany with a good medical degree. One morning, this doctor was taken to examine a patient, Naseem, the ailing daughter of Ghani Sahib, a landlord in Kashmir. He treated her and later on married her. He got a job at Agra University. When he was shifting his family to Agra, he witnessed the Jallianwala Bagh Massacre in Amritsar. "I confess . . . I have noticed a thin crack, like a hair, appearing in my wrist, beneath the skin. . . . No matter. We all owe death a life." (36)

Aadam Aziz was surprised to see Nadir Khan at his residence, one fine morning. He wanted to save his life as he fled from assassins. He expressed his love towards Mumtaz, the second daughter of Aziz, but Major Zulfikar was assigned a job to capture Nadir Khan, whom Nadir avoided skilfully. In the meantime, a wealthy businessman from Delhi Ahmed Sinai married Mumtaz, later on known as Amina.

Soon after the communal riots in Delhi, Ahmed shifted to Bombay where Saleem was born on the midnight stroke of August 15, 1947 at the time when India became independent. Saleem says that "the children of midnight were also the children of the time fathered . . . by history." (118) Saleem said that his birth was prophesied by a fortune-teller and a Sadhu, greeted by the press. Saleem bagged the prize from *The Times of India*. The then Prime Minister Nehru sent his parents a letter praising him and his attitude. Nehru also wrote in the letter that Saleem would become the mirror of the nation.

Part One of the novel chiefly narrates the events that took place in India from 1915 to 1947. Therefore it deals with the early life of Saleem's grandfather Aadam Aziz.

Part Two of the novel begins with the never-ending crisis faced by the family of Ahmed Sinai. The family decided to migrate to Pakistan. But they became the victims of 1965 war. Saleem thought that he was creating a world. He says:

> Because the feeling had come upon me that I was somehow creating a world; that the thoughts that jumped inside were mine, that the bodies I occupied acted at my command; that, as current affairs, arts, sports, the whole rich variety of a first class radio station poured into me, I was somehow making them happen—which is to say, I had entered into the illusion of the artist and thought of the multitudinous realities of the land as the raw unshaped material of my gift. (207)

Illusion of responsibility was of power and not of any guilt. Saleem was neither innocent nor was the only person who was guilty. In *Midnight's Children*, we observe the patches straightaway taken from history. These patches are correspondingly related by direct allusions to practical politics. The readers are supposed to decipher on their own.

The class tension is portrayed in the scene where boatman Tai Bibi and Aadam Aziz have hot discussion. It goes on when we notice the conflict of the poor accordion-player Wee Willie Winkie and the Methwold household. Saleem and Shiva fight over the birthright of India itself. Saleem puts before us the mirror of Indian history. The reader finds number of episodes from the past which are tied together by Saleem. The fiction and the fact go side by side in order to create astonishing effect on the readers. The tension between the two countries is described in this passage along with other vital facts:

> Entirely without my help, India conquered Goa. . . . I played no part in the acquisition of large-scale US aid for Pakistan, nor was I

> to blame for Sino-Indian border skirmishes in the Aksai-Chin region of Ladakh; the Indian census of 1961 revealed a literacy level of 23.7 percent . . . and in the elections of 1962, the All India Congress won 361 out of 494 seats in the Lok Sabha, and over 61 percent of all State Assembly seats. (351)

Timothy Brennan describes *Midnight's Children* as "repeatedly recalling the sectarian violence of contemporary Indian Political Life": "*Midnight's Children* therefore elides an older view of the nation with a contemporary and neo-colonial one, in which national 'mythos' merges with a humanist critique of the 'polis.' The familiar 'nativist' rhetoric of much Third-World fiction is therefore both appropriated and parodied. Although much of *Midnight's Children* upholds within a modern and political mode, repeatedly recalling the sectarian violence of contemporary Indian political life and the class tensions against which any national unity is artificially constructed, it is nevertheless designed to suggest the living presence of India's mythical past, not as 'vital tradition' but as 'false consciousness.'

India's mythical past is felt everywhere in the novel. Ganesh is perhaps the most central of all the images. He is a God of good fortune. From the opening pages to the concluding chapter His reference is there. Aadam Aziz is said to have a nose 'comparable only to the trunk of the elephant-headed Ganesh.' (8) In the last pages, Saleem's 'son' Aadam Sinai is described as 'the true son of Shiva-and-Parvati—(the) elephant-headed Ganesh.' (500) Aadam has the qualities of Ganesh i.e. ability to overcome difficulties. Ganesh is 'the typical embodiment of success in life and its accompaniments of good living, prosperity and peace.'[3]

The character of Shiva in the novel has nothing to do with the Shiva myth. For example, Shiva's 'gift of war' is narrated like this: '[Shiva] the god of destruction, who is also most potent of deities; Shiva, greatest of dancers; who rides on a bull; whom no force can resist.' (264) But Shiva in the novel is fallible. He intentionally frightens weaker people. He uses offensive language. He has criminal mind. His action cannot be justified. We cannot expect metamorphosis in his character. He expresses no regret for whatever he does. Shiva joins the election fraud. The rivalry of Saleem and Shiva may have its roots in the legendary rivalry between Shiva and Brahma. Saleem imagines the whole of Indian history and correlates it with his life and other characters. His impotency (lack of practical political power) is in no way an obstacle to his becoming a writer. Saleem acts himself a kind of Big Brother when he narrates how his mental transmissions had the power of entering minds at will. "No never mind chief, just think of me as a . . . a big brother, may be." (273)

Padma is called Saleem's 'interlocutrix' who plays an important role in the novel. She calls Saleem 'city boy.' The word 'Padma' means lotus "and in the traditional Indian consciousness, the lotus symbolises one who was born in slime and mud but is able to reach out to the higher things of life. In other words, the name is suggestive of the ability to capture the essence of both worlds, the sordid and the beautiful."[4]

Padma's relationship with Saleem is often strained. The graphic description of her relationship with Saleem makes us feel that she is an enchantress.

> How I admire the leg-muscles of my solicitous Padma! There she squats, a few feet from my table, her Sari hitched up in fisher woman-fashion—my admiration extends also to her arms, which could wrestle mine down in a trice, and from which, when they enfold me tightly in futile embraces, there is no escape. Past our crisis now, we exist in perfect harmony: I recount, she is recounted to; She ministers, and I accept her ministrations with grace. (324-25)

Padma is a servant, who is narrated at the beginning of this novel like this: "thick of waist, somewhat hairy of forearm."' (21) Saleem later on says, "I must go to bed. Padma is waiting; and I need a little warmth." (36) Saleem cannot extract that heavenly pleasure from her as he is impotent. He is unable to make love to her but he is not indignant. Saleem is sexually attracted towards Padma, but it is the same monotonous 'cold respect.'

Saleem totally disapproves Padma's aesthetic counsels. He is rather sniffy about her suggestions. He thinks that he is superior in his thoughts. He knows the limitations of her advice. Syllogism of her advice is noticed by Saleem. Therefore, he temperamentally sometimes avoids her advice. Padma is not vociferous. Her strength of story telling is superb.

Padma's plebeian strength of story telling is repeated in the story proper by several characters. Mary Pereira, Saleem's Christian ayah, whose gift of preserving memories he compares to Padma's making of Chutney (252), and above all, by the boatman Tai, whose chatter, says Saleem, was fantastic, grandiloquent and ceaseless (9) whose age no one could remember, whose verbiage was endless and his talk 'magical' and who was illiterate."[5]

Padma avoids any contentious argument with Saleem as she dislikes any breaking of the narrative spell:

> I must interrupt myself. I wasn't going today because Padma has started getting irritated whenever my narration becomes self-conscious, whenever, like an incompetent puppeteer, I reveal the hands holding the strings. (72)

She is an illiterate and she regards Saleem as a person who gives more time to his writing. She feels that she is in a very difficult or unpleasant situation. But she never overacts though she understands the nothingness in her life. Her masterful control over Saleem can be felt when we see that she is Saleem's typical audience. She is true critic of Saleem. But there are certain limitations to her criticism.

Salman Rushdie's *Midnight's Children* is a postmodern fantasy. It is a novel which is confessional, but it is an humble effort to gravitate towards the history of India, though the incidents are not in clear chronological order. There is a feeling of inertia sometimes in Saleem's character. He recalls the halcyon days of his early days.

According to Rosemary Jackson, fairytale creates a world which is safely removed from the 'real' world, and so it never threatens the real world, but fantasy is constantly challenging our notion of real world. Fantasy is without any kind of principle or design. *Midnight's Children* is a postmodern fantasy as it is experimental in nature. The narrator admits that he is 'destroying the unities and conventions of fine writing.' (236) The novel opens thus:

> I was born in the city of Bombay—once upon a time. No, that won't do, there's no getting away from the date. I was born in Doctor Narlikar's Nursing Home on August 15th, 1947. And the time? The time matters, too. Well then: at night. No, it's important to be more—On the stroke of midnight, as a matter of fact.

The phrase 'once upon a time' is a beginning of fantasy.

The narrator wishes to narrate the things in its maximum truest form. But he is aware of the problems:

> I must describe, as nearly as possible in spite of this filmy curtain of ambiguities, what actually happened. (87)

Saleem's dexterity is felt everywhere. Though he promises to reveal everything still most part of the details remain wrapped in the 'filmy curtain of ambiguities.' He knows that memory is illusory. He prevaricates sometimes and his rudimentary details amuse the readers. This amusing state does not last for a long time. He explains the role of memory:

> Memory's truth, because memory has its own special kind. It selects, eliminates. alters, exaggerates, minimizes, glorifies and vilifies also; but in the end it creates its own reality, its heterogeneous but usually coherent version of events; and no sane human being ever trusts someone else's version more than his own. (211)

Saleem's dramatic fragmented style of narration could have been inherited from his grandfather who had a habit of seeing all things in piecemeal way. His grandfather Aadam Sinai was a trained medical doctor. In his earlier days, when he was a young man, he was asked to treat a young and sexually attractive girl of a Muslim family.

But he was not allowed to examine the girl fully, instead the girl's female attendants held a sheet, which had a hole in it. The doctor was supposed to inspect the body of his young patient through the hole. In a few years the doctor was able to know the different areas of her body. But as he had never seen her in full form he was never able to guess how she would look if all parts were fitted together. The intermittent look of the patient made the doctor curious about the patient. The only interlink between the patient and the doctor was the hole in a sheet. This is a link between Saleem and his grandfather who both had a habit of seeing the things in a piecemeal way, never in a full form. Saleem had no pre-cognition, therefore he could not predict anything at an early stage. The fragmented style of narration might have been inherited from his grandfather but there is an instance where his mother too is unable to express her affection towards her mother in full. She loves her husband in segments. Saleem feels the existence of "ghostly essence" throughout his life:

> and above all the ghostly essence of perforated sheet, which doomed my mother to learn to love a man in segments, and which condemned me to see my own life—its meanings its structures—in fragments. (107)

Saleem is able to remember the incidents prior to his own birth. The elaboration of the events makes Saleem elated. The hole in the sheet symbolically clears out many ideas in the novel. One day Saleem's mother notices a dark hole in the centre of her father's body (139). Even Saleem too feels a hole at the centre of himself. (193) At the end of the novel the Reverend Mother (Saleem's grandmother) looks down at Saleem "through a hole in a perforated cloud." (461) Saleem himself seems to have some idea of the meaning of these things, it is not altogether clear how these holes contribute to the overall meaning of the story. The parallelism between and the inter-relatedness of Saleem's own life and the history of modern India force the readers to find out metaphorical meaning. There are situations pregnant with several interesting possibilities.

Midnight's Children, of course, as Salman Rushdie himself pointed out in an interview, is a metaphor. Though Saleem had earlier named 'optimism' as a dangerous virus, he at last managed to cure himself of the optimism. He is complaining and anxious in the novel about the plight of midnight's children. He expresses his dissatisfaction and discomfort about the shocking incidents. He sharply expresses his views as if he has been unsuccessful in his efforts:

> It is the privilege and curse of midnight's children to be both masters and victims of their times, to forsake privacy and be sucked into the annihilating whirlpool of the multitudes and to be unable to live or die in peace. (463)

You may call Saleem hypocrite, eccentric, a pensive thinker or a promising brilliant person who plays a central role in the novel. His rambunctious behaviour is closely related to the statements he makes. He claims he is responsible for the birth of a separate Maharashtra State, for the overthrow of the Pakistani Government. He further claims that he is indirectly responsible for the death of Pandit Jawaharlal Nehru. Relatively speaking, some of the statements sound self-respecting to Saleem. Saleem gives self-importance and tries to establish link between his own life and the events in India. He tries to find correspondences or parallels. He says:

> Born amidst correspondence, I have found it continuing to hound me . . . while Indians headed blindly towards a military debacle. I, too, was nearing (and entirely without knowing it) a catastrophe of my own. . . . While Indians attacked under cover of artillery, Amina Sinai planned my downfall, protected by a lie. (300-1)

Sometimes we may feel that the episodes from the history of India may be coincidences as the incidents in his life sway suspiciously.

The novel is a strange blend of autobiography, history and fantasy. The readers may be baffled for sometime noticing extraneous references or links. Saleem's nebulous ideas about his life and the history of India are correlated by him. Saleem's representation of the midnight children born on the night of 15 August 1947 is honest, open and truthful. His stupendous effort to narrate the happenings from the storehouse of memories are experienced throughout the novel. *Midnight's Children* is sufficiently charged with posivitism, fantasy and restatement of Indian history with a sweetener of Saleem's autobiography.

NOTES

1. *Midnight's Children* (Picador, 1982), p. 256
2. *Midnight's Children* (New York: Avon, 1980), p. 112.
3. Stanley Wolpert, *A New History of India* (London: Oxford University Press, 1982), p. 18.
4. Wimal Dissanayake, "Towards a Decolonized English: South Asian Creativity in Fiction," *World Englishes*, Vol. 4, no. 2 (1985), p. 240.
5. Brennan Timothy, *Salman Rushdie and the Third World: Myths of the Nation* (London: Macmillan, 1989), p. 104.

Change as Constant: Of Monsters, *Dayans* and *Djinns*: The Bizarre and Fantastic in *Midnight's Children*

NANDINI BHATTACHARYA
Hooghly Mohsin College, Hooghly

Rushdie's fiction abounds in weird and fantastic creatures and his characters remain in a constant state of change. Nandini Bhattacharya traces the origin of these bizarre transformations to the Menippean tradition of writing to which, she thinks, Rushdie belongs. According to her, the bizarre and fantastic blurs the boundaries between the real and the improbable in the novel, problematizes the identities of gender, parenthood and nationality, and compels the reader into a position of radical uncertainty.

Editor

One of the interesting features of Rushdie's novels is the predominance of fantastic and mythical creatures, beast-human hybrids, witches and djinns coexisting within the human self, multiple, conflicting selves jostling to find space within these bag of skins. Moreover, all his characters are in a constant state of change and metamorphosis, adding to the reader's confusion and a sense of moral uncertainty. So we have Saleem who is transformed into a she-dog CUTIA, "Canine Unit for Tracking and Intelligence" to sniff out enemies with his extraordinary nose (*Midnight's Children*), the bizarre change of Sufiya Zinobia into a man eating beast (*Shame*), the mysterious metamorphosis of Saladin Chamcha into a devilish goat-like beast, or for that matter the mass transformation of illegal immigrants at the Detention Centre (*The Satanic Verses*).

Bizarre as these transformations may seem, they are central to the Menippean tradition, to which Rushdie clearly belongs. The carnival sense of the world according to Bakhtin[1] came into the literature of the modern world through the conduit of Menippean satire. This genre had its origin in the third century B.C. partly in parodic response to tragic and epic seriousness. The fullest development of this genre is to be found in Petronius's *Satyricon* and Apeleius's *Metamorphoses* or *The Golden Ass*. While the Menippean satire abounds in the carnivalesque elements, it freely uses the fantastic, the mythical and absurd as a deliberate defiance of "normality," "wholeness," "order" and sacralized absolute, of any kind. One such mode of defying normality is to effect transformation or metamorphosis of a normal human being into a fantastic human-beast hybrid. Mikhail Bakhtin notes in his *The Dialogic Imagination* that "the folktale image of man—throughout the extraordinary variety of folkloric narratives—always orders itself around the motifs of transformation and identity." (112) The classic work of Menippean human-animal metamorphosis, Apeleius's *The Golden Ass*, is used as an intertext in *The Satanic Verses* Muhammad Sufyian quotes from Apeleius when he sees the transformed Chamcha for the first time. (343) That Rushdie is acutely aware of his debt to the Menippean tradition is apparent in his essay entitled "Journey with a Golden Ass," in his collection of critical writings, entitled *Imaginary Homelands* (284-367), where he registers a need to make a new journey with the ass to detect and expose the follies of modern American civilization. According to Bakhtin "Metamorphosis serves as the basis for a method of portraying the whole of an individual's life in its important moments of crisis: for showing how an individual becomes other than what he was." (1115)[2] Rushdie's predecessors in this form are Rabelais, Swift and Sterne, and his contemporaries are Thomas Pynchon and Gunter Grass. It is equally important to trace his affiliations to the Modernist practitioners of this form such as Joyce, Ionesco and Kafka.

The narrator Saleem reminds the reader that his story is about

> a mythical land, a country which would never exist except by the efforts of a phenomenal collective will—except in a dream we all agreed to dream. . . . India, the new myth—a collective fiction in

> which anything was possible, a fable rivalled only by the two other mighty fantasies: money and God. (112)

In this fabulous land, where anything is possible, monsters, dayans, djinns abound and the distinction between the real and the dream worlds is.persistently blurred, forcing the reader into a position of perpetual and radical uncertainty. It is a world where an angelic little girl, begging to peep into Lifafa Das's magic-box, can, at a moment's notice, transmogrify into a terrible basilisk figure, indicting the dugdugee-man as a Hindu transgressing Muslim space and therefore suitable candidate for public lynching. She is now the midget-queen, the "pony-tailed, one-eyebrowed valkyrie" (76) inciting bloody, communal riots. The charming "dilli-dekho" man can transform, within minutes of such indictment, into a monster and rapist, and an entire community of peace-loving, normal people into bloodthirsty hounds. It is a world where the traditional Nordic Jesus, with an aquiline nose and emaciated body can transform into the fat, balding, Falstaff-like 'Isa,' in the imagination of the Kashmiri boatman Tai (16), or into a Krishna-like blue Christ, in the imagination of a liberal priest who wants to build bridges between religions. (103)

One of the sections of Book One of *Midnight's Children* is actually entitled "Many-headed monsters" (78), which begins innocuously enough with Amina Sinai embarking upon a journey to the soothsayer Ramram Seth, who has promised to make predictions about her coming son. But, the many monsters the reader encounters is quite different from the one predicted by Ramram. The relatively sheltered Amina is unable to come to terms with the monsters created by poverty, disease and oppression in the interiors of the city of Delhi.

> Look, my God, those beautiful children have black teeth! Would you believe . . . girl children baring their nipples . . . sweeper women with . . . collapsed spines, . . . and cripples everywhere, mutilated by loving parents to ensure them of a lifelong income from begging . . . yes, beggars in boxcars, grown men with babies' legs, in crates on wheels. (81)

There are also beggars who are white and therefore terrible oddities because "begging was not for white people." (82)

At the centre of the design is, of course, the terrible monster predicted by Ramram Seth, the son that is to be born to Amina Sinai. Because the prediction has remarkable similarities with many literary predecessors such as the opaque pronouncements of the Delphic oracle in Sophocles' *Oedipus Rex*, or the equivocating predictions of Witches in Shakespeare's *Macbeth*, it is worth quoting at length. Ramram, who is himself an oddity, surrounded by screaming monkeys and lapsing into frequent trances, teases and he belies all reader expectations. To the Indian reader, he is typical of the exotic, levitating 'sadhu,' so frequent in the Westerners' readings of India. To the Western reader he is an example of India's mystic powers. Yet he is patently a fraud who sits on a jutting-out shelf to give the impression of levitation. His predictions—typical mumbo-jumbo and yet uncannily correct. He predicts a son

> A son, Sahiba, who will never be older than his motherland—neither older nor younger. . . . There will be two heads—but you shall see only one—there will be knees and a nose, a nose and knees. Newspaper praises him, two mothers raise him! Bicyclists love him—but crowds will shove him! Sisters will weep; cobra will creep. . . . Washing will hide him—voices will guide him! Friends mutilate him—blood will betray him. . . . Spittoons will brain him—doctors will drain him—jungle will claim him—wizards reclaim him! Soldiers will try him—tyrants will fry him. . . . He will have sons without having sons! He will be old before he is old! And he will die . . . before he is dead. (87-88)

Ramram's monster prediction does come true, as Saleem with the nose is actually Shiva with the knees. Saleem is the child of the departing colonialist Methwold and the low-caste Vanita who has been changed places at birth, by nurse Mary Pereira, with Shiva who is really the son of Amina and Ahmed Sinai. But then, Saleem is really the hydra-headed, born of multiple parents, monster—called India, born as he is at the midnight hour and therefore never older than his country. Like the newborn nation he has multiple parents because he is also the child of a new dream.

> So: there were knees and a nose, a nose and knees. In fact, all over the new India, the dream we all shared, children were being born who were only partially the offspring of their parents—the children of midnight were also the children of the time: fathered, you understand, by history. It can happen. Especially in a country which is itself a sort of dream. (118)

If Amina encounters a prophecy about monsters, Ahmed actually goes to keep a date with one. The Ravana gang as Mr. Kemal explains is not the mythical many-headed demon but "a dastardly crew," "a band of incendiary rogues" (71) out to intimidate and blackmail Muslim businessmen into paying protection money. Ahmed actually sees one, a grotesque, pajama-clad figure, "in the head-dress of a demon, a papier-mache devil-top which has faces grinning on every side of it." (85) In a comic aside, the narrator notes that though there were certified monsters like the Ravana gang, there were also camouflaged ones like the excessively polite Mr. Kemal who hoarded his rice, lentils and tea 'as a form of protection against the many-headed many-mouthed rapacious monster that is the public, which, if given its heads, would force prices so low in a time of abundance that god-fearing entrepreneurs would starve while the monster grew fat." (7I)

Unfortunately the hush-money, paid by Ahmed Sinai, never reaches the devil (intercepted as it is, comically, by a monkey) and the Ravana gang carry out their threat of burning down his factory. The violence kicked off by this demonic gang can only be matched by the unnatural frenzy that grips the country on the eve of Independence. As the midnight hour approaches, the many-headed monster of the masses begins to roar, and India prepares for a blood-letting exercise and pre-Partition violence that only a demon could incite.

> The monster in the streets has already begun to celebrate . . . while trains burn in the Punjab, with the green flames of blistering paint and the glaring saffron of fired fuel. (115)

Saleem is a monster that defies all definition because of his protean ability to change shapes and sizes. As a baby he is almost gargantuan, growing at an enormous speed, with blue alien eyes that never blink, eating and defecating in monumental amounts. His nose is alternately denoted as a monstrous cucumber, a wooden shikh-kebab, the trunk of an elephant. Saleem's large nose aligns him with the elephant-god Ganesh, so revered in the city of Bombay where Saleem grows up. He is further disfigured and mutilated by the sadistic teacher Zagallo. At the age of nine he is revived to life by snake poison. Still later he is rendered impotent by the Widow and finally struck on his head with a spittoon, which leads to schizophrenia, which literally means becoming two people at the same time. He is employed by the Pakistani army as a sniffer-dog and designated the title CUTIA (an acronym for Canine Unit for Tracking and Intelligence Activities), which literary means a bitch, in Hindi.

In *Midnight's Children*, the fantastic transmogrified figures define and problematize all identities including those of gender, nationality and parenthood. Women are frequently threatening, masculine and bizarre just as men are weak, impotent, djinnladen. Naseem, the beautiful daughter, is seen through a perforated sheet held by muscular and threatening masculine women. After marriage, Naseem soon transforms from a lissome young girl into a bloated, imposing figure with enormous moles like witches' nipples on her face (40) and fearsome ability to invade her daughter's and husband's dreams (55). With 'whatsitsname' as her leitmotif, she is appropriately called the Reverend Mother. Mothers are a problematic category in Rushdie's novels and most likely to be demonized. *Midnight's Children* abounds in demonic mothers from Naseem Aziz to the Widow who calls herself Mother India. The metamorphosis of mothers into terrible witch-like figures must be seen in the context of the deeply schizophrenic mother-construction in the Indian psyche. In an essay entitled "Adorno in India: Revisiting the Psychology of Fascism," in his book *At the Edge of Psychology*, Ashis Nandy notes: "In terms of organization of personality . . . the Indian lives in his inner world less with a feared father than with a powerful, aggressive and unreliable mother. Manifestly he idealizes her and sees her as the repository of all nurture and motherliness. Underneath this, there are deep doubts about the nurture and the way she might use her powers to aggress. Contrarily, the father is seen as non-interfering, inefficacious, distant and a co-victim of the castrating mother figure." (107)

Naseem's absolute controls over kitchen and pantry and alternately refusal to serve food, which brings Dr. Aziz to the point of death, is an example of the mother's alternately nurturing and destructive qualities. The cook Daaud, burning his feet with hot gravy, unnerved by the Reverend Mother's glare, is convinced "that the old hag had power of witchery." (58-59)

If Naseem is only a comic witch, *Midnight's Children* has the black and green Widow at the centre of its design, calculated to arouse fear even in the dauntless of hearts. She simultaneously occupies the dream and actual space though one is not too sure in her case whether nightmare is reality or reality is a nightmare. She first makes an appearance on Saleem's tenth birthday in a feverish nightmare. (207-8) When she appears in reality as the Mother India with the 'gomata' (mother cow) and the calf as her election symbols, the fear she evokes can equal no nightmare. She imposes the infamous Emergency, launches a programme of forcible vasectomy in the name of family planning and bulldozes slums in the name of civic beautification programme. Reality comes to resemble a nightmare as Saleem is thrown into the Widow's Hostel and forced to undergo vasectomy while his castrated genitals are fed to pie-dogs.

> Yes, perhaps a nightmare: green and black the Widow's hair and clutching hand and children muff and little balls go flying green and black her hand is green her nails are black as black. (422)

According to Sudhir Kakar, in his *The Inner World; A Psycho-Analytic Study of Childhood and Society in India*,

> the sexual presence of the "bad mother" looms large in the unconscious experience of male children in India. . . . Certainly all societies call upon witches, vampires, ghosts and other spectres to symbolize the forbidding, negative aspect of a real mother . . .

> these are familiar figures in individual and collective fantasy across cultures, and the *dayans, jinns and bhoots* who people the Indian night . . . are unexceptionable. (95-96)

Mother India comes to resemble those fantastic figures such as "*dayans, jinns and bhoots.*" (*Inner World*, 96)

If mothers are monstrous so are fathers as parenting is a problematized space in Rushdie's novels. As Ahmed Sinai's assets are frozen by the government, his genitals are frozen and he is possessed by djinns in the bottle. Saleem obviously refers to a defeated and frustrated man's increasing dependence on bottled, alcoholic drinks like gin. The comic narrator would of course like to pun on the idea that in the *Arabian Nights* tales, djinns frequently appeared in bottles waiting to be released from their captivity. The young Saleem, as usual blaming himself for his father's degeneration, describes the metamorphosis of a happy father into a spirit-encumbered, red-eyed monster.

> And so it was my doing that Ahmed Sinai fell, in those days after my birth, into the twin fantasies which were to be his undoing, into the unreal worlds of the djinns and of the land beneath the sea. . . . At six o'clock every evening, Ahmed Sinai entered the world of the djinns; and every morning, his eyes red, his head throbbing with the fatigue of his night-long battle, he came unshaven to the breakfast table; and with the passage of the years, the good mood of the time before he shaved was replaced by the irritable exhaustion of his war with the bottled spirits. (131-32)

Saleem's real father, Methwold, also undergoes a remarkable transformation. From a Samson-like figure, irresistibly attractive to women, he changes into what Padma calls "a baldie." (114) His change is undoubtedly related to the overnight transformation of the almighty British Empire on whom the sun never set, into merely another European country.

> Samson-like, William Methwold's power had resided in his hair; but now, bald patch glowing in the dusk, he flings his thatch through the window of his motor-car, . . . and drives away. (114)

Introduction of hybrid monsters is an oft-used technique to problematize gender identity. Both Padma, Saleem's subaltern audience, and the women who hold up the perforated sheet (behind which Naseem hides) are muscular and threatening women, who gave a lie to the stereotype of feminine frailty. Padma is also at times a beast-human hybrid under the spell of the teller of tales, Saleem.

> She, my squatting glimpser, is captivated, helpless as a mongoose frozen into immobility by the swaying, blinkless eyes of a hooded snake. (121)

Saleem's sister is a tomboy and called Brass Monkey because of her aggressive and destructive nature. Most men, like Saleem, Ahmed, Aadam, and Nadir Khan are impotent or weak and inactive. Even the most potent of them all, Shiva, is ultimately killed by a so-called weak woman.

National identity is a problematic space where the monster paradigm is frequently employed. What adds to Saleem's peculiarity are his 'alien' blue eyes. Though they are attributed to his supposed grandfather Aadam Aziz, the reader knows that they are a British inheritance. Yet, this very Kashmiri heritage will also soon be considered alien as Pakistan and India embark on a disastrous war over Kashmir. As Aadam Aziz worries, will he be considered an Indian or a Kashmiri? Ironically, he had been regarded as alien and monstrous by the indigenous Kashmiri, boatman Tai, because he had been educated in Germany and therefore tainted by 'abroad' in his youth. It is interesting to note that aliens, immigrants and marginals have traditionally been considered as monstrous, unnatural and hence the wonderfully suggestive term naturalization[3] is used to describe the process of integration into the mainstream of the nation. The entire imperial exercise of the nineteenth century was sustained by the belief that non-Europeans are actually sub-humans, alien monsters who needed to be humanized. Therefore, colonization was not simply an exploitative exercise but a just and missionary one, bringing the fruits of human civilization to the semi or anti-human world. Racism in Hitler's Third Reich or apartheid in South Africa was sustained by a belief that the discriminated individuals are not human at all and therefore did not deserve humane treatment.

Hence, Shylock is finally condemned as a bloodthirsty monster in Shakespeare's *The Merchant of Venice* because he is perceived as an alien, plotting against the life of a citizen of Venice. As Portia notes: 'If it be proved against an alien/That by direct or indirect attempts/He seek the life of any citizen/The party 'gainst which he doth contrive/ Shall seize one half his goods/ . . . and the offender's life lies in mercy/Of the Duke." (75) In *The Satanic Verses*, all immigrants transform into mythical creatures or human-beast hybrids. (104) The three soldiers, Ayooba, Shaheed arid Farookh, consider East-Pakistanis to be sub-humans, sort of jungle-bunnies, to be slaughtered indiscriminately. The Sunderban episode is full of ghosts and phantoms encountered by people who consider each other alien.

Monster paradigm is central to Rushdie's approach to literature in general. Rushdie believes that the fantastic, the unreal and magical are far more reliable modes of storytelling, especially when one describes a country like India where reality is stranger than fiction. Like the Latin-American novelists who employ magic realism as a mode, Rushdie believes that the fantastic and the bizarre are often a more accurate mirror of truth. The magical and fantastic has a special place of honour in *Midnight's Children*. Uncle Hanif is successful as a filmmaker when he adopts this fantastic, blatantly unrealistic mode of storytelling in his film, *The Lovers of Kashmir*. His realistic attempt to tell stories of pickle-factories and wives of labourers falls flat because it is in the fantastic that our deepest desires and innermost anxieties are captured. Hanif is of course a projection of the author himself. So is Saleem who abandons Padma's demand for realistic 'whatnextism' for a bizarre mode of storytelling. The midnight's children are all in possession of magical qualities like the new-born land itself born in the midnight hour. As Saleem says just before independence, "myths, nightmares fantasies were in the air." (111) The magical and fantastic are symptomatic of the new hope and powers of regeneration that are granted to the midnight's children.

> During the first hour of August 15th, 1947—between midnight and one a.m.—no less than one thousand and one children were born within the frontiers of the infant sovereign state of India. . . . What made the event noteworthy . . . was the nature of these children, every one of whom was, through some freak of biology, or perhaps owing to some preternatural power of the moment, or just . . . by sheer coincidence . . . endowed with features, talents or faculties which can only be described as miraculous. It was as though . . . history, arriving at a point of the highest significance and promise, had chosen to sow, in that instant, the seeds of a future which would genuinely differ from anything the world had seen up to that time. (195)

Hence there are boys who can walk through mirrors and girls who can multiply fish, and children with great powers of transformation such as turning into werewolves or becoming giants and dwarfs at will and a child who can change gender at the drop of a hat or children who can divide water and children whose words can actually inflict cuts and wounds (a reference to Rushdie's own art as a satirist?) and some one who has literal green fingers and grows aubergines in deserts. (198) The fantastic is at the heart of a new-born nation, transforming it daily.

Rushdie is frequently of the opinion that it is only in dreams that we may re-mould and re-make the world. Therefore, the dictator or fascists' first task is to destroy dreams and imaginative bodies. In *Haroun and the Sea of Stories*, Khattam Shud is the Prince of Silence, the arch-enemy of dreams and expressions. In *Midnight's Children*, the Widow is the arch-enemy of the magical and the fantastic. Hence, she attacks the magicians' colony in Delhi, bulldozes them and puts them to flight. She also arrests most of the midnight's children (because they symbolize hope for change), literally castrates them and figuratively makes them impotent. In this context it is worthwhile to look at Rushdie's essay entitled "The Location of Brazil" in his *Imaginary Homelands*.

> This idea—the opposition of imagination to reality, which is also of course the opposition of art to politics—is of great importance, because it reminds us that we are not helpless; that to dream is to

> have power . . . the other great tradition in art [is] the one in which techniques of comedy, metaphor, heightened imagery, fantasy and so on are used to break down our conventional, habit-dulled certainties about what the world is and has to be. Unreality is the only weapon with which reality can be smashed, so that it may subsequently be reconstructed. (122)

The power of change and transformation is indeed a fearsome one.

The entire novel is ultimately placed in a space, which is advertised as a city of dreams. Bombay, India's premier Film City, abounding in dream-merchants, aggressively sells the nation's secret desires and fantasies. (215) Bombay's popular dream-merchandise, the popular Bombay cinema, forms the subtext of *Midnight's Children*. The novel consciously simulates the Bombay talkies' fantastic and melodramatic mode, incorporating conventions like mistaken identities, changes at birth, doubles, fantastic coincidences, melodramatic cloak and dagger affairs, proliferation of semi-magical beasts (in the Indian consciousness) like snakes, monkeys and elephants invading the human world. Saleem rightly notes that world of *Midnight's Children* has "melodrama, piling upon melodrama: life acquiring the colouring of a Bombay talkie." (I48) In *Midnight's Children*, the fantastic and the real ultimately cannot be distinguished as they erase each other's boundaries. Rapid transformation of identity, space and time makes *change* the only *constant* in the novel.

NOTES

1. Carnivalization, in Bakhtin's usage, is the process whereby "a carnival sense of the world"—arising in the ancient and medieval worlds out of a lived mass experience of the festive, ritual pageantry of carnivals such as the Saturnalia—was transposed into the language of literature. These ideas are to be found in Bakhtin's *Problems of Dostoevsky's Poetics*, p. 107.
2. The idea of Menippean satire to describe Rushdie's novels was first used by lb Johansen in his essay "The Flight from the Enchanter: Reflections on Salman Rushdie's *Grimus*" and subse-

quently by M. Keith Booker in his essay "Beauty and the Beast: Dualism as Despotism in the Fiction of Salman Rushdie."

3. I am indebted to Benedict Anderson's *Imagined Communities; Reflections on the Origin and Spread of Nationalism* (p. 145) for this idea.

Works Cited

Anderson, Benedict, *Imagined Communities; Reflections on the Origin and Spread of Nationalism* (London and New York: Verso, rev. 1991).

Apeleius, Lucius. *The Golden Ass*, trans. Jack Lindsay (Bloomington, Indiana University Press, 1962).

Bakhtin, Mikhail, *The Dialogic Imagination; Four Essays,* ed. Michael Holquist, trans. Caryl Emerson and Michael Holquist (Austin: University of Texas Press, 1981).

Bakhtin, Mikhail. *Problems of Dostoevsky's Poetics*, trans. Caryl Emerson (Minneapolis: Minnesota University Press, 1984).

Booker, Keith, M. "Beauty and the Beast; Dualism as despotism in the Fiction of Salman Rushdie," in M.D. Fletcher.

Fletcher, M.D., ed. *Reading Rushdie; Perspectives on the Fiction of Salman Rushdie* (Amsterdam, Rodopi Press, 1994).

Johansen, lb. "The Flight from the Enchanter; Reflections on Salman Rushdie's *Grimus*," in M.D. Fletcher.

Kakar, Sudhir, *The Inner World; A Psychoanalytic Study of Childhood and Society in India* (New Delhi: Oxford University Press, 1981).

Nandy, Ashis. *At the Edge of Psychology; Essays in Politics and Culture* (New Delhi: Oxford University Press, 1980).

Rushdie, Salman. *The Midnight's Children* (1981; London: Vintage, 1995).

______. *Shame* (1983; London: Vintage, 1995).

______. *The Satanic Verses* (The Consortium, 1992).

______. *Haroun and the Sea of Stories* (London: Granta Books in association with Penguin, 1991).

______. *Imaginary Homelands; Critical Essays 1981-1991* (London: Granta Books in association with Penguin, 1991).

Shakespeare William, *The Merchant of Venice*, ed. Roma Gill (New Delhi: Oxford University Press, 1997).

Shakespeare William, *Macbeth*, ed. Roma Gill (New Delhi: Oxford University Press, 1997).

The Emergency as Another Midnight in Salman Rushdie

O.P. MATHUR
Banaras Hindu University

Mathur's paper examines Rushdie's treatment of the Emergency in the novel. According to him, Rushdie has imaginatively recreated Indian history from Independence to Emergency, focusing on two momentous midnights—those of August 15, 1947 and June 25, 1977 which channelled the flow of history in two opposite directions. The ironic and censorious portrayal of the second midnight, he thinks, completes the author's political message in the book.

Editor

Salman Rushdie's prismatic handling of the Indian Emergency (1975-77) against the vast background of Time, though mostly ignored by critics, forms a significant part of the vehicle through which he conveys his profound message to mankind. In *Midnight's Children* Salman Rushdie has attempted to restore his Indian past and its values to himself by making his narrative run along with the period of Indian history from the freedom struggle to the Emergency and its end, chiefly concentrating on two momentous midnights which turned the current of history in two different directions. One was the midnight of August 14-15, 1947 in which India awoke into freedom, and the other was the midnight of June 24-25, 1975 in which President Fakhruddin Ali Ahmad, at the instance of Prime Minister Indira Gandhi, signed the declaration of the state of internal Emergency which greatly damaged the achievements of freedom, at least temporarily, by extinguishing the rights of the people.

The narration of *Midnight's Children* runs at two levels simultaneously—history and imagination. The fictitious narrative of Saleem Sinai, explicating and commenting on the historical events, allegorizes India's emergence into a massive and democratic order through the birth of 1001 (i.e. a very large number, in common parlance) children born around that historic midnight. Representing freedom of speech and discussion, these children occasionally meet for free discussion in the imagination of Saleem who, having been born exactly at that hour is their natural leader and convener. The strong olfactory power of his nose stands not only for his own sharp and perceptive sensibility but also for the curiosity for the acquisition of knowledge.

Interestingly, in the nursing home, there was a clandestine exchange of the two babies, Saleem and Shiva, both born exactly at the stroke of midnight.

But the inherent potentialities of the two are so different that either the 'exchange' was just a 'show' or there was another exchange unknown to everybody, including Saleem, or they have merged and emerged in their true selves from the novelist's imagination based upon the materialistic theory of the governing role of environment over heredity. The last guess is probably the most likely.

In any case, the germs of the second and a sinister midnight, which is our main theme, are present in Saleem himself. Shiva, gifted with powerful knees suggesting thoughtless physical strength, becomes the arch-rival of Saleem. In the first midnight the nose has it, in the second, which comes about twenty-nine years later, it is knees that prevail, though their varying strengths culminate in a figure which ironically belongs to both.

The symbol of the second midnight, Aadam Sinai, is an interesting figure. His parentage, as suggested above, is shrouded in a mystery. He is the son of Parvati, who marries Saleem on the Republic Day of 1975, already impregnated by Shiva. Saleem knows it, but accepts the situation, meekly "trapped by the lie of his impotence." (495) He can only store the riddle of the mysterious fatherhood and genealogy of his son in one of his pickle jars: "Once again a child was born to a father who was not his father, although by a terrible irony the child would be the true grand-child of his father's parents." (495) Like Saleem himself, his son is handcuffed to history even before his birth. The progress of Parvati's pregnancy is accompanied by events in the country's politics, foreshadowing a new phase of history. Even before Saleem's marriage to Parvati, there is an historical omen, the death of L.N. Mishra, the then minister for railways, in an explosion at Samastipur. The events on the political front are mirrored in the progress of Parvati's pregnancy. As the clash between the people's front, formed by a union of various political parties grows, Parvati's belly also goes on expanding till the flash point is reached at 2 p.m. on June 12, 1975 when the judgement against Indira Gandhi is delivered and Parvati's labour begins, and at the midnight of June 25, when Parvati's labour reaches the climax of the baby's birth, "elsewhere the Prime Minister was giving birth to a child of her own":

> The labour of both came to a successful conclusion and at the precise instant of the birth of new India and the beginning of a continuous midnight which would not end for two long years, my son, the child of the renewed ticktock, came out into the world. . . . The birth of his father Saleem was not only quick and easy, but it was also welcomed with clock hands joined together, while his child is born after a thirteen-day-long labour. One led to the gay dawn of independence, the other to "a continuous midnight" full of "silence and fears across the country." (499-500)

The contrast between Saleem and his child Aadam is also marked. Saleem's long and highly sensitive nose is in his child converted into large ears and big eyes, and the ears "flapped so high and wide that they must have heard the shootings in Bihar and the screams of lathi-charged dock-workers in Bombay." (501) Saleem's meandering verbosity, going round, backward and forward, in his child becomes absolute frozen silence. The characteristics of Saleem are those of a vibrant democracy—curiosity of and freedom to acquire knowledge and the freedom of expression; while his son's physical features are a prism of the Emergency. An important fact, often overlooked, is that Aadam is really the child divine of "Shiva-and-Parvati." (500) Who could he be except "the elephant-headed Ganesh." (500) With his large flapping ears and the hidden invincible strength of a god, the lord of the people ('gana + 'eash')? This is revealed partly in his determination to resist evil and not to speak, in spite of strong medication.

His 'bimbi' (i.e. navel) protruding from the belly is another interesting symbol. His resentment and anger at all the grunts and groans of the people are ingested through his large ears, but remain unexpressed in words or action. Simmering within him with a strong determination to resist evil and tyranny, they are expressed in a way unknown to the public through the 'bimbi.' It is his voice, potency and potentiality. Thus, he is one of a generation of "fearsomely potent kiddies, growing, waiting, rehearsing the moment when the world would become their plaything (How these children may, in the future, be identified "their bimbis stick out instead of in).' (535)

Aadam is also suffering from Tuberculosis, a wasting deadly disease which is cured by itself with the lifting of the Emergency. In fact, there is something "darkly metaphorical" (504) in all the abnormalities of Aadam, the child of his times which badly damaged reality so much that nobody ever managed to put it together again (500). Saleem is right in insisting, "While the Emergency lasts, he will never become well." (504) He is thus a pioneer of the democratic order, "a torch in a long dark tunnel . . . a child of dignity." (536) The first word he utters after the Emergency is 'abracadabra' which may have been meant to be a cabalistic or magical incantation to rid the country of its evil, the Emergency, and possibly also to prevent its recurrence.

The Mother of the Emergency is Indira Gandhi who in this novel has been repeatedly called 'Widow' (with capital 'W')—an appellation that often signifies the drying up of emotions, harshness, cruelty and, above all, supreme uncontrolled power over the household, i.e. the country. Saleem says,

> We the magical children of midnight, were hated feared destroyed by the Widow who was not only Prime Minister of India but also aspired to be Devi, the Mother-goddess in her most terrible aspect, possessor of the shakti of the gods, a multi-limbed divinity, with a center-parting and schizophrenic hair. (522)

Rushdie makes one of her devotees called 'Widow's Hand' describe her as "a manifestation of the OM," whom all the people of India worship like a god and of which all the three hundred and thirty million gods of Hinduism are manifestations." (521) Such a gross exaggeration makes her seem almost ridiculous—a Demon instead of a Devi. Her hair style, so characteristic of her is also described with a mischievous relish:

> If the Mother of the Nation had had a coiffure of uniform pigment, the Emergency, she spawned might easily have lacked a darker side. But she had white hair on one side and black on the other; the Emergency, too, had a white part—public, visible documented, a matter for historians—and a black part which being secret macabre untold, must be a matter for us. (501)

Rushdie does mention Sanjay Gandhi, but the responsibility is squarely placed on his mother, who is the perpetrator and the presiding deity of the Emergency and later on also its political victim, illustrating the truth that the actions are ours but their results none of our own.

As confessed in the lines quoted above, Salman Rushdie is concerned with the dark side of the Emergency, though its brighter aspects are also mentioned in passing:

> All sorts of things happen during an Emergency: trains run on time, black-money hoarders are frightened into paying taxes, even the weather is brought to heel, and bumper harvests are reaped. (517)

Rushdie himself is not a historian nor an eye-witness of the events. But he makes his persona Saleem Sinai witness a few, as largely a commentator who keeps his stance shifting from sympathy and appreciation to amusement, irony, satire and outright condemnation, as the occasion demands. In treating the Emergency his focus is mainly on bringing out its spirit and not on acting as a chronicler. The core of the Emergency consists in what Indira Gandhi does or allows Sanjay or her other lieutenants to do. The main thrust of the Emergency was on 'beautification' by demolition, sterilization and imprisonments under MISA. Saleem describes all of them with irony. The infamous bulldozers pour out people who display unusual physical uniformity as if they were clones:

> all the men had the same curly hair and lips-like-women's-labia, and the elegant ladies were all identical, too, their features corresponding precisely to those of Sanjay's Menaka, whom newsscraps had described as a "lanky beauty," and who had once modelled nighties. for a mattress company . . . the ruling dynasty of India had learned how to replicate itself. (511-12)

The demolitions of houses and jhuggis are open to public gaze, but what happens in sterilization camps is secret. Sterilizations are often castrations in disguise. In Banaras, Shiva's town, Saleem is sterilized under the orders of Major Shiva, his archrival. Suggesting the secrecy, fear and the dark intent of the perpetrators, the atmosphere inside the camp is eerie: "a table with a hanging lamp, and doctors, nurses green and black, their robes were green and their eyes were black . . . who, with knobbly irresistible knees, escorted me to the chamber of my undoing." (522) In these camps all the midnight's children, already imprisoned, are operated upon in a way that they "were denied the possibility of reproducing themselves." (523) Shiva also gets himself voluntarily vasectomised. So that seems to be the end of the race of midnight's children. But is it so?

> I laughed because Shiva, destroyer of the midnight children, had also fulfilled the other function of Shivalingam, of Shiva the procreator, so that at this very moment, in the boudoirs and hovels of the nation, a new generation of children, begotten by midnight's darkest child was being raised towards the future. Every Widow manages to forget something important. (525)

It is supreme irony, for Aadam Sinai, Shiva's natural son begotten on Parvati before her marriage, was growing up carrying onwards the characteristics of Midnight's Children of whom Saleem and not Shiva was the true representative. Silent genetics ironically prevails over human intentions and planning. Saleem's "Sperectomy: the draining-out of hope" (521) is only partially and temporarily true. When he, along with the other midnight's children is in prison, he talks to them at length through a thin wall, telling them about himself and about the steep depletion in their number, but cheers them up at the end:

> Yes, here is optimism, like a disease: one day she'll have to let us out and then, and then, wait and see, maybe we should form, I don't know, a new political party, yes, the Midnight Party, what chances do politics have against people who can multiply fishes and turn base metals into gold? Children, something is being born here, in this dark time of our captivity; let Widows do their worst unity is invincibility! *Children, we've* won! (520)

His optimism is substantiated not only by their ultimate invincibility, but later on in their continuity also through Shiva's 'natural' child, but now his own 'son'—Aadam Sinai.

His optimism receives a jolt even after Indira Gandhi loses at the polls and a six-hundred-and-thirty-five-day-long midnight" (529) is over, for what follows is hardly an enthusing dawn:

> the tattered hopes of a nation had been placed in the custody of an ancient dotard who ate pistachios and cashews and daily took a glass of "his own water." Urine-drinkers had come to power. The Janata Party, with one of its own leaders trapped in a kidney-machine, did not seem to me (when I heard about it) to represent a new dawn. (525)

The Emergency has ended at last, but depressingly, "not with a bang but a whimper." But the gloom is brightened by the return of Aadam to his father Saleem after his release. Aadam, bearing the same name as that of his great grandfather and also that of the progenitor of mankind in more faiths than one, and wearing "a tee-shirt decorated with pink guitars" is a heart-warming symbol of life, hope, enlivement and the continued survival of mankind, maybe with "shadows of imperfection." (548) The novelist's one empty jar in the novel will always remain empty, ready to receive the future products of the "chutnification of history" (548) in which one hungry generation treads down another:

> Yes, they will trample me underfoot, the numbers marching one two three, four hundred million five hundred six, reducing me to specks of voiceless dust, just as, all in good time, they will trample

> my son who is not my son, and his son who will not be his, until the thousand and first generation, until a thousand and one midnights have bestowed their terrible gifts and a thousand and one children have died, because it is the privilege and the curse of midnight's children to be both masters and victims of their times, to forsake privacy and to be sucked into the annihilating whirlpool of the multitudes and to be unable to live or die in peace. (552)

This world is progressing neither towards a utopia nor a dystopia. It is condemned to survive with this mild diseases of pale optimism and 'sperectomy' (draining out of hope). This is the best product of the "chutnification of history" that Rushdie can pulp out. It is twilight and a chameleon-like world in which both good and evil are inextricably and unrecognizably woven, one sometimes quietly transforming into the other. One set of Midnight's Children will be kaleidoscopically replicated a thousand times along with the ambiguity of the identity of a Saleem and a Shiva. *Midnight's Children,* with such a different replication of the children of two midnights only illustrates this observation. One midnight might have made a highly readable novel, but the consummation of the novelist's view of world, life and time is reached by the portrayal of another midnight, that of the Emergency. Ironical, hilarious and condemnatory it is, but only on the surface, the profound message of the novelist is completed by the second midnight of the Emergency without which the novel might have been a highly interesting reading, but without the spire of a meaning.

NOTE

1. Salman Rushdie, *Midnight's Children* (1980; New York: Avon Books, Alfred A. Knopf, 1982).

The (Hi)Story of Padma's 1001 Different Faces

Pier Paolo Piciucco
University of Turin

This well-researched article by Piciucco offers an absorbing analysis of the multifaced and ambivalent character of Padma and her role in the novel through a series of different—often unconventional—readings of the text, each reading featuring her as the main character. His perceptive analysis not only contradicts Rushdie's claim that his books do not function as allegories but also refutes some commonly accepted theories and critical opinions about the novel. The article will help the reader to appreciate the text in a new light.

Editor

I usually resist the idea of allegory. In India there is too much of it, allegory is a kind of disease. People try to decode everything, every story or text allegorically, and although clearly there are elements that you could call allegorical in *Midnight's Children* and *Shame*, the books are not allegories in the way that *The Pilgrim's Progress* is, where everything stands for something and the real story is a story that is not told. Allegory asks readers to make a translation, to uncover a secret that has not actually been told. In that sense I don't think my books operate as allegories.[1]

Salman Rushdie is a fictional character created by the ingenious mind of Saleem Sinai, who made him a very unreliable narrator and speaker. Although his idea quoted above can in fact be easily understood if the parallel with *The Pilgrim's Progress* is implied, the core of the message, his reluctance to explain the fundamental tenets in *Midnight's Children* in terms of an allegorical code, is surprising, to say the least. Many of the critical debates on his novels over the years would lose their substance and *Midnight's Children* itself, in my personal opinion, could hardly have achieved the international resonance it has enjoyed since publication, should we read the book without referring to a symbolic convention. In the present paper I aim at illustrating a theory on a new reading of the novel, focussing on the character of Padma, "an ambivalent figure within the novel,"[2] but taking for granted that allegories work as a main agent informing various characters, events and perspectives with significant meanings and/or interpretations. While I attempt at analyzing the multifacedness of this very peculiar character and therefore propose a series of different readings, I discourage the reader from taking the individual interpretations as neatly distinguished one from the other, but rather to perceive the assortment and amalgamation—or should we say the chutnification?—of these patterns to be the crux of the issue.

As has been often underlined, *Midnight's Children* is a container of stories and my reading has simply followed the one featuring Padma as the main character. While other stories are much shorter, Rushdie has chosen this particular one to stretch for the whole length of the novel, although obviously interrupted by various stops and continuous digressions. What seemed interesting to me was that, although she remains the same character from the beginning, Padma undergoes a significant change in the eyes of the reader towards the end of the book. *Midnight's Children* is the acrobatic unfolding of tales and anecdotes by a talented narrator who writes/tells these stories from his desk. Since his task is all-absorbing, he needs another figure to materially take care of him while he completely devotes himself to narrating anecdotes. Hence the creation of Padma, "nurse and cook,"[3] whose nature and function soon appear ambivalent: she is not the real author of the stories but, say, the author's "vital collaborator." Considering the intimacy between these two figures ("I must go to bed. Padma is waiting; and I need a little warmth"[4]), that her brief parting from him is to be viewed as an exceptional case and due to her hot temper, and her total dedication to her man, the reader may reasonably presume that they are husband and wife. This is never stated but, since no different solution is suggested, it would not be a completely wild guess on the reader's part: a further element justifying such a hypothesis is that together Saleem and Padma seem a very traditional couple, spouses who have lived together for a very long time and whose union is now governed by inertia. It is not before the end of the novel that the reader is informed of the whole truth: they are simply partners, allegedly not even very long-standing ones at that. She tries to convince him to marry her, but he seems to resist. It is in the very last pages of the novel that Saleem meets again his ayah, Mary Pereira, and through their dialogue the reader is made aware that Saleem has finally decided to surrender: "'Why you getting married so sudden sudden?' Because Padma wants. No she is not in trouble." (459) In the fashion of many Rushdie's stories, this one, too, has an open ending and the reader does not witness Padma's much awaited celebration. To complicate matters, the finale's gloomy atmosphere leaves more than a simple doubt about such a romantic evolution.

Much has been said about both the similar representation of female characters in the fiction of Rushdie and the symbolic role of Padma in the novel, at various levels. It is my opinion that the role she plays could be seen in relation to that of the other women described in *Midnight's Children*; more in detail, I suggest that she be seen as a surrogate of femininity. Likewise, Saleem would be representative of masculinity. Needless to say, Rushdie's approach to this canon is considerably altered by a distortion lens and sarcasm. Elsewhere[5] I have dealt with the stereotypical representations of female and masculine characters, indicating that Indian writers are very inclined to apply a peculiar cultural code to fictional discourse when referring to similar prototypes: *Midnight's Children* would be another example reinforcing that theory. Without entering into details, I will simply say that an Indian philosophical and aesthetic principle directly inherited from a traditional view, but still in keeping with the modern times, the Samkhya concept, views the whole universe as the creation of two complementary agents: *purusha* and *prakrti*. The former is generally associated with spirits; it is a concept implying plurality, inaction, thought, air, manliness. The latter is nature, activity, earth, femininity. They are to be considered as two equally important forms of energy whose final union leads to the creation of the universe. Whether or not Rushdie intentionally alluded to this philosophical bipolarism while sketching the figures of Saleem and Padma is hard to say (I would be more inclined not to believe so), but the number of parallels linking Padma to prakrti and Saleem to purúsha is striking. Each perspective will illustrate them as perfectly complementary agents, following a canon which, if not directly relating to the Samkhya concept, is only slightly different from it. What is relevant here, though, is not a philosophical explanation of the events described but an interpretation of these two figures as the primordial man and woman. Their union (or should we say simply their relationship, considering the final pessimistic tone of the novel?) would lead to the creation of the novel. This perspective would provide a key of interpretation to various behaviours and characteristics of these two characters I will discuss later: suffice it to say now that it may explain Saleem's powerful verbosity countered by Padma's more evident sexual urge, a cliché much contested by a feminist reading (see Verma, 1991: 158).

Both the characters in fact appear extremely well-endowed with particular features, totally lacking other attributes at the same time. Whereas Saleem is in fact a fertile story-teller, he is emasculated: while Padma is illiterate, she seems driven by very intense physical urges. In this context, *Midnight's Children* can also be seen as the challenge between wordiness and desire. The ironical allusion to his sex, called "my 'other pencil'" (121) by Saleem, would find further implications here. Incidentally, we may remember that psychoanalysis verged on very similar results. Sigmund Freud in fact explained the mechanisms leading the artist to the creative process as the effect of instinctive unsatisfied longings, which he deemed very akin to the libido.[6] In this perspective, the desire to tell and the sexual impulse would prefigure as the two parallel forces which we would find personified as Saleem and Padma in *Midnight's Children*. In a particular instance his act of writing appears explicitly as a surrogate of a sexual intercourse:

> Is it possible to be jealous of written words? To resent nocturnal scribblings as though they were the very flesh and blood of a sexual rival? I can think of no other reason for Padma's bizarre behaviour; and this explanation at least has the merit of being as outlandish as the rage into which she fell when, tonight, I made the error of writing (and reading aloud) a word which should not have been spoken . . . ever since the episode of the quack doctor's visit, I have sniffed out a strange discontent in Padma, exuding its enigmatic spoor for her eccrine (or apocrine) glands. (121)

This is exactly in keeping with the structure of *Arabian Nights*. Sheherazade, in fact, uses the nights at her disposal in order to entertain her king with tales rather than with sexual pleasure.

Debates on the relevance of intertextual strategies in the fiction of Salman Rushdie have always been a central topic. Contaminations by Marquez's *One Hundred Years of Solitude,* Grass's *The Tin Drum*, Sterne's *Tristram Shandy* and *Arabian Nights*, among various others, are either highlighted in the course of narration or have been acknowledged by the writer in various interviews. Although they sooner or later emerge in the plot adding more spice to Saleem's "chutney," they do not share the same weight in the general plan of the book. Of the texts listed above, the only one which candidly appears in *Midnight's Children* is *Arabian Nights* and its importance has already been stressed in the work of other scholars.[7] However, I would stretch the analogies between the two texts a bit further than this, by suggesting an interpretation of *Arabian Nights* functioning as a macrotext to *Midnight's Children*. This fact is crucial to our debate in that in the process of appropriation of the medieval collection of stories, Rushdie adopts a sex-switching strategy. Saleem, the archetypal man, is reproposed as the young virgin Sheherazade, while Padma, the feminine principle, is turned into the terrifying king Shahriyar. Structurally, in fact, both *Arabian Nights* and *Midnight's Children* are love-stories. Implausible, paradoxical, allegorical, exaggerated, but nonetheless love-stories. As far as *Midnight's Children* is concerned, it is a strange relationship which develops between the two characters, a relationship which illustrates a tragi-comic dichotomy. As

Hutcheon rightly argues, "instead of satisfaction, he offers her sublimation."[8] And, as we know, sublimation of desire is also the strategy employed by Sheherazade with king Shahriyar to win his thirst for blood and become his wife. Of course, Rushdie makes use of irony to represent the dramatic destiny of Saleem-Sheherazade: till Saleem tells stories, he can keep Padma at a safe distance and control her. And what longer is there to narrate than the (hi)story of the Indian republic? Padma's victory, on the other hand, lies in her patience: she lets Saleem unfold all his stories and exhaust his power. When he is about to finish, he is weak and abruptly capitulates: he accepts the marriage proposal. This reading may provide an explanation to Padma and Saleem's different discoursive strategies: his digressive penchant juxta-posed to her "what-happened-nextism." (39) In the strange chal-lenge between the two, it is always Saleem who feels threatened by some danger or another. Padma-Shahriyar is in fact safe whatever happens to her, at least in comparison to him. This is why Saleem, beyond adopting a digressive discoursive strategy, tries, significantly towards the very end of his narration, to dis-suade her with various motivations that their union is impossible: it is then that he tactically reveals his emasculation to her and it is again only towards the end that he warns her against the tragic end she would meet, should she marry him. Women are in fact dogged by a perverse doom with him. Yet, Padma easily over-comes all these fears and wins him in the end.

The slightly pessimistic part of this strange love-relationship is the unbalanced emotional commitment for each other. Padma in fact is deeply in love with Saleem: "Padma fell for me from the first, seeing in me an outlet for her vast reservoir of pent-up solicitude." (460) On the other hand, he, who is surely affected to her, does not necessarily share her same feelings. Rather than love, he seems regulated by a kind of a habit, a part of a ritual, a sort of a self-centred disposition at times; Saleem's moves are therefore governed by a fair amount of coldness. Discussing the whole fictional corpus of Rushdie, Ahmad rightly points out: "for all its marvellous humour, Rushdie's imagined world is, in its lovelessness, almost Orwellian."[9]

I understand at this point that my reading is quite original as it disputes various other commonly accepted theories. First, it emphasises that the architecture of *Midnight's Children* is structured on the myth of *Arabian Nights*. Scholars, on the other hand, have often missed such a clue, maybe because searching for mythical references in the Hindu or Muslim pantheon: "In *Midnight's Children*, myth functions as a kind of a shorthand to convey concepts though it is rarely fully and elaboratively worked out, unlike in Joyce's *Ulysses* and Eliot's *The Waste Land* which use myth as a framework."[10]

Secondly, it opposes the commonplace that Padma is not part of the story proper but occupies selected "asides" in which she participates with Saleem in composing the novel we are reading. Her relationship is not with Saleem the character, but with Saleem the narrator and author.[11]

Finally, it contradicts the opinion that Rushdie's treatment of female characters always denotes implied strategies of male dominance (Ahmed, 142-52). My theory would in fact propose the reading of the plot as a sort of an open challenge between Padma and Saleem within a strange love relationship. Padma's final victory, or at least Saleem's surrender considering that the story is deliberately left open-ended, would eschew such a conclusion. That is far more significant in that, if Rushdie firstly adopts a sex switching code when applying *Arabian Nights*' model to his novel, he later comes back to the original situation when establishing who is the winner. In both the texts, in fact, it is the woman who prevails in the end. What is more important, in this context, is that Padma's victory is not so much associated with a personal victory, but rather with that of a gender: "most of the male characters are weak (it is not only Saleem who has to say: "women have made me: and also unmade") whereas most of the women are strong and independent. They invariably get what they want because they have the strength or willpower."[12]

If we then refer to the allegorical meaning of such a peculiar construction, these interpretations of the two protagonists may appear to be the most important. Actually, this is not exactly what happens in *Midnight's Children*. Rushdie in fact subverts the priorities generally assumed in *Arabian Nights*; his act of appropriation implies that the private (love-)story of the two heroes be relegated to a secondary role by their telling of the stories. What substantially distinguishes *Midnight's Children* from *Arabian Nights* in terms of structural approach, is that Sheherazade's tales, although extremely entertaining, remain a set of discoursive agents isolated from her personal predicament, while Saleem's story is deeply amalgamated with his present development with Padma and, more relevantly still, the choice of the subject discussed makes it the focal point of the book. Whereas, say, a reader of *Arabian Nights* could equally do without some of Sheherazade's fabulous stories, a reader of *Midnight's Children* is totally absorbed by Rushdie's rewriting of Indian history and can partially ignore Saleem and Padma's liaison. That is why the structural corpus of *Midnight's Children* and the mythological frame end up being a section of lesser weight, in comparison to the central tale. The following interpretations of Padma are to be placed outside her emotional commitment for Saleem and, more importantly, outside the structural frame referring to *Arabian Nights*; they are those which more consistently fuelled the theoretical debates around the reception of *Midnight's Children*.

A Marxist reading of *Midnight's Children* has emphasizec Padma's symbolical value as a plebeian commentator next tc Saleem, illustrative of the local élitism (Brennan, 100-9). This interpretation has therefore focussed on the hegemonic prevalence of the central/bourgeois/male agents over the liminal/plebeian/female identity. What is particularly engaging and original about this reading is that this theory avoids acknowledging in Saleem alone the emblem of India, but it demonstrates that a complete national identification is to be searched for in the combination of Saleem and Padma. Yet, in *Midnight's Children* we can detect that Rushdie deliberately focuses his attention on Saleem's story only, totally overlooking Padma's background. The reader's conclusions about Padma plebeian lineage, although manifest, cannot be supported by the evidence of her story in the text because that is totally abrogated.

Gender criticism has not generally been extremely soft with Rushdie, to use a delicate euphemism. Outside the code of reference to *Arabian Nights*, and the parallel with king Shahriyar-Sheherazade, Padma seems to be modelled on the traditional Indian wife. Her world is the domestic sphere, she is totally dedicated to her husband and it is assumed that patience is her most characterising trait. She is supposed to live in the shadow of her husband and, as Parnell argues, "like most of Rushdie's women she is not a shaper of events but an adjunct to her male" (Moore-Gilbert, 250). Furthermore, the huge gap between his high-level education and her illiteracy, which induces Saleem to tag her as "my one disciple," (149) have become an unhappy caricature of a sad social reality. What has justifiably most irritated gender criticism is that Padma has been clearly sketched out as a stereotype, as a character representative of a whole gender. This is the context in which I would place the criticism to Rushdie's alleged misogyny. The fact that this interpretation of Padma's figure may radically contrast with the one illustrated at the beginning of this paper should not surprise us too much, because they pertain to two different registers of discourse. Apart from evaluating such contradictions within the set of norms generally accepted by the postmodern cliché, I am much inclined to view paradoxical ideological ambiguity as a trademark of Rushdie's writing.

An analysis of Padma's role in terms of narratological discourse is not likely to lead us towards a more straightforward result. This is doubtless one of the fields in which Rushdie revealed himself as a master of shuffling cards. Other scholars have treated the subject with significant insight and I cannot hope to solve the matter briefly. I will just point at some strategies enabling Rushdie to create such an anarchic construction.

To begin with, the evident dichotomy between the implied orality of Saleem's speech and his being at at his table writing his tales, a strategy perceptively discussed by Brennan as "written orality" (Brennan, 139), consequently introduces the first ambiguity of role for Padma. Is she a listener or a reader? Apparently, she must paradoxically cover both the functions at the same time, implying in such a contradiction in terms also that she is a "primitively illiterate"[13] "reader's surrogate."[14] We may then explain the strident haziness about her role in two different ways: firstly, since Rushdie imagines a reader completely different from her, Padma's function as a narratee is simply allegorical, as Wilson argues (Fletcher, 65-66). Secondly, her role is limited to that of the listener only in that the implied reader is a figure different from her. Saleem's narration, in fact, is not necessarily directed at her only, but to a (much) more educated kind of readership, if not to other subjects still.[15]

Padma, in addition, is strategical to Rushdie's deconstruction of a narration responding to a set of pre-established norms. Once more, contradiction is the privileged medium of resistance to conventional narration. Padma's widely acknowledged passivity as a traditional Indian wife turns out to be extremely productive to the text, in that her presence is essential to the economy of the novel. The reader is explicitly made aware that Saleem has only a short-lived independence in the brief interval when she is missing. Various theories credit her with different strategical roles which are always of primary importance and, significantly, at odds with her status of an illiterate: Batty maintains that "Padma's role as Saleem's 'necessary ear' (149) should not obscure her status as co-creator of the narrative,"[16] Cundy affirms that "Padma is a vital spur and judge of Saleem's autobiography,"[17] while Brennan argues that "Padma is not only a passive receptor, or disembodied voice of the national conscience, but a literary *critic*." (Brennan, 101) However we choose to classify her, her identity is almost to be defined in terms of opposition to Saleem's.

A variety of different interpretations have divided critics on Padma's alleged identifications within the Hindu pantheon, too. Whereas Saleem is quite clearly associated with the figure of Ganesha for a number of reasons, Padma's reference to the Hindu mythology seems more flexible. Her traditional role of patient Indian wife, "just one step behind her husband," would indicate in Sita a possible prototype for her character: this parallel would then probably apply to those engaged in gender criticism, being the figure of Sita among the privileged banners for women emancipation in India today. Significantly, Uma Parameswaran, who is more inclined to favour her prevailing identity on Saleem, prefers to associate her to Durga, the archetypal Mother Earth. Goonetilleke, on the other hand, considers Padma a sort of Saleem's Muse and he equates her to Saraswati, the goddess of creative arts (Goonetilleke, 41). The mythical association of Padma with a deity, anyway, is much more the effect of Saleem's jokes with the significance of her name: "her mother told her, when she was only small, that she had been named after the lotus goddess, whose most common appellation amongst village folk is 'The One Who Possesses Dung.'" (24)

The Lotus-Goddess in Hindu mythology is Lakshmi,[18] the goddess of Beauty and the equivalent of Aphrodites in Greek mythology. She is commonly associated with desire and fertility, attributes which Rushdie would deform into a grotesque. In addition, Lakshmi's notorious appellative of Shri suggests general well-being, material prosperity and ruling majesty, all features which are completely reversed in Padma. This may further prove how pertinent is Brennan's Marxist interpretation of the character.

Since *Midnight's Children* is a novel which constantly implies cross-references with other literary texts, we may evaluate Padma's allusions in that perspective, too. Fortunately, the possible parallels to similar characters in other novels drastically limit the wide range of connections to other literary works originally entailed by *Midnight's Children*. Significantly, there seems to be no association with the traditional Sanskrit epics—at least with the most important ones—although the practice of oral story-telling is quite common in that context. Alter convincingly stresses that "Saleem's Padma plays a role analogous to Tristram's Jenny, though she is more a dramatised naive reader of the narrative than is Jenny."[19] A proclivity for triviality and gossip, as well as the narrator's titanic amount of self-centredness, in fact, assert undeniable links with Sterne's masterpiece. Merivale, on the other hand, analyses *Midnight's Children* in reference with Grass's *The Tin Drum* and she draws a parallel between Bruno and Padma, establishing a correspondence on the narratological ground: "Saleem and Oskar are writing, telling, or reading out their stories with a frame narrative, to a clearly delineated listener, a "narratee," who is a stand-in for the implied reader and a perpetual reminder of the present tense of narrating time. Bruno [. . .] and Padma [. . .] are both permitted to interrupt and even to contribute short sections of their own."[20]

Last but not the least, a psychological analysis may reveal further interesting aspects of Padma's character. Contrary to what her traditional role of Indian wife may suggest at first, she is quite unusual if compared to other characters in *Midnight's Children* and not necessarily subject to its internal code. The fragmented experience—Saleem resisting his own fragmentation and the perforated sheet are the most evident metaphors of this process—seems to be one of the constants which regulate the aesthetic principles at the base of *Midnight's Children*'s creative thrust. Significantly, Padma escapes this norm. Similarly, she evades the principle assigning various names to each character as the plot unfolds; in that respect, her identity remains undisturbed by the events. This notwithstanding, as much of the previous discussion has shown, her identity and/or function is to be defined only in strict relationship to that of Saleem. Since she is involved as an opponent/accomplice in all his tasks, she becomes a sort of "alter ego" for him in the whole course of narration. Regardless of the critical perspective employed to analyze her connection with Saleem, it remains indisputable that her relationship with him is founded on a strictly complementary code. Substantially, *Midnight's Children* is the final result of the sum: Saleem + Padma. It is their union, rather than their being associated as different identities, which leads to a fruitful and fertile combination. As also Banerjee appropriately underscores, "together they make history." (25) Considering the vast amount of cross-references to autobiographical elements that spice the pages of *Midnight's Children*,[21] and the discounted association Rushdie/Saleem, one should not be surprised to discover that Padma bares significant symbolical similarities to a real woman, although I would hasten to add that this may hardly be a flattering parallel. After all,

Shandy's "dear, dear Jenny"—one of Padma's prototypes—was the fictional personification of a real maiden, Catherine de Fourmentelle.

As the present study is likely to illustrate, Salman Rushdie elegantly shows a mastery of two different cultural codes and implies the creation of a third cultural pole, eschewing the polarization of the postcolonial era. *Midnight's Children*, as well as the other novels he has written, is therefore an authentic reservoir of intertextual allusions and a rich and complex system of symbologies. This is why, I suppose, it is more fun writing a paper on his fiction than reading his novels.

NOTES

1. W.J. Weatherby, *Salman Rushdie: Sentenced to Death* (New York: Carroll and Graf, 1990), p. 18.
2. Tim Parnell, "Salman Rushdie: from Colonial Politics to Postmodern Poetics," *Writing India 1757-1990*, ed. Bart Moore-Gilbert (Manchester and New York: Manchester University Press, 1996), p. 250.
3. Ashutosh Banerjee, "Narrative Technique in *Midnight's Children*," *The Novels of Salman Rushdie*, ed. G.R. Taneja and R.K. Dhawan (New Delhi: Indian Society for Commonwealth Studies, 1992), p. 25.
4. Salman Rushdie, *Midnight's Children* (1991; London: Vintage, 1995), p. 37.
5. Pier Paolo Piciucco, "Woman in the Fiction of Arun Joshi," *Cross-Cultural Voices*, ed. Claudio Gorlier and Isabella Maria Zoppi (Roma: Bulzoni, 1997); "Femininity in the Fiction of R.K. Narayan: A Study," *Indian Writings in English*, ed. Manmohan K. Bhatnagar and M. Rajeshwar (Delhi: Atlantic, 2000), for instance.
6. See Sigmund Freud, *Freud Library 14: Art and Literature* (London: Penguin, 1990).
7. See for instance: Wendy B. Fabris, "Sheherezade's Children: Magical Realism and Postcolonial Fiction," *Magical Realism: Theory, History, Community*, ed. Zamora and Fabris (Durham and London: Duke University Press, 1995).
8. Linda Hutcheon, *A Poetics of Postmodernism* (London and New York: Routledge, 1988), p. 162.

9. Aijaz Ahmed, *In Theory. Classes, Nations, Literatures* (London and New York: Verso, 1992), p. 151.
10. D.C.R.A. Goonetilleke, *Salman Rushdie* (New York: St. Martin's Press, 1998), p. 19.
11. Timothy Brennan, *Salman Rushdie and the Third World* (London: Macmillan, 1989), p. 100. See also Charu Verma, "Padma's Tragedy: a Feminist Deconstruction of Rushdie's *Midnight's Children*," *Feminism and Recent Fiction in English*, ed. Sushila Singh (New Delhi: Prestige, 1991), p. 154.
12. Uma Parameswaran, *The Perforated Sheet. Essays on Salman Rushdie's Art* (Delhi: Affiliated East-West, 1988), p. 20.
13. Harish Trivedi, "Salman the Funtoosh: Magic Bilingualism in *Midnight's Children*," *Rushdie's Midnight's Children: A Book of Readings*, ed. Meenakshi Mukherjee (New Delhi: Pencraft, 1999), p. 82.
14. Keith Wilson, "*Midnight's Children* and Reader Responsibility" in *Reading Rushdie: Perspectives on the Fiction of Salman Rushdie*, ed. M.D. Fletcher (Amsterdam-Atlanta: Rodopi, 1994), p. 64
15. To the Midnight's Children at p. 480, for instance.
16. Nancy Batty, "The Art of Suspense: Rushdie 1001 (Mid-)Nights," in Meenakshi Mukherjee, p. 100.
17. Catherine Cundy, *Salman Rushdie* (Manchester and New York: Manchester University Press, 1996), p. 30.
18. See David Kinsley, *Hindu Goddesses: Visions of the Divine Feminine in the Hindu Religious Tradition* (Delhi: Motilal Banarsidass, 1987), pp. 19-29.
19. Robert Alter, "*Midnight's Children* and *Tristram Shandy*," in Meenakshi Mukherjee, p. 113.
20. Patricia Merivale, "Saleem Fathered by Oskar: Intertextual Strategies in *Midnight's Children* and *The Tin Drum*," in Meenakshi Mukherjee, p. 124.
21. See Goonetilleke, pp. 1-5.

'Chutnification': The Dynamics of Language in *Midnight's Children*

SISIR KUMAR CHATTERJEE
Hooghly Mohsin College, Hooghly

This article examines the extent to which Rushdie succeeds in abrogating the 'classical' English and linguistically dragging the peripheral to the central. It also explores the strengths and weaknesses of Rushdie's innovativeness in the use of language in Midnight's Children *and points out the relevance of his inventiveness to the novel's postcolonial and postmodernist perspectives.*

Editor

Ever since it was declared the 'Booker of Bookers' (i.e., the best book in 25 years of Booker history) in 1993, Rushdie's *Midnight's Children* has been at the centre of critical attention. Critics have focussed their interest on various aspects of Rushdie's art in the novel. Ashutosh Banerjee, for example, has dealt with the narrative technique employed in the book; Ron Shepherd and M.L. Pandit have discussed the novelist's use of fantasy in the work; Tariq Rahman has written on the treatment of politics in it; R.S. Pathak explores Rushdie's delineation of the relation between history and the individual in the novel. Neil Ten Kortenaar discusses *Midnight's Children* as an allegory of history. Goonetilleke takes up the subject of Rushdie's use of myth in the novel. Many critics have also paid attention to Rushdie's intertextual strategies in the work. Nancy E. Batty, for instance, brings out the novel's affinities with the *Tales of Arabian Nights,* while Robert Alter has done a comparative study between *Midnight's Children* and Sterne's *Tristram Shandy*. What, however, has not as yet received adequate critical attention is Rushdie's use of language in *Midnight's Children*. This article attempts to address the issue of the dynamics of Rushdie's language in the novel on the assumptions that first, what contributes, perhaps more than anything else, to the popularity, controversiality and complexity of the work is its language and, more importantly, all the important shades of the novel's perspective—which is evidently postcolonial and postmodernist—can be profitably searched for in the novelist's use of language which, it should be made clear right at the outset, is here understood as a narratorial/strategic complex that subsumes much more than what is ostensible, i.e., mere vocabulary and syntax.

In a sense, the history of Indian fiction in English is a history of the evolution of the English language used by novelists, and *Midnight's Children* is a prominent milestone in this respect. The grandmasters in the field—R.K. Narayan, Raja Rao and Mulk Raj Anand—wrote their novels in what was essentially chaste or pure English which is another name for imperial English, the English of the 'centre.' Even those who succeeded the great maestros—e.g., Anita Desai and Arun Joshi—did not show any fundamental departure from the basic principles that constitute the chastity of British English. As a consequence, there was a wide disparity between the novelist's subject and his/her medium of writing, the subject being *Indian* society and the language being English. The end result of this was that the Indian novel in English, unlike that in the Indian regional languages, only too often seemed to be a coterie-confined literary entity, studied principally by the academics of English departments and read by very few, either in India or abroad, for entertainment. There then emerged in the arena of Indian fiction in English, a group of young novelists—most of them born around 1947—who appeared to feel for the first time that it is important to indigenize the medium of writing, to project a comprehensive vision of the highly complex, multilingual and multicultural society that India is. The novelist to leave the most significant and revolutionary contribution in Indian fiction in English in this respect is Salman Rushdie who has written his novels in a language that deserves more probing critical attention than it has so far received. This article, however, will remain confined to the functionality of Rushdie's language in *Midnight's Children* only.

Rushdie believes that if he has to convey his vision of Indian culture in an original way with English as his medium of writing, he has "to break up the language and put it back together in a different way . . . to destroy the natural rhythms of the English language . . . [and] to dislocate the English and let other things into it." (Goonetilleke, 43) Rushdie does not find the task of dislocating the English language much of a problem. In an interview, he explicitly states: "The English language is, I think, less of a problem than people make it out to be." He mildly accuses the 'earlier generation of writers' "who were basically just about adult at the time of Independence, who were very heavily influenced by the English, the classical English, writing." He contends that "that was their formation, and I think that their instinct was to write in that way. But I think also," he maintains, "that by now English is very domesticated in India." Rushdie desires "that Indian writers will become much freer with the English language . . . use it more and more . . . unproblematically and without that kind of echo of the colony . . . [and] use it with more verve, more confidence, more ease, and with more Indianness." (Vijay Kumar, 223) And *Midnight's Children* best illustrates Rushdie's strategy or method of Indianising, revitalising and decolonising the English language.

Rushdie's defiance of the "classical," which for him means "colonial," English is manifest at the lexical level in the following features:

1. He inserts a considerable number of Hindi, Urdu and Hindustani lexical items into his English, e.g. 'ekdum,' 'angrez,' 'phut-a phut,' 'nasbandi, 'dhoban,' 'feringhee,' 'baba,' 'garam masala,' 'rakshasas,' 'fauj,' 'badmaas,' 'jailkhana,' 'baap-re-baap,' 'hai hai,' 'sab kuch,' 'bas,' 'chi-chi,' 'yaar,' 'gora,' 'pyar kiya to darna kiya,' 'goondas' 'hubshee,' 'ooper neechay,' 'sarpanch,' 'kahin,' 'bhai-bhai,' 'it,' 'zenana,' 'buddha,' 'crorepatis,' 'ayah,' 'nimbu-pani,'

'paan,' 'khichri,' 'chutney,' 'gur,' 'rasgullas,' 'gulabjamuns,' 'jalebis,' 'barfi,' 'bhel-puri' etc.

2. Rushdie's language at the lexical level is marked by the sudden intrusions of esoteric Latin and classical Arabic, e.g. 'mucuna pruritis,' 'feronia elephanticus,' 'sunt lacrimae rerum,' 'kan ma kan,' 'fi qadim azzaman,' 'tilk al-gharaniq al, ula wa inna shafä ata-hunna la-turtaja,' etc.
3. Rushdie presses a bunch of English words belonging to a particular grammatical category occur together without either punctuating or conjugating them so that they form a simulacrum of complex compounds. There are such compounds of nouns (e.g., 'murder rape greed war,' 'animals peasants brutes,' 'mother sister lover sibyl friend,' etc.); of verbs (e.g., 'yelling jabbering arguing giggling,' 'chased arrested dragged,' 'kick stamp trample,' etc.); of Noun Phrases having adjectives or classifiers (e.g., 'rotting coconuts abandoned cigarette packets pony turds non-degradable bottles fruit peelings jellyfish'). In all these compounds the items all belong to a related set.
4. Phrases are made to frequently run together (e.g., 'overandover,' 'updownup,' 'downdowndown,' 'suchandsuch,' 'noseholes,' 'birthanddeath,' 'whatdoyoumeanhowcanyousaythat,' 'getoutofitsillyoldmooitsthesoddingbeach,' 'blackasnight,' 'nearlynine,' 'nearlynineyearold,' 'almostseven,' 'godknowswhat,' 'dirtyfilthy,'etc.
5. Rushdie generates the effect of onomatopoeia with sounds typically Indian (e.g. 'wham bamshot,' 'doomboombadoom,' 'Thaii! Thaiii!,' 'khrikk-khrikk,' 'dharrraaammm,'etc.
6. Rushdie demolishes the notion of the purity or centrality of English, (i) by inventing new forms of existing English words as well as of Indian lexical items through audaciously creative hybridization (e.g., 'mediocrely,' 'dislikeable,' 'alienness,' 'writery,' 'doctori,' 'suicidally,' 'unbeautiful,' 'sonship,' 'memoryless,' 'historyless,' 'dupatta-less,' 'Bombayness,' 'chutnification,' etc.); (ii) by accommodating outrageously clipped sentences that are made to function as classifiers (e.g., 'long-ago-letter,' 'once-upon-a time wife,'

'long-ago desire,' 'by-now-constant itch,' 'film-poster-trolley pushers,' 'long-time-no-see-smile,'etc.); (iii) by transforming clipped sentences into nouns (e.g., 'excuse-mes,' 'next-attractions,' 'coming-soons,' 'what-happened-nextism,' etc.); (iv) by forging new compound words through the remoulding of English phrasal verbs (e.g., 'a looker-after'); (v) by reshaping English idioms (e.g., 'to put the cart before the bullock'); (vi) by transplanting Indian concepts into equivalent English expressions (e.g., 'our little piece-of-the-moon,' 'four hundred and twenty, the number of trickery and fraud,' 'whatnextism,' etc.); (vii) by including Indian slang words (e.g., 'funtoosh,' 'goo,' etc.); (viii) by creating new slang words (e.g., 'other pencil' for male sex organ as in Padma's words to Saleem Sinai: "Now that the writery is done, let's see if we can make your other pencil work!" (39) or 'cucumber' to refer to the same object as in the phrase "the useless cucumber hidden in my pants" (141), or 'soo-soos' as in "now I saw him and Cyrus behind a bush, doing such funny rubbing things with their soo-soos!" (18), or 'spittoon' to refer to the female sex organ as in Saleem's candid admission: "despite everything she tries, I cannot hit her spittoon" (39); (ix) by incorporating mis-spellings (e.g., ' straaange,' 'hopeyu guessma nayym,' 'unquestionabel,' 'existance,' 'ees,' etc.); (x) by making room for those Indian forms of English words which are traditionally looked upon as incorrect (e.g., 'informations,' 'mens,' 'lifeliness,' etc.); (xi) by encompassing habitual linguistic mannerisms that distinguish characters (e.g., the Reverend Mother's use of the expression 'whatsitsname'), or even their stammers (e.g., 'rah rah wrong,' 'hiss hiss history,' 'caw corpses,' 'ist ist is-tiff,' etc.) and (xii) by using nonsense back-up words which is a typically Indian language habit (e.g., 'writing-shiting,' 'writery-shitery,' 'club-shub,' joke-shoke,' 'pumpery-shumpery,' etc.).

No critic should be so naïve as to misconstrue all this as mere gimmick(ry). It is part of a deliberate anti-colonial strategy. By using language "unproblematically," Rushdie on the one hand enhances the process of abrogating and re-placing the English language and on the other hand forges a multilingual medium to capture the 'polyglossic'[1] and multicultural reality of India. Since language is a primary titan of defining the self, Rushdie, as an avowedly anti-colonial writer, seizes the language of the centre and replaces it in a discourse fully adapted to the cultural ambience of India. By re-moulding the colonial English to new, inventive, need-based usages, he gives a jolt to the notion of the illusory standard of normative or 'correct' usage. He forces the language of the centre to bear the burden of communicating the cultural experience of the periphery. It is, as Raja Rao puts it in *Kanthapura,* to 'convey in a language that is not one's own the spirit that is one's own." (EWB, 39) By conveying the syncretic and hybridized nature of his postcolonial experience, Rushdie thus refutes the privileged position of a standard code in the English language and any monocentric view of human experience. So, Rushdie's re-lexification of the English language through his innovative, imaginative use of it is a step in the process of the dismantling of the imperialist centralism as established through the privileged centrality of the English language. Thus viewed, *Midnight's Children* may be regarded as a paradigmatic demonstration of the abrogating and appropriating impetus of a postcolonial writer—his attempt at promoting the peripheral to the status of privileged centrality.

Thematically, besides reflecting an 'inclusive' mode of writing of the novelist, this re-orientation of language not only enables the novelist to perceive and communicate his experience of a hybridized and complex cultural reality but also to lend it an impact of immediacy, to help capture the natural rhythms of Indian speech habits and of the basic tenor of sub-continental life manifest in its bewildering multiplicity and its non-exclusive cultural modality. This "chutnification" of language shows how Rushdie is concerned with depicting his experience with utmost honesty, exploiting all the resources he can wield. When, for example, Padma admonishes Saleem for his 'writery-shitery' and urges him to be attentive to more basic activities by saying "eat na, food is spoiling" or when the boy Saleem goes spying on his mother to a "real rutputty joint" which advertises its "Lovely Lassi, Funtabulous Falooda and Bhelpuri Bombay Fashion," Rushdie is attempting to deploy all the linguistic resources available to him for evoking the plurality of urban India for which no single language is adequate. The very texture of life in the Indian sub-continent, particularly in the urban areas, is multilingual. The young generation who speak English as a second language or a surrogate first language very often mix it up with the vocabulary items taken from many other Indian languages, particularly Hindi, Urdu and the speaker's mother tongue. In other words, they treat English as an everyday peer-group language and therefore use it in creative, though playful and impure, ways. They do it constantly in college campuses, coffeehouses, playgrounds and other places where they meet. Rushdie weaves this multilingual warp and woof of life in India into his concern in *Midnight's Children* and negotiates it at different levels—ranging from Naseem Aziz's resistance ("If God meant people to speak many tongues . . . why did he put only one in our heads?" [48]) to the Pakistani soldiers' incomprehension of the Mukti Bahini's song "Amar Sonar Bangla" which "protected [them] from the insidious subversion of the lyric, although their feet did inadvertently tap to the tune." (424)

Interestingly enough, much more polyglossic than Rushdie's language in the rest of the novel is Saleem's treatment of the midnight's children themselves:

> The voices babbled in everything from Malayalam to Naga dialects, from the purity of Lucknow Urdu to the Southern slurrings of Tamil. I understood only a fraction of the things being said within the walls of my skull. Only later, when I began to probe, did I learn that below the surface transmissions, language faded away, and was replaced by universally intelligible thought-forms which far transcended words. (200)

Here language, as Meenakshi Mukherjee rightly observes, "may be seen as a metaphor for the rich profusion of India's multiple culture which is more an asset than a problem except when state policy decides to demarcate the differences." (19) In the text

Rushdie mentions the redrawing of India's map in 1956 in which the boundaries of states "were not formed by rivers, or mountains, or any natural features of the terrain, they were instead walls of words. Language divided us." (225) Judged from this point of view, Rushdie's multilingual medium in the novel may be considered a plea for resisting the artificial divisions or partitions of Indian democracy and for embracing fluidity and multiplicity, which is the ultimate reality about India.

However, Rushdie's vocabulary in *Midnight's Children* is not as strong and strategically flawless as the above discussion may tend to suggest. While he uses the technique of "selective lexical fidelity" (Ashcroft 64) which is evident in his daring to leave some Hindi, Urdu and Hindustani words unglossed in the text, he cannot consistently maintain this position. There are many words and expressions taken from Indian languages "dugdugee-drum," "dia-lamp," "hey phaelwan, hey little wrestler," "Hey, bahenchud! Hey, little sister-sleeper," "chand-ka-tukra, . . affectionate piece-of-the-moon," "formality—takalluf," "Jehad, Padma! Holy war!," "chhi-chhi! Filthy," "Ravana, the ten-headed monster," "Rama, the hero of the Ramayana," "the Devil, the Great Beast, Shaitan himself,' "pagal-zagal, crazy Zagallo," "chamcha (literally a spoon, but idiomatically a flatterer)," etc. Rushdie himself once remarked: "to do footnotes or to do notes at the end was a kind of defeat. The story has to tell itself, it mustn't rely on explanations. If it needs footnotes, it's a failure." (Vijay Kumar 217) It is true that in *Midnight's Children* Rushdie has not used 'footnotes' or 'endnotes' as such. But the purpose of 'footnotes' is served by his parenthetic explications which foreground the continual reality of cultural distance. In fact, these authorial intrusions betray a two-fold weakness: first, they helplessly accord a superior status to the translated words, and therefore to the language translated into, over the original ones; and secondly, they expose the writer's failure to completely trust the native words as having power enough to bear the burden of effectively conveying experience. It is this tacit acknowledgement of the unreliability of words and expressions borrowed from marginal (Indian) languages which frequently leads the writer to explicate Indian concepts. This vulnerability in Rushdie's strategy of making his writing multilingual, thus, reflects his unconscious admission of and surrender to the sense of the superiority of the language of the masters. One wonders whether it does not tend to make his language more neo-colonial than anti-colonial.

This impression gains further ground when one comes to Rushdie's syntax in *Midnight's Children.* Rushdie's operation at the level of syntax is far less audacious and militant than it is at the lexical level. It is to be admitted that he does show a distinctive inventiveness and boldness in (i) the use of punctuations (particularly dots, hyphens, exclamatory signs and interrogative marks); (ii) effecting sudden changes of person (as in "Saleem Sinai came to terms with himself. I will not say he was not sad; refusing to censor my past" (378); or in "After this, the boy soldiers waited for the man-dog to die; but I was stronger than the snake-poison" (436); (iii) executing abrupt changes of tense within a single verbal group (e.g., "I cannot will not say how," "night is falling has fallen," "we were are shall be the gods you never had" etc.); (iv) making four or five sentences run together without separating them by stops or other punctuation marks as in "No colours except green and black the walls are green the sky is black (there is no roof) the stars are green the Widow is green but her hair is black as black" (249); (v) abrupt switching from reported to direct speech or vice versa, at times doing away with the grammatical means that distinguish one from the other as the following passage illustrates:

> that's my father thinking, MY FATHER, now he's looking at me all funny What's the matter son don't you feel well Yes fine Abba fine, must go now GOT TO GET AWAY homework to do, Abba, and out, run away before he sees the clue on your face (my father always said that when I was lying there was a red light flashing on my forehead). . . . He's butting into my thoughts, hey phaelwan, hey little wrestler, what's dragging your face down, it looks longer than a bad movie, you want channa? Pakoras? what? And me shaking my head, No, nothing, Hanif mamu, so that he relaxes,

> turns away, starts yelling Ohe come on Dara, that's the ticket, give him hell, Dara *yara!* (202-3)

But these have hardly anything to do with the strategy of de-colonising English language. The English stream-of-consciousness novelists, particularly Joyce and Woolf, for example, very often resorted to syntactic experimentation of this type. Indeed, Rushdie hardly effects any significant departure or deviation from the fundamental syntactic principles of British English. And since syntax is the more elemental level of a language than lexis, Rushdie cannot be said to have achieved any remarkable feat of re-placing the English language in *Midnight's_Children.* Since the basic Subject-Verb-Object/Complement syntactic pattern of British English is followed more or less uniformly throughout the novel, Rushdie's language here, all said and done, remains fundamentally classical English. The only typically Indian syntactic features that may be said to have been exploited by the novelist in the text are the plethora of relative clauses heaped upon one another and the frequent breakings off in the middle of sentences. While the former feature is related to the writer's narrational strategy of recapitulating all that was related earlier, the latter feature is exploited to create an atmosphere of gossip and fun in the telling of the tale. But, the very fact that a writer who is so blatantly defiant in his use of language at the lexical level is so disappointingly tame in his handling of syntax points to the elemental unalterability of English, or, for that matter, any language in the world. Ironically, even at the level of lexis whatever indigenisation a postcolonial writer encodes in his writing can be decoded by a native English speaker only after he/she translates the experimented items into the equivalents of his/her language. For instance, Rushdie may deliberately misspell the word 'listen' as 'lissen,' but a British reader will not understand the word before translating it back into 'listen.' This applies equally invariably to all other lexical innovations. This unavoidable reality of the process of the human act of decoding language in fact tends to thwart the very purpose behind a postcolonial writer's effort at de-colonising a language. The greatest irony underlying the situation is that the extent of Rushdie's success in abrogating British English—his dragging of the marginal to the central—has to be examined in an English which is more or less classical and pure.

This is not to argue that Rushdie's language in *Midnight's Children* lacks in functionality. On the contrary, it operates with its own aesthetic dynamics which assumes a richly complex edge within the narratorial framework of the novel. A few examples should be enough to establish the point. Rushdie's language at the very opening of the novel functions in a self-expository manner, serving as a brilliant introduction to the work and indicating the novelist's thematic and technical preoccupations:

> I was born in the city of Bombay . . . once upon a time. No, that won't do, there's no getting away from the date; I was born in Doctor Narlikar's Nursing Home on August 15th, 1947. And the time? The time matters, too. Well then: at night. No, it's important to be more. . . . On the stroke of midnight, as a matter of fact. Clock-hands joined palms in respectful greeting as I came. Oh, spell it out, spell it out: at the precise instant of India's arrival at independence, I tumbled forth into the world. There were gasps. And, outside the window, fireworks and crowds. A few seconds later, my father broke his big toe; but his accident was a mere trifle when set beside what had befallen me in that benighted moment, because thanks to the occult tyrannies of those blandly saluting clocks I had been mysteriously handcuffed to history, my destinies indissolubly chained to those of my country. (3)

The novel, in other words, begins in an autobiographical vein ("I was born in the city of Bombay"). This is followed by the phraseology of a fairy tale ("once upon a time," an expression that occurs repeatedly in the novel and assumes the proportion and takes on the effect of a leitmotif), suggesting the mode of fantasy. But this is rejected in favour of a recording of an actual historical year, date, and time, suggesting the novelist's sense of responsibility to history. The insertion of the image of "clock-hands joining palms" brings out Rushdie's brilliant metaphoric imagination and thinly veils his vulnerability to the thought of partition. His father breaking "his big toe" right at the hour of

Saleem's birth and India's attaining independence (which obviously means the birth of a nation too) foreshadows how cataclysmic the two births are going to prove. The phrases "handcuffed to history" and "my destinies indissolubly chained to those of my country" reveal the basic narrative strategy the writer is going to adopt in the novel: the synchronization of the history of an individual with that of a nation. And it is significant that the language of this passage is repeated, almost verbatim, in the passage later in the book where Saleem's description of his son's birth duplicates his description of his own:

> He was born in Old Delhi . . . once upon a time. No, that won't do, there's no getting away from the date: Aadam Sinai arrived at a night-shadowed slum on June 25th, 1975. And the time? The time matters, too. As I said: at night. No, it's important to be more. . . . On the stroke of midnight, as a matter of fact. Clock-hands joined palms. Oh, spell it out, spell it out: at the precise instant of India's arrival at Emergency, he emerged. There were gasps; and, across the country, silences and fears. And owing to the occult tyrannies of that benighted hour, he was mysteriously handcuffed to history, his destinies indissolubly chained to those of his country. (500)

In fact, repetition is an unmistakable feature of Rushdie's language in *Midnight's Children*. Certain words keep on recurring throughout the novel (e.g., 'recurrence,' 'form,' 'shape,' 'fragments,' 'broken,' 'cracks,' 'pieces,' 'centre-parting,' 'spittoon,' black,' 'white,' optimism,' 'nose,' 'knees,' 'snake,' 'ladder,' 'chutney,' etc.), and sometimes even a whole sentence is repeated (e.g., "What can't be cured must be endured," "there is no escape from form/recurrence," etc.). These recurrent words, phrases and sentences are viscerally related to the novel's theme and technique. For example, 'spittoon' functions in the book as a receptacle of memory which holds variegated events together. 'Chutney' with its primary association with Mary Pereira seems to form the novel's thematic axis since it is her change of birth-tag which is at the centre of all that happens in the book. Also, if 'black' and 'snake' conjure up images of evil, 'white' and 'ladder' provide a potent antithesis to these by implying good; and, taken together they figure the inclusiveness which characterises the basic tenor of Indian philosophy. Again, 'centre-parting,' 'cracks,' 'fragments,' 'pieces,' 'broken'—all these form the bulk of the vocabulary descriptive of partition which is one of the major thematic concerns of the work. In sharp contrast to this group of words, however, there is another group consisting of such words as 'form,' 'shape,' and 'recurrence' which convey the idea of an attempt to define a symmetry amidst the formlessness and fragmentation all around. Indeed, the historical forces or political events as depicted in the novel—from India's partition to Indira Gandhi's proclamation of the Emergency—as well as the different layers of the story told in it all exude a sense of disintegration, of centrifugality. Yet, throughout the novel the narrator strives to impose on these disintegrating phenomena a pattern of centripetality by using various devices, the most effectively functional of which is the recurrent iteration of certain key words, phrases, expressions and sentences which are thus made to form a complex pattern of leitmotifs that really hold the novel together. The recursive property of Rushdie's language in *Midnight's Children*, thus, may be said to be an expression of (to use Rushdie's own words in the novel) "a sort of national longing for form—or perhaps simply an expression of our deep belief that forms lie hidden within reality; that meaning reveals itself only in flashes." (359)

Finally, the very texture of Rushdie's language in *Midnight's Children* shows an amalgamation, or, to use Rushdie's own neologism, 'chutnification' of various narrational registers which are happily assimilated. For instance, the book embodies spiralling, involved, epic interrogatives as evident in the following passage:

> What weight, falling, created such an almighty crash? Whose hand wrenched a door open; in whose heel are visible two red, flowing holes, filled with a venom for which there is no known antivenene, a poison which has killed stablefuls of worn-out horses? Whose body is carried out of the tower by plain-clothes men. . . ? Why, when the moonlight falls upon the dead face, does Mary Pereira fall like a sack of potatoes to the floor, eyes rolling upwards in

> their sockets, in a sudden and dramatic faint? . . . Why are there so many bottles with rags stuffed into their necks? (174)

If the use of these interrogatives shows Rushdie's adherence to the tradition of the comic epic, Rushdie's work also encompasses filmy language as the following instances reveal: 'zooming out slowly into long-shot. . . . Merrily it rolls along, rolls along, rolls along. . . . (Fade-out)" (283), or "I permit myself to insert a Bombay-talkie-style close-up—a calendar ruffled by a breeze, its pages flying off in rapid succession to denote the passing of the years; I superimpose turbulent long-shots of street riots, medium shots of burning buses," (414) or perhaps most effectively:

> Close-up of my grandfather's right hand: nails knuckles fingers all somehow bigger than you'd expect. Clumps of red hair on the outside edges. Thumb and forefinger pressed together, separated only by a thickness of paper. In short: my grandfather was holding a pamphlet. It had been inserted into his hand (we cut to a long-shot—nobody from Bombay should be without a basic film vocabulary) as he entered the hotel foyer. (31)

This use of film language shows up Rushdie's absorption of popular/mass culture. Correspondingly, the novel is also marked by frequent use of verbal fantasy. For instance, Boatman Tai is described as "a watery Caliban"; Naseem Aziz could even dream her daughters' dreams, just to know what they were getting up to. But the most remarkable illustration of Rushdie's use of verbal fantasy can be found in the passage describing Dr. Aziz's nose:

> My grandfather's nose: nostrils flaring, curvaceous as dancers. Between them swells the nose's triumphal arch, first up and out, then down and under, sweeping in to his upper lip with a superb and at present red-tipped flick. An easy nose to hit a tussock with. I wish to place on record my gratitude to this mighty organ—if not for it, who would ever have believed me to be truly my mother's son, my grandfather's grandson?—this colossal apparatus which was to be my birthright, too. Doctor Aziz's nose—comparable only to the trunk of the elephant-headed god Ganesh—established incontrovertibly his right to be a patriarch. It was Tai who taught him that, too. When young Aadam was barely past puberty the di-

> lapidated boatman said, "That's a nose to start a family on, my princeling. There'd be no mistaking whose brood they were. Mughal Emperors would have given their right hands for noses like that one. There are dynasties waiting inside it,"—and here Tai lapsed into coarseness—"like snot." (8)

This kind of language testifies to the fervour of Rushdie's imaginative vivre and his creative mode of the fantastification of reality. It is also noticeable that at other places too, Rushdie's language in *Midnight's Children* evinces a distinct journalistic flavour as in the following passage:

> It is a matter of record that the States Reorganization Committee had submitted its report to Mr. Nehru as long ago as October 1955; a year later, its recommendations had been implemented. India had been divided anew, into fourteen states and six centrally-administered "territories." . . . Kerala was for speakers of Malayalam, the only palindromically-named tongue on earth; in Karnataka you were supposed to speak Kanarese; and the amputated state of Madras—known today as Tamil Nadu—enclosed the *aficionados* of Tamil. Owing to some oversight, however, nothing was done with the state of Bombay; and in the city of Mumbadevi, the language marches grew longer and noisier and finally metamorphosed into political parties, the Samyukta Maharashtra Samiti ("United Maharashtra Party") which stood for the Marathi language and demanded the creation of the Deccan state of Maharashtra, and the Maha Gujarat Parishad ("Great Gujarat Party") which marched beneath the banner of the Gujarati language and dreamed of a state to the north of Bombay City, stretching all the way to the Kathiawar peninsula and the Rann of Kutch. (225-26)

This language points to the writer's insistent fidelity to history and relates his work to the postmodernist form of the Non-fiction novel. Finally, *Midnight's Children* also incorporates a considerable amount of analytical and critical idiom which can be traced in the use of certain words, phrases and expressions scattered throughout the novel (e.g., "the feasibility of the chutnification of history," (548) "synchronistic birth," "a countdown for building suspense," etc.). But this is best illustrated in the following passages:

> Reality is a question of perspective; the further you get from the past, the more concrete and plausible it seems—but as you approach the present, it inevitably seems more and more incredible." (197)

> How, in what terms, may the career of a single individual be said to impinge on the fate of a nation? I must answer in adverbs and hyphens: I was linked to history both literally and metaphorically, both actively and passively, in what our (admirably modern) scientists might term "modes of connection" composed of "dualistically-combined configurations" of the two pairs of opposed adverbs given above. This is why hyphens are necessary: actively-literally, passively-metaphorically, actively-metaphorically and passively-literally, I was inextricably entwined with my world. (285-86)

If this is a type of language that uses a typically critical idiom, it also displays a fundamental self-reflexive, even self-parodying quality. In other words, Rushdie's critical-analytical phraseology serves as a vehicle of a self-conscious, self-reflexive. metafictional method of writing. And ultimately, it is these multidimensional aspects of Rushdie's language in *Midnight's Children* that make the novel a protean and inexhaustibly attractive postmodernist text.

NOTE

1. The authors of *The Empire Writes Back* opine that India is a 'diglossic society.' (39) But, it seems more appropriate to categorize India as a 'polyglossic' society because here a multitude of languages "interweave to form a generally comprehensible linguistic continuum." (39)

Works Cited

Ashcroft, Bill, et al. *The Empire Writes Back: Theory and Practice in Postcolonial Literatures* (1989; London: Routledge, 1993).

Banerjee, Ashutosh. "Narrative Technique in *Midnight's Children*," in *The Novels of Salman Rushdie*, ed. G.R. Taneja and R.K. Dhawan, pp. 23-32.

E. Rege, Josna. "Victim into Protagonist? *Midnight's Children* and the Post-Rushdie National Narratives of the Eighties," in Meenakshi Mukherjee, pp. 182-211.

Goonetilleke, D.C.R.A. *Salman Rushdie* (Macmillan Modern Novelists Series; Houndmills: Macmillan, 1999).

Kortenaar, Neil Ten. "*Midnight's Children* and the Allegory of History," in Meenakshi Mukherjee, pp. 28-48.

Mukherjee, Meenakshi, ed. *Rushdie's Midnight's Children: A Book of Readings* (Delhi: Pencraft International, 1999).

Nair, Rukmini Bhaya. "History as Gossip in *Midnight's Children*," in Meenakshi Mukherjee, pp. 49-68.

Natarajan, Nalini. "Woman, Nation and Narration in *Midnight's Children*," in Meenakshi Mukherjee, pp. 165-81.

Page, Norman, ed. *The Language of Literature* (Casebook Series, Houndmills: Macmillan, 1984).

Pandit, M.L. *New Commonwealth Writing* (New Delhi: Prestige, 1996).

Rushdie, Salman. *Midnight's Children* (New York: Avon, 1982).

Shepherd, Ron. "*Midnight's Children* as Fantasy," in G.R. Taneja and R.K. Dhawan, pp. 33-43.

Taneja, G.R. and R.K. Dhawan, ed. *The Novels of Salman Rushdie* (New Delhi: Indian Society for Commonwealth Studies, 1992).

Vijay Kumar, T. "'Doing the Dangerous Thing': An Interview with Salman Rushdie," in Meenakshi Mukherjee, pp. 212-27.

Postmodernism and *Midnight's Children*

SUBIR DHAR
Rabindra Bharati University

The level of engagement of Midnight's Children *with the tropes of postmodernism has been a major concern of critics. In this article, Subir Dhar matches some distinctive features of the novel with an array of practices which are acknowledged to be postmodern, and contends that Rushdie's novel shares and embodies some fundamental preoccupations of postmodernist discourse.*

Editor

'Postmodernism' is a word that many love to hate, or at least regard with unease and suspicion. Worldwide, the range of critical reaction to this term has extended from caution to unbridled hostility. Hence there have been such reactions as the one that cautions:

> To come to postmodernism is to come to the great Serbonian bog where whole armies have sunk. In the first place the word is semantically anomalous. Then, how can something which is a contemporary phenomenon come *after* the present? To say "I am postmodern would sound like saying "I am dead."[1]

or the one that reacts more unrestrainedly:

> The new illiterate who espouse the postmodern condition are, of course, extraordinarily agile in the composition of the age of decomposition. . . . The paradox here is grounded in their own socio-economic dilemma. As members of a class whose literacy privileges them even more in the stage of late capitalism than it did in the modernist period, they are obliged to catch up with an intensification of sensationalism that has exceeded anything Baudelaire or Benjamin might have imagined. Just as rock musicians drown language in the auto-copulatory gestures performed before bodies without carnal knowledge, so postmodern theorists destroy knowl-

> edge by separating language in gestures that play out sensation without context or sense.[2]

Such attitudes to postmodernism are however symptomatic of more than a simple reactionary instinct to a term that has today invaded a whole army of disciplines in the arts and social sciences—literature and history, political science and philosophy, cultural studies and anthropology, communication theory, sociology, the visual arts, as well as architecture and television. The unease with which many regard postmodernism may indeed be traced to the very indefiniteness of the term, its refusal to remain restricted semantically within the straitjacket of a definitive matrix of meaning or signification. Postmodernism may in fact be used to describe a cultural state, stage or condition, denote the time-frame of an intellectual and cultural epoch that started somewhere in the 50s of the twentieth century, indicate a neo-epistemological trend of enquiry or mode of awareness or thought, or refer to a phase in the development of late capitalism.

However, perhaps the easiest way to look at postmodernism is to see it as an outgrowth of modernism, to note that postmodernism shares certain genetic features with its progenitor while remaining essentially different from what preceded it. By itself modernism as a movement in art and culture is generally recognized as a trend that began as a reaction against realism, the most favoured form of aesthetic expression during the nineteenth century. As Malcolm Bradbury, writing in a popular critical lexicon, has indicated, modernism entails and is expressive of 'the tradition of the new.'

> It is experimental, formally complex, elliptical, contains elements of decreation as well as creation, and tends to associate notions of the artist's freedom from realism, materialism, traditional form and genre, with notions of cultural apocalypse and disaster. Its social content is *avant-garde* or bohemian; hence specialized.[3]

Modernism, in short, set its face against the cultural hegemony of the bourgeois, valorized abstraction and symbolism, rejected the time-hallowed norms of consistency in characterization and linearity and coherence in plotting, and foregrounded artistic technique as an end in itself. Writing about the genre of fiction in what may legitimately be described as a manifesto of the modernist movement, Virginia Woolf thus poured scorn on such premodern novelists like Arnold Bennet (and those of his ilk) who conformed to the norms of realistic representation to the slavish extent of describing characters dressed 'down to the last buttons on their coats in the fashion of the hour,'[4] and refused to think beyond the thraldom of having 'to provide a plot, to provide comedy, tragedy, love interest and an air of probability.' Against such conformists, Woolf cited with approval the practice of such modernists as James Joyce who, 'concerned at all costs to reveal the flickering of that innermost flame which flashes its message through the brain . . . disregard[ed] with complete courage whatever seem[ed] to him adventitious, whether . . . probability, or coherence, or any other of these signposts which for generations have served to support the imaginations of a reader when called upon to imagine what he can neither touch nor see.' (394)

It would not be an exaggeration to say that such concerns and responses brought about wide-ranging transformations in the literary and cultural scene in the early twentieth century. Whether the neoplasticist art works of Piet Mondrian, the poetry of T.S. Eliot, the novels of James Joyce, or even Ludwig Mies van der Rohe's International Style in architecture, modernism bravely set out to ring out the old and the familiar and to replace the known with radically *new* ideas, forms and expressions. Yet it is important to note that entropy was not slow in catching up with modernism. As technological innovations in such diverse fields as warfare and medicine, leisure and personal transport, entertainment and communications began to impinge upon and thus effectively transform the texture of human life on a hitherto unprecedented scale, the erstwhile novelties in the sphere of the arts began to lose the edge of their newness. As Jim Collins has argued, modernism's "need to develop radically new styles that would provide the shock of the new, and thereby transform consciousness, depended on the rejection of the familiar (specifically nineteenth century realism and twentieth-century mass culture). Yet that very rejection led to a semiotic/ideological impasse. The avoidance of the familiar and the celebration of innovation produced bold new forms of personal expression, but these styles failed to be very effective forms of communication. . . . By the 1960s, modernism was thoroughly institutionalized, no longer 'revolutionary' except within the self-enclosed worlds of the art market and academia."[5]

II

Published in 1980, Salman Rushdie's *Midnight's Children* has been widely seen as a paradigmatic postmodern text. One critic has, for instance, described it as 'the quintessential fictional embodiment of the postmodern celebration of de-centring and hybridity. The novel's insistence that realism was no longer an adequate mode for describing today's world in which there [is] no consensus about the nature of reality, also fits in with postmodernist impulses.'[6] However since a great many discussions of postmodernism are more theoretical than applied, and so generative of only a small amount of textual analysis or appreciation, it may be a useful exercise to examine the novel as a sample of postmodernist writing, to match the distinctive features of the text with an array of practices that are acknowledged to be postmodern. At the same time, it is well to keep in mind that in such a strategy there is always the danger of neglecting the simple yet vital truth that postmodernism is as much a matter of technique and its applications as an attitudinal or theoretical orientation. In other words, it is not enough to simply relate a list of itemized features to be found in the text with a skew of technical data, but also to reflect upon such larger dimensions of the postmodern sensibility as attitude, perspective, ideological bias or ground. The former are directed toward and concern the actual working practices of the postmodern artist, while the latter is related to the ontology, the identity and status of the artist as a creator and as a person.

To take the last point first, it is an acknowledged fact that postmodernism effectively debunks the modernist concern in the creation of what is generally called an 'artistic aura.' At its simplest, this entailed a glorification of the author as a genius of sorts and as a creator of a cultural space, alternative to and independent of socio-economic and geo-political 'realities,' an autonomous world of literature that was independent of (though capable of being contingent upon) the material arena. Hence it is that T.S. Eliot could unambiguously declare: "I do not deny that art may be affirmed to serve ends beyond itself; but art is not required to be aware of these ends, and indeed performs its functions, whatever they may be, according to various theories of value, much better by indifference to them."[7]

Hence too can Joyce's prototypal artist Stephen Dedalus beguile himself into thinking that 'The pages of his Horace never felt cold to his touch even when his own fingers were cold,' and finally decide to fly by the nets of 'nationality, language, religion'[8] that had threatened to tie him down to his roots.

It is precisely against one aspect of this valorization of the special identity of the Author-God (to use Barthes' term) that postmodernism reacted. In the new theoretical regime the author has diminished, as Barthes expresses it, 'like a figure at the far end of the literary stage,' preempted from his position at the center stage byte 'Scriptor' who is nothing more than 'a multidimensional space in which a variety of writings, none of them original, blend and clash."[9] As Barthes further persuasively argues, since the Author is dead, "*writing* can no longer designate an operation of recording, notation, representation, 'depiction' (as the Classics would say); rather it designates exactly what linguists, referring to Oxford philosophy, call a performative, a rare verbal form (exclusively given in the first person and in the present tense) in which the enunciation has no other content (contains no other proposition) than the act by which it is uttered.'" (170) This in turn led Barthes to postulate the theory that 'The text is a tissue of quotations drawn from innumerable centers of culture. . . . [T]he writer can only imitate a gesture that is always anterior, never original. His only power is to mix writings, to counter the ones with the others, in such a way as never to rest on any one of them." (170) This logic led Barthes to declare the death of the author and to propose what Donald Pease has explained as 'a new definition of literature: a discursive game always arriving at the limits of its own rule, without any author than the reader . . . who is defined as the effect of the writing game he activates.'[10] The story does not end here, however, for also within the margins of postmodernist thought, Michel Foucault opposed this postulate by arguing that the author could not so simply be written off as so irrelevantly deceased. According to Foucault, "An author's name is not simply an element in a discourse (capable of being either subject or object, of being replaced by a pronoun or the like); it performs a certain role with regard to narrative discourse. . . . The author's name serves to characterize a certain mode of being of discourse: the fact that the discourse has an author's name, that one can say 'this was written by so-and-so' or 'so-and-so is its author,' shows that this discourse is not ordinary everyday speech that comes and goes. . . . The author's name manifests the appearance of a certain discursive set and indicates the status of this discourse within a society and a culture. . . . The author-function is therefore characteristic of the mode of existence, circulation, and functioning of certain discourses within a society.'"[11]

There are two ways in which this stand-off between Barthes and Foucault engages with Rushdie's 'writery-shitery' or compositional strategy in *Midnight's Children.* In the first place, Barthes' postulation of the text as 'a tissue of quotations' signposts us immediately into what Umberto Eco has typified as one of the most fundamental aspects of the postmodern tendency—to that of rearticulation and intertextuality.'[12] Instances of such practice abound in *Midnight's Children*—for instance in the passage at the beginning of the novel where, reflecting upon his mnemonic icon, "a large white bedsheet . . . stained . . . with three drops of old faded redness,' Saleem quips, citing a passage from the Quran: *'As the Quran tells us: Recite, in the name of the Lord, thy Creator, who created Man from clots of blood.'* Or to cite two other examples, note the Hollywoodian intertext in

> Salt water washes the confessional floor . . . and now, is there a new dilemma for the young father? . . . In short, would this bishop-ridden, stomach-churned young father behave like, or unlike,

> Montgomery Clift in *I Confess?* (Watching it some years ago at the New Empire cinema, I couldn't decide).[13]

And the Hindu contexts in

> How are we to understand my too many women? As the multiple faces of Bharat-Mata? Or as even more . . . as the dynamic aspect of maya, as cosmic energy, which is represented as the female organ?
>
> Maya in its dynamic aspect is called Shakti; perhaps it is no accident that, in the Hindu pantheon the active power of a deity is contained within his queen! Maya-Shakti mothers, but also "muffles the consciousness in its dream-web." Too-many-women: are they all aspects of Devi, the goddess—who is Shakti, who slew the buffalo-demon, who defeated the ogre Mahisha, who is Kali Durga Chandi Chamunda Uma Sati and Parvati. (485)

On another level, *Midnight's Children* clearly relates to Foucault's valorization of the role of the author in Rushdie's fictional relegation of his own authorial identity to Saleem Sinai. Throughout the fiction, Saleem gathers together the odds and ends of his reminiscences in order to constitute what Foucault calls 'a certain mode of being of discourse' that is his story (or *history)*. In opening the narrative, Saleem seems to reflect upon just this paradigm when he muses:

> And there are so many stories to tell, too many, such an excess of intertwined lives events miracles places rumours, so dense a commingling of the improbable and the mundane! I have been a swallower of lives; and to know me, just the one of me, you'll have to swallow the lot as well. Consumed multitudes are jostling and shoving inside me; and guided only by the memory of a large white bedsheet with a roughly circular hole some seven inches in diameter cut into the center, clutching at the dream of that mutilated square of linen, which is my talisman, my open-sesame, I must commence the business of remaking my life from the point at which it really began, some thirty-two years before anything as obvious, as *present,* as my clock-ridden, crime-stained birth. (4)

These circuits of intertextuality and narrativai enclosure are also further symptoms of what is generally called the hyperconsciousness of postmodern literary productions, a phenomenon that has been well described by Jim Collins as 'a hyperawareness on the part of the text itself of its cultural status, function and history, as well as of the conditions of its circulation and reception.' As Collins adds, 'Hyperconsciousness involves a different sort of self-reflexivity than that commonly associated with modernist texts. Highly self-conscious forms of appropriation and rearticulation have been used by postmodern painters, photographers, and performance artists. . . . The self-reflexivity of these popular texts of the late eighties and early nineties does not revolve around the problems of self-expression experienced by the anguished creative artist so ubiquitous in modernism but instead focuses on antecedent and competing programs." (335) Insofar as *Midnight's Children* is concerned, the effect of such hyperconsciousness is revealed in two distinct formats—one purely technical or embodied in and through the text, and the other more ideational or attitudinal, lying resident within the general shape and thrust of the narrative. The former is indicative of what is described in recent critical theory as Fabulation and Surfication, terms which denote literatures characteristic of much postmodern writing in which the writer consciously draws the reader's attention to his artifice as the creator of a text. Instances of such practices abound in *Midnight's Children:*

> Other men have recited stories before me; other men were not so impetuously abandoned. When Valmiki, the author of the *Ramayana,* dictated his masterpiece to the elephant-headed Ganesh, did the god walk out on him halfway? He certainly did not. (Note that, despite my Muslim background, I'm enough of a Bombayite to be well up in Hindu stories, and actually I'm very fond of the image of the trunk-nosed, flap-eared Ganesh solemnly taking dictation!) (177)

Such stylistic or compositional features also illustrate the postmodern recognition that all narratives are more social and human constructs than value-free representations of immutable realities. For as Linda Hutcheon has indicated, narratives are basically modes of 'totalizing' representations, the term 'totalizing' indicative of the fact that all writers—whether of fiction, history, or theory—structure their narratives consciously in order to impart to them order and meaning.[14]

Neil Ten Kortenaar has acutely observed that 'Rushdie's novel is a mediation on the textuality of history, and, in particular, of that official history that constitutes the nation.'[15] The point at issue here is the central thesis of the novel, that the life of a midnight's child born on 15 August 1947 is coterminous with that of the evolving history of the nation born at the same instant, and that the telling of the 31 year old story of an infant-boy-man is the same as chronicling the history of the nation. Metaphors of gestation underline the parallel between the birth of the nation and the delivery of a child. As Saleem puts it,

> Our hero is greatly affected by being shut up in confined spaces. Transformations spring upon him in the enclosed dark. As a mere embryo in the secrecy of a womb (not his mother's), did he not grow into the incarnation of the new myth of August 15th, the child of ticktock? (456)

Since postmodernism (Linda Hutcheon and Benedict Anderson in particular[16]), it is easy to see today that the making of a fictional narrative and the making of a nation are both sourced in essential(ly similar) acts of imagination. In a key passage in the novel, Rushdie has Saleem reflect precisely on this:

> This year—fourteen hours to go, thirteen, twelve—there was an extra festival on the calendar, a new myth to celebrate, because a nation which had never previously existed was about to win its freedom, catapulting us into a world which, although it had five thousand years of history, although it had invented the game of chess and traded with Middle Kingdom Egypt, was nevertheless quite imaginary; into a mythical land, a country which would never exist except by the efforts of a phenomenal collective will—except in a dream we all agreed to dream; it was a mass fantasy shared in varying degrees by Bengali and Punjabi, Madrasi and Jat. (129-30)

Apart from this, there is also yet another feature of postmodern theory that *Midnight's Children* conforms to, and that is of the concept of a Self different and divergent from that of the Desecration (Romantic and Modern) notion of a unitary consciousness informed within the limits of a single mind. At the core of the new postmodern conception lies the realization that the Self is *not a* singular, but rather, as Chantal Mouffe has indicated, 'always multiple and contrary subjects, inhabitants of a diversity of communities . . . constructed by a variety of discourses and precariously and temporarily sutured at the intersection of those subject positions.'[17] This idea of the postmodern man as multiple in his identity has clear affinities with Saleem's characterization in *Midnight's Children.* He is, after all, so many subjects simultaneously:

> Who what am I? My answer: I am the sum total of everything that went before me, of all I have been seen done, of everything done-to-me. I am everyone everything whose being-in-the-world affected was affected by mine. I am anything that happens after I've gone which would not have happened if I had not come. Nor am I particularly exceptional in this matter; each "I," every one of the now-six-hundred-million-plus of us, contains a similar multitude. (457-58)

These functions further direct our attention to yet another feature of postmodernism, that is its matter-of-fact acceptance and even celebration of differences and diversities within traditions of representation, with contestations between discourses and registers thereof. This is one way of accounting in the large variety of styles that one comes across in *Midnight's Children.* To take a few random examples, there is the juxtaposition of history and fantasy in a passage like:

> Today, the papers are talking about the supposed political rebirth of Mrs. Indira Gandhi, but when I returned to India, concealed in a wicker basket, "The Madam" was basking in the fullness of her glory. . . . On December l6th, 1971, I tumbled out of a basket into an India in which Mrs. Gandhi's New Congress Party held a more-than-two-thirds majority in the National Assembly. (460-61)

the fusion of national chronicles and personal memories:

> While astrologers make frantic representations to Congress Party bosses, my mother lies down for her afternoon nap. While Earl Mountbatten deplores the lack of trained occultists on his General

> Staff; the slowly turning shadows of a ceiling fan caress Amina into sleep. While M.A. Jinnah, secure in the knowledge that his Pakistan will be born in just eleven hours, a full day before independent India, for which there are still thirty-five hours to go, is scoffing at the protestations of horoscope-mongers, shaking his head in amusement, Amina's head, too is moving from side to side. (126-27)

and the blend of the low and trivial with the high and serious:

> In the summer of 1956, when most things in the world were still larger than myself, my sister the Brass Monkey developed the curious habit of setting fire to shoes. While Nasser sank ships at Suez, thus slowing down the movements of the world by obliging it to travel around the Cape of Good Hope, my sister was also trying to impede our progress. (178)

At the same time, while endorsing *Midnight's Children* as a postmodern text, it is important to realize that such a reading also opens it up to critiques of postmodernism as that of Fredric Jameson who has argued that postmodernism is a cultural byproduct of late-capitalistic socio-economic and political drives, the need to create new markets for consumption. The narratival diversity, the perspectival ambiguities, the generic and tonal multiplicity of the text, may be looked upon in this light as a ploy as invidious as the repackaging of a commodity. But it may also be recognized that Rushdie's novel shares in and bodies forth some of the fundamental preoccupations of postmodern theory because both literature and theory today are responses to the complexities of being and essence that confront all thinking human beings.

NOTES

1. Mohit K. Ray, 'The Genealogy of Postmodernism," *Postmodernism and English Literature*, ed. M.K. Bhatnagar and M. Rajeshwar (New Delhi: Atlantic, 1999), p. 13.
2. John O'Neill, *The Poverty of Postmodernism* (London: Routledge, 1995), p. 198.

3. Malcolm Bradbury, "Modernism," *A Dictionary of Modern Critical Terms,* ed. Roger Fowler (London: Routledge and Kegan Paul, 1997), p. 151.
4. Virginia Woolf, "Modern Fiction," *English Critical Essays: Twentieth Century,* First Series, Selected with an Introd. by Phyllis M. Jones (London: OUP, 1964), p. 392.
5. Jim Collins, "Television and Postmodernism," *Channels of Discourse, Reassembled,* ed. Robert C. Allen (Chapel Hill: University of North Carolina Press, 1992), pp. 329-30.
6. Meenakshi Mukherjee, "Introduction" to *Rushdie's Midnight's Children: A Book of Readings* (Delhi: Pencraft International, 1999), p. 9.
7. T.S. Eliot, "Criticism" in *Selected Essays* (London: Faber and Faber, 1980), p. 24.
8. James Joyce, *A Portrait of the Artist as a Young Man* (Harmondsworth: Penguin, 1969), pp. 179 and 203.
9. Roland Barthes, 'The Death of the Author," rpt. in *Modern Criticism and Theory: A Reader,* ed. David Lodge (New York: Longman, 1989), p. 170.
10. Donald E. Pease, "Author," *Critical Terms for Literary Study,* ed. Frank Lentricchia and Thomas McLaughlin (Chicago: University of Chicago Press, 1995), p. 112.
11. Michel Foucault, "What is an Author?" Rpt. in David Lodge, pp. 201-2.
12. Umberto Eco, *The Name of the Rose* (New York: Harcourt Brace Jovanovich, 1984).
13. Salman Rushdie, *Midnight's Children* (New York: Avon, 1982), p. 121.
14. Linda Hutcheon, *The Politics of Postmodernism* (London: Routledge, 1995), pp. 61-62.
15. Neil Ten Kortenaar, "*Midnight's Children* and the Allegory of History," in Meenakshi Mukherjee, p. 29.
16. See Linda Hutcheon, *A Poetics of Postmodernism: History, Theory, Fiction* (New York: Methuen, 1987) and Benedict Anderson, *Imagined Communities: Reflections on the Origin and Spread of Nationalism* (London: Verso, 1983).
17. Chantal Mouffe, "Radical Democracy: Modern or Postmodern?" *Universal Abandon*, ed. Andrew Ross (Minneapolis: University of Minnesota Press, 1988), p. 44, qtd. Jim Collins, p. 337.

Rushdie's Novel of Novels: *Midnight's Children*

K. VENKATA REDDY
S.K. University, Anantapur

Midnight's Children *was adjudged the 'Booker of Bookers' (i.e. the best book in the 25 years history of the Booker Prize) in 1993. It was a recognition of the worth of this novel and a tribute to the genius of Rushdie, one of fiction's finest practitioners. In this article Prof. Reddy analyses the salient features of the book which have contributed to its extraordinary success and made it 'the novel of novels.'*

Editor

It is quite heartening to note that Salman Rushdie, the world-famous novelist living under an Iranian death-threat, accused of blasphemy against Islam on account of his novel, *Satanic Verses,* has won the "Booker of Bookers" award, marking the 25th anniversary of Britain's most prestigious literary prize. (*The Hindu,* Sept. 22, 1993) This is the greatest compliment paid to the writer. Rushdie got this most covetous award on the basis 1981 novel, *Midnight's Children,* which was adjudged "the best of his books that have won the annual Booker prize since 1968. To his own surprise, Rushdie has been picked from a list of Booker winners including such stalwarts as Kingsley Amis, Iris Murdoch, William Golding and Nadine Gordimer.

But, those who have fully grasped the extraordinary scale and fertility of *Midnight's Children*—its span of styles from free buoyant fantasy to murderous social invective, its mixture of radical aesthetic experiment and political courage, its power of illuminating the English language with the metaphors, myths and sheer loquacities of Indian writing—are not surprised over the kind of distinction that has been bestowed on it. What makes the novel so extraordinarily important and so vertiginously exciting a reading experience is 'the way it takes in not just the whole applecart of India and the problem of being a novel about India, but the business of being a novel at all." (Valentine Cunningham in *TLS)* What is more, it burgeons with life, exuberance and fantasy. It has the same effect on the eyes and ears of the reader as a magnificent circus performance—a scene that is filled with colour, zest, dare-devilry and loud bravado. Small wonder, therefore, if *Midnight's Children* was unanimously received both in India and abroad with an overwhelming and breathless mood of acclaim and a spontaneous overflow of enthusiasm.

Rushdie himself has corroborated this view, when in an interview he was asked to explain the extraordinary success of *Midnight's Children.* He said that the appeal for the Western readers lay in the adventurous, the exotic, the comic, the unexpected and the strange. So, for the West, specially Britain and the United States, it is not only the colourful fictional world of *Midnight's Children,* but, to a high degree, the exoticist image of India itself that accounts for the literary quality and sensational success of the novel.

Few novels in recent years have unleashed so much praise and criticism as Rushdie's *Midnight's Children* did when it won the 1981 Booker McConnell Award. According to the *New York Times,* the novel "sounds like a continent finding its voice." *The New York Review of Rooks* hailed it as "an extraordinary novel," incorporating as it does "the stupendous Indian past with its pantheon, its epics, and its wealth of folklore and fairy tales, while at the same time playing a role in the tumultuous Indian present."

Midnight's Children marks quite a radical departure from what has been written by Indian novelists in English to date. With the exception of writers like G.V. Desani, Raja Rao and Sudhin Ghose, Indian writing in English has not been overly concerned with experimentation. *Midnight's Children* differs from this earlier fiction in that most of the usual ground rules associated with the older form of fiction are broken. The unities of time and place and character are, at best, unstable. The narrative fluctuates uncertainly between first and third person. What is more, ordinary notions of fictional realism are subverted, natural law becomes unnatural or supernatural even though the novel is not in any straightforward sense religious or metaphysical. The novel is full of cryptic clues, archaic utterances, and seems always on the point of offering some important explanation and of arriving at some goal or conclusion. But what this conclusion is we can never be quite sure. It is a novel of signs, gestures and sleight-of-hand, narrated with a passion for narrating rather than for clarifying meaning.

In writing *Midnight's Children,* the novelist's avowed purpose is "to relate private lives to public events and to explore the limits of individuality in a country as big, as populous and culturally variegated as India." *Shame* does the same thing for Pakistan, to some extent. Rushdie is "centrally involved" with "aspects of the most crucial critical/theoretical debates of his day." He is deeply concerned with the politics of the Indian subcontinent, and his commitment and sense of urgency are really remarkable. He presents realities of public history influencing, and getting influenced by, individual's actions and aspirations, with exceptional honesty.

Midnight's Children is Rushdie's interpretation of a period of about seventy years in India's modern history dealing with the events leading to the partition and beyond. It encapsulates the experience of three generations of the Sinai family, living in Srinagar, Amritsar and Agra and then in Bombay, and, finally, migrating to Karachi. Saleem Sinai, the narrator engaged in the actual writing of the story, works at a pickle factory by day and records his experiences by night, hoping that "one day, perhaps, the world may taste the pickles of history."

The novel has an epic sweep extending in time and space, covering some six decades, and the entire Indian sub-continent and its history. Though the narrative chronologically covers over a period of sixty-three years (from the spring of 1915 to 1978) it effectively begins in the midnight of August 15, 1947 and ends again on the midnight of August 15, 1978. Thus, Time is cyclical and regenerative. It ends where it begins. The temporal world is hoisted with a momentous urgency and resolved in an open-ending manner.

Like *Grimus, Midnight's Children* is tripartite in structure, presenting a cross-section of humanity, of Indians—Muslims—Anglo-Indians. Book One covers the time from Jallianwallah Bagh up to Saleem's birth on August 15, 1947; Book Two up to the end of the Indo-Pakistan War in September 1965; and Book Three up to the end of Emergency in March 1977. Rushdie succeeds in presenting the past and the present of Saleem in alternating bits of narration in a captivating manner. We find in the novel virtually all of the twentieth century Indian history—the Jallianwallah Bagh tragedy, Quit India movement, Cabinet Mission, freedom movement, Muslim League and its role, riots and bloodshed subsequent to the independence, Five Years Plans, reorganization of Indian states and language riots, Chinese aggression, the theft of the sacred relic from the Hazratbal mosque, Pakistan war, liberation of Bangladesh, the Emergency and various other historically important events. There are also typically Indian divisions and dissents, chaos and disillusion, communal tensions, religious fanaticism besides traditional values and modernizing efforts. *All* these are "preserved" in the novel to evoke the truth of India and make the novel, in Maria Couto's words, "an extraordinary saga of epic dimensions and resonances."

In *Midnight's Children,* the 'Children' stand for humanity in the essentialist sense of the word. They are exposed to strong political (and other) forces which strip them of their illusions, alienate them from others and from themselves for a short time and finally exterminate them. Saleem Sinai, the symbol of the human spirit, retires to the privacy of a retired life. Politics now leaves him alone because, like the others, he acquiesces to its demands. His individuality has been eliminated and the moral courage which is imperative for opposing tyrannical government is no longer there.

Midnight's *Children* is alternately classified and characterized picaresque novel, "a Bildungsroman in the negative sense," a very modernist mixture of naturalist background and surrealist foreground," "an eminently political novel between myth, irony, magic and the flair of an oriental fairy-tale," "a political elegy on disappointed hopes" and "a continuation of Indian oral traditions combined with a superb handling of the Western novel genre." It has been observed and praised that Rushdie does not present a cynical image of India as V.S. Naipaul has done with his two novels—*An Area of Darkness* (1964) and *India: A Wounded Civilization* (1977). Instead Salman Rushdie is said to present, almost immerse the reader in a throbbing, pulsating, warm-blooded, colourful world.

The ingredients of the "European" novel—realism, satire, structural unity, fantasy, prophecy, pattern and rhythm can all be traced in *Midnight's Children,* but they are colourfully overgrown or, as it were, interwoven into the pattern of a magic carpet, by the pungent spices of the Indian cuisine: analogy, repetition of the same ambiguity. The result is a novel that is at the same time a carefully constructed allegory for artistic creation, "chutnification," selection, preservation and spicing of reality, and a magic tale of 1001 children, 1001 episodes, anecdotes, 1001 adventures, told by Saleem, the protagonist, who is man, demon and demi-god in one, a male Scheherzade, "an Indian Tin-drummer straight out of the *Ramayana*."

Select Bibliography

Books by Salman Rushdie

Grimus, London: Grafton, 1975.

Bibliography

Books by Salman Rushdie

Grimus, London: Grafton, 1975.

Midnight's Children (1980), London: Picador, 1981.

Shame, Calcutta: Rupa, 1983.

The Jaguar Smile: A Nicaraguan Journey, London: Picador, 1987.

The Satanic Verses, London: Viking, 1988.

Haroun and the Sea of Stories, New Delhi/London, Penguin India/Granta, 1990.

Imaginary Homelands: Essays and Criticism 1981-1991, London: Granta, 1991.

The Wizard of Oz: A Short Text about Magic, BFI Film, Classics. London, BFI, 1992.

East, West, London: Jonathan Cape, 1994.

The Moor's Last Sigh, London: Jonathan Cape, 1995.

The Vintage Book of Indian Writing (ed. with Elizabeth West), London, 1997.

The Ground Beneath Her Feet, London: Jonathan Cape, 1999.

Fury, London: Jonathan Cape, 2001.

Step across this Line: Collected Non-Fiction 1992-2002, London: Jonathan Cape, 2002.

Interviews by Rushdie

Interview with Chandrabhanu Pattanayak, *The Literary Criterion*, 18:3(1983), pp.19-22.

Interview with David Brooks, *Helix*, 19 (1984), pp. 55-69.

Interview with John Haffenden in Haffenden, ed., *Novelists in Interview*, London: Methuen, 1985, pp. 231-61.

Interview with Rani Dharkar, *New Quest*, 42 (Nov.-Dec., 1983).

'Free at Last,' Salman Rushdie's interview with Shrabani Basu, *Sunday* (11-17 October 1988), pp. 18-21.)

'My real prize in India,' Salman Rushdie's interview with Swapan Dasgupta and Ashok Malik, *India Today*, May 1, 2000, pp. 71-74.

"'Doing the Dangerous Thing': An Interview with Salman Rushdie," T. Vijay Kumar in *Rushdie's Midnight's Children: A Book of Readings*, ed. Meenakshi Mukherjee, Delhi: Pencraft International, 1999, pp. 212-27.

Selected Rushdie Criticism

Ahmad, A. (1992) *In Theory: Classes, Nations, Literatures*, London: Verso.

Ashcroft, B., G. Griffiths, H. Tiffin, ed. (1989) *The Empire Writes Back: Theory and Practice in Post-colonial Literatures*. London: Routledge.

Brennan, Timothy. (1989) *Salman Rushdie and the Third World: Myths of the Nation,* London: Macmillan.

Cundy, Catherine. (1996) *Salman Rushdie*, Manchester and New York: Manchester University Press.

Dingwaney, Anuradha. (1992) 'Author(iz)ing *Midnight's Children* and Shame' in S. Emanuel Nelson, ed. *Re-Worlding: The Literature of the Indian Diaspora,*Westport: Greenwood, pp. 157-68.

Dissanayake, W. (1985) 'Towards a Decolonized English: South Asian Creativity in Fiction,' *World Englishes*, 4:2, pp. 233-42.

Durix, Jean-Pierre. (1985) 'Magic Realism in *Midnight's Children*,' *Commonwealth Essays and Studies*, 8:1, pp. 57-63.

Fletcher, M.D., ed. (1994) *Reading Rushdie: Perspectives on the Fiction of Salman Rushdie*, Amsterdam: Rodopi.

Goonetilleke, D.C.R.A. (1998) *Salman Rushdie*, London: Macmillan.

Harrison, James. (1992) *Salman Rushdie*, New York: Twayne.

Kirpal, Viney, ed. (1990) *The New Indian Novel in English: A Study of the 1980s*, New Delhi: Allied.

Mukherjee, Meenakshi, ed. (1999) *Rushdie's Midnight's Children: A Book of Readings*, Delhi: Pencraft International.

Parameswaran, Uma. (1988) *The Perforated Sheet: Essays on Salman Rushdie's Art*, Madras: Affiliated East-West Press.

Price, David W. (1994) 'Salman Rushdie's Use and Abuse of History in *Midnight's Children*,' *Ariel*, 25: 2, pp. 91-107.

Rao, Madhusudhana. (1992) *Salman Rushdie's Fiction: A Study*, New Delhi: Sterling.

Rushdie, Salman. (1985) '*Midnight's Children* and *Shame*' (Lecture/ Interview), *Kunapipi*, 7:1, pp. 1-19.

Shepherd, Ron. (1985) '*Midnight's Children*: The Parody of an Indian Novel,' *SPAN*: 21, pp. 184-92.

Srivastava, Aruna. (1989) 'The Empire Writes Back: Language and History in *Midnight's Children*,' *Ariel*: 20 (4).

Suleri, Sara. (1992) *The Rhetoric of English India*, Chicago: Chicago University Press.

Taneja, G.R. and R.K. Dhawan, ed. (1992) *The Novels of Salman Rushdie*, New Delhi: Indian Society for Commonwealth Studies.

Walsh, William. (1983) "India and the Novel," *The New Pelican Guide to English Literature*, vol. 8, ed. Boris Ford, London: Penguin, pp 256-58.

Wilson, Keith. (1984) '*Midnight's Children* and Reader Responsibility,' *Critical Quarterly*, 26:3, pp. 23-37.